Individualism Reconsidered

DAVID RIESMAN was born in Philadelphia on September 22, 1909. After his graduation from Harvard Law School he was law clerk to Justice Brandeis and later became Deputy Assistant District Attorney of New York County. Since 1946, Mr. Riesman has been teaching at the University of Chicago, and in 1949 he became a Professor of Social Sciences there.

He has written *Civil Liberties in a Period of Transition*, 1942; *The Lonely Crowd* (with the collaboration of Nathan Glazer and Reuel Denney), 1950; *Faces in the Crowd* (with the collaboration of Nathan Glazer), 1952; *Thorstein Veblen: A Critical Interpretation*, 1953; and *Individualism Reconsidered*, 1954.

The Lonely Crowd was published in an abridged edition by Anchor Books in 1954.

This edition of *Individualism Reconsidered* contains a selection of the essays from the volume originally published by The Free Press in 1954.

SELECTED ESSAYS FROM

Individualism Reconsidered

BY DAVID RIESMAN

Doubleday Anchor Books

Doubleday & Company, Inc., Garden City, New York

COVER BY MIRIAM WOODS

TYPOGRAPHY BY EDWARD GOREY

To my wife

CONTENTS

Introduction

In selecting from the original Free Press volume for this paper-back edition, some of my preoccupations have had to be left out. Thus, save for the rather speculative essay on the aging process, originally prepared as a memorandum for discussion among colleagues, there is very little here which is the direct fruit of organized research activities, though to be sure the two essays bearing on changes in attitudes towards leisure and consumption have benefited from seminars carried on at the University of Chicago with Reuel Denney and, more recently, Nelson Foote. Continuing concern with interviewing and public opinion polling as a social process is not represented in this book, nor are other specifically methodological interests. The articles that are included here are taken over in full from the Free Press edition, occasional dots representing minor cuts from the version of first publication. I am indebted to the various journals and symposia, named in a footnote at the beginning of each article, which have permitted these reprintings.

In the first half dozen articles of this collection, I am defending individualism (of a certain sort) and being critical of conformity (of a certain sort). Yet I am perfectly sure that I would not be attacking "groupism" in America if I could not rely on its durable achievements—it is just these that make individualism possible. I attempt to deal with such shifting contexts for judgment in the first article, "Values in Context," in which I set forth the motto of William Blake, which I took as my own when I first began writing: "When I tell any Truth, it is not for the sake of Convincing those who do not know it, but for the sake of defending those that do."

This implies a defense of people from themselves, as well

as from outside pressures. To do this I must know something about the audiences reached by what I say. For instance, when I published in 1942 a monograph on "Civil Liberties in a Period of Transition," in which I criticized a number of traditional civil liberty assumptions (such as the "clear and present danger" test), I was writing for those already on the side of civil liberties, not for the unenlightened. And so I was very happy when I learned that the American Civil Liberties Union had distributed copies to its board; but when asked to debate with Roger Baldwin in a public meeting I declined because I felt that before a large lay audience I would prefer to support Baldwin on certain major issues rather than to attack him on minor ones. Indeed, I believe that when issues are complex, one must write for a special audience, because one can't say everything at once.

Not long ago *The Lonely Crowd* brought me a critical letter from a woman in North Dakota who complained of my difficult and twisted style; she wrote:

"I am not a Dr. I never went to college, I have not even finished High School, I am only a nurse's aid, and I like things simple and clear. All really great things, characters and thoughts are simple and clear . . ."

Lack of clarity may sometimes be the result of confused ideas. But it may also be the result of an attempt to speak to some audiences to the exclusion of others. A writer may pitch his discourse at a certain level, in a certain vocabulary or metaphoric language for that purpose. Indeed, for reasons just given, there have been times when I regretted that *The Lonely Crowd* was not more inaccessible. Thus, there is a section in it dealing with tendencies in a now traditional sort of progressive education: I criticize the frequent "groupiness" of teachers, their lack of concern for intellectual content, their preoccupation with watery, presumably tolerance-breeding "social studies." As it happened, publication of the book coincided with a renewed drive against "Deweyism" and progressive education generally; I was dismayed to find myself quoted (or misquoted) by angry people in their all too easy onslaught against "new-fangled" notions in the public schools. Dismayed because of all occupational groups, schoolteachers are among the most vulnerable; under attack, often from virulent reactionaries, they were hardly in a mood for truly critical self-examination. Despite what seemed to me reasonable caution, I had furnished ammunition against them.

Such hazards of communication arise in some measure because of the fact that parts of American society move much more rapidly than other parts. I sometimes think of our society as of a great snake, the head of which (the avant-garde) has turned while the main body is still slowly following where the head once was. If the body should try to anticipate matters and move suddenly to where the head now is, it would perhaps overreach itself: one has to explore certain positions in order that later positions can be moderate, differentiated, and firm. To return to my previous example: one is best able, and best entitled, to criticize progressive education if one is fully aware of its achievements and knows at first hand the sort of cruel and crushing education that often preceded it. Intellectuals debating among themselves about which way the head of the snake should now turn have occasionally to lend a hand to see that the body catches up with the enlightenment now stale to them—rather than to short-circuit that enlightenment for the rest of society because they have discovered certain limitations or qualifications in it.

Naturally, I do not alter my critical appraisals of contemporary schools because reactionaries are also on the warpath; rather I try to present my views in such a way as to carry challenge to the complacency of both camps. But I know I am far from successful in doing so, and that the fate of ideas, like that of people and nations, is unpredictable.

The articles on Freud present another sort of problem of context. Their original audiences were largely sympathetic to Freud—for the first three, the audience was the students and staff in the College at the University of Chicago, to whom I lectured in 1946; for the fourth, it was the Channing Club, a Unitarian student group at the university, to whom I spoke in 1950 as one participant in a series on "Attack and Counter-Attack in Religion," a series covering such figures as Nietszche, Marx, Malinowski, Reinhold Niebuhr, and Toynbee. Freud was not news to a majority of my hearers, many of whom seemed to be inclined to swallow him whole as part of their progressivism. The situation was very different from my own student days when no course I took had Freud on a reading list and when the only classroom reference to him I heard was a sneering reference to "Saints Sigmund and Karl," who were presumably up to no good. For these Chicago audiences I did not have to worry lest I give cause for new sneers at Freud, nor was this a problem when the articles were published in *Psychiatry, The American Scholar,* and *The Chicago Review.*

In the last few years, however, it is my impression that students and academic people generally neither resist Freud nor fall for him; his work and criticisms of it such as mine are taken for granted; he is simply one of a host of figures in a downgraded pantheon. In the social sciences there are signs of a retreat from the use of psychoanalytic theory in research, in favor of "sounder" work, but Freud is not rejected (which might lead some young people to him); he is, in Harold Lasswell's phrase, "resisted by partial incorporation." These essays of mine were not intended to please the dwindling band of orthodox Freudians, but neither were they intended to encourage glib unconcern with the persistent vitality of Freud's work; the essays themselves, as well as much of my other writing and that of my colleagues, are a tribute to that work.

"Individualism Reconsidered," the essay which has lent this book its title, may also serve to exemplify my contextual view of the intellectual's role. If one should compare it with the monograph of 1942 on civil liberties, one would find an effort to show some of the limitations of laissez-faire liberalism and individualism in the realm of ideas. The earlier essay emphasizes the cultural conditioning of thought; it aims to put civil liberties doctrines in the perspective of the sociology of knowledge. To some extent I have changed my views since 1942; to some extent the world has changed, and "groupism" has become ever more of a danger; but also, to some extent, my audiences have changed. The earlier essays were written when I was still a law professor, addressing colleagues who appeared slow to recognize the social-psychological roots of opinion—colleagues, often enough, still immured in the heavenly city of the eighteenth-century philosophers. In contrast, "Individualism Reconsidered," like most of the essays in this volume, was written with an audience of social scientists (including historians and philosophers) mainly in mind—groups which, as I see them, have sometimes been all too inclined to overemphasize the values of collective or folkish life and to damn the individualism they find rampant in bourgeois, industrial, urban society.

Indeed, some anthropologists and sociologists, focusing on the group and the culture, tend to take a conservative position as far as individual rights are concerned even when, as citizens, they affiliate with the "left." Where the left is collectivist, hostile to middle class individualism, there is no contradiction in spirit between the lack of concern with individual rights and the leftism of such social scientists, even if there is some contradiction between the belief in cultural determinism and the hope for drastic political reorganizations of society. In August Comte, "father" of sociology, these paradoxes can be clearly seen: Comte's work seems to be unmatched as a blueprint for a totalitarianism which is full of altruism and free of terror, but is nonetheless profoundly hostile to individualism. My own sympathies lie, though not wholly unequivocally, with Comte's great contemporary, Alexis de Tocqueville, who, taking for granted and in many ways sympathetic to the coming of a more democratic, more equalitarian social order, devoted his energies to seeing how individual liberty might yet be preserved in the interstices of that order.

As I read over "Individualism Reconsidered," which appeared in a volume edited by liberal churchmen, I feel again the hazards of dealing in a brief essay with such complex themes in history and ethics: I can attempt it only because I assume in my readers a certain fund of shared knowledge and argumentation.

The relation of social science to its audience, who are

also its subjects, forbids any easy, undialectical answer to the problems of communication—a process that involves "noise," redundance, and overtones. A generation ago, when social science was still struggling to free itself from theology and social work (from socialism, too), even the oversanguine efforts to establish an "operational" and "value-free" science made good pragmatic sense. Social scientists, finding their professional passion to lie in casting a cold eye, could in this way disassociate themselves from American reformism and the optimism about the social process it usually implied and could free themselves from overt sentimentality and blatant ethnocentrism. However, contrary to the situation of a generation ago, we live, I am inclined to think, in an era of a "safe and sane" Fourth of July and a "safe and sane" sociology, though the world has hardly got safer in the interim. Hence, the tasks and tensions of sociology are not what they were, and a retreat into a deadpan vocabulary which studiously avoids intellectual excitement would appear to be less useful; readers will in any event pursue the professional even into such symbolic lairs of refuge, and will perhaps take his devices as a judgment upon the reader and the world—conceivably as a manipulative, frightened, or unsympathetic one.

In these remarks I have invited the reader to share certain problems of the writer—just as many novels and short stories today have writers as protagonists. Not only must we all, as Lionel Trilling has said, become amateur sociologists to defend ourselves, perhaps against manipulation and certainly against misinterpretation, but we may all do so in order to share in a form of self-exploration which, among its other functions, has taken its place alongside the novel.

Chicago, Illinois D. R.
April, 1955

Values in Context

I. Lyman Bryson, examining a few weeks ago the papers submitted for the annual [1952] Conference on Science, Philosophy and Religion, observed that only four out of forty-five dealt with values in any concrete and empirical way; the rest were hortatory, many of them assuming that the academicians there assembled understood each other and needed only some formula of belief to impose values on a world that had presumably lost them. Reading a number of these same papers, I also was struck by the frequent assumption that values in general, not merely some values or the speaker's values, had gotten lost or dissipated; moreover, that without consensus on values, our democratic society would not hold together. I see no convincing evidence for either of these assumptions. It seems plain to me that men cannot live without values, without preferences and choices, without the vocabulary of motives that we partly learn and partly teach ourselves. Those who bewail the loss of values seem disingenuously to bewail the loss—that is, the replacement—of their own values; and in many cases I believe this applies quite literally: for many of the men whom I find to be most hysterical about the loss of values appear to me to lack confidence in their own ongoing processes of valuation; they do not enjoy making choices, and their effort to escape from freedom is writ larger than life in their overly subjective appraisal of the society as a whole.

Something of this sort, I think, must lie behind the sec-

"Values in Context" was first delivered as an address at a conference on Science and Human Values at Mount Holyoke College, October 1952. It was first published in The American Scholar, *Vol. 22, No. 1, 1952.*

ond assumption also, namely, that agreement on fundamental values is essential for democratic functioning. The attempt to enforce such agreement seems to me a good way to bring on civil war; and it is important to study those institutions in our society which allow society to function precisely in the face of profound disagreements on fundamentals. One of these institutions, I suggest, is the city bosses and their machines: these act as brokers among competing urban values, based as they are on religious, ethnic, regional, occupational and other identifications. These bosses can trade a park in a middle-class section for a symbolically important Italian judgeship, and otherwise keep a tolerable peace by appropriate pay-offs from the spoils of American productivity. The current attempt to unify the country against municipal patronage and bossism seems to me dangerous, because by enforcing an ideological unity on politics we threaten with extinction a few men, soaked in gravy we can well spare, who protect our ideological pluralism.

To be sure, there is a fundamental value underlying my own view, which is that men should not be forced by the needs of society to give more than conditional cooperation to specific, short-term goals. Thus, I think we can ask people to be vaccinated, but not to believe in its efficacy, or in science, or in long life. And on the whole I prefer that we win people's cooperation by offering concrete advantages—including such personal growth as they may gain from the cooperation itself—without asking them what their fundamental values are. (Incidentally, the Communists in our midst have made this program difficult, not only because their fellow-workers in the usual front organizations naively assume that since the Communists share the work they also share the liberal and humane values alleged to be involved in the joint enterprise, but even more because the country at large assumes that it is always the fellow-workers and never the Communists who are the dupes: the fact often is that the Communists are gulled into doing the work on the improvident speculation that they will win converts or make some other gain.) To put the matter another way, I believe it a fallacy to assume that people can cooperate only if they understand each other (this is the illusion of many semanticists), or if they like each other, or if they share certain preconceptions. The glory of modern large-scale democratically-tending society is that it has developed the social inventions—such as the market, the practices and skills of negotiation, and the many other devices which allow us to put forward in a given situation only part of ourselves—which allow us to get along and, usually, not to kill each other while retaining the privilege of private conscience and of veto over many requests made of us by our fellow men. No doubt, for this to occur there has to be some *procedural* consensus, some shared values of a very general sort like due process, and among sufficient people in strategic locations, some less-than-fanatical attitude toward compromise and even corruption. But this is far from saying that we would be better off if we could go forward by going back to some partly mythical state of value-agreement based on choicelessness.

II. The psychoanalytic psychologist can come at this same problem in another way. His clinical work makes him aware that in an individual values are contextual, with each value-element having a very different loading depending on the *Gestalt,* on the whole. It did not, of course, take Freud to teach us that, for instance, the morally indignant person is often a sadist whose own impulses were his first victims. But the analytic method does allow us to delineate such observations in more detail and in more complexity. Let me take as an illustration the virtue of sincerity, which is becoming a salient and unquestioned value, so far as I can see, among a whole generation of young people. One gifted boy of fifteen, whose interview I have analyzed in detail elsewhere, stated that his best trait was sincerity, and proved the point by a gallant effort to be totally frank with the interviewer. It did not occur to him that such sincerity puts pressure on others in a social situation to be equally sincere: it is coercive, and tends to break down etiquettes which we use to protect our emotional life from strangers, from over-inquisitive relatives and friends, and at times from ourselves. Nor did it occur to him that his very frankness concealed some of its driving motives, not only this coercive one but also another equally coercive insistence that he be regarded and valued for his truth-telling. He tells us everything about himself without reserve—everything but what he doesn't know, namely, that he wants the credit, or at least some response, for this very frankness.

In this connection, it is interesting to note the study of values made in Vienna some years ago by Else Frenkel-Brunswik. She asked people what values they thought they possessed and then asked their associates to rank them on the same values. And she discovered, for example, that people who said they were sincere were not thought to be so by their friends; rather, those who said "I try to be sincere but I am often insincere," were regarded by others as sincere. Such observations confirm my feeling of wanting to be particularly cautious when meeting someone who says, "I am going to be frank with you."

But of course it would be going much too far to say that the contemporary cult of sincerity is simply negative, a regression from the superior age of manners. The *opportunity* to be sincere, particularly between men and women, is a tremendous achievement over the past; the *opportunity* to convert a stranger into a friend in a Pullman car or academic convention is an American blessing; the growth, through the practice of sincerity, of the One Big Union, the union of sinners, has lifted intolerable burdens of moral underprivilege from the isolated and the inarticulate. Moreover, in a big rich country, lifted above the needs of peasant guile and tenement-house suspiciousness, millions of us can afford sincerity, just as in many parts of the country we can afford to leave our cars unlocked and would in any case suffer—unlike the Italian victim of *The Bicycle Thief* —only moderate discomfort from an instance of misplaced confidence.

My point rather is to show how a trait like sincerity must be studied in the life-plan of given individuals and of society as a whole before we conclude that it is a value we want to encourage or discourage. My own guess is that sincerity is today so much taken for granted as an unequivocal blessing that it becomes important, as it never was at an earlier historical point, to discover some of its ethical ambiguities and limitations. To do so may help curb the tyranny of the self-styled sincere over the rest of us.

III. I want to turn now from the problem of appraising the values of an individual or of an age to the analogous problem of evaluating the ethical positions of the great thinkers of the past and present. For here, too, I believe a contextual analysis is necessary if we as intellectuals are to live in some productive tension with our times and not merely to ride the waves of the past or of the future. Let me begin by taking as an illustration the great controversy opened up by the debate between Condorcet and Godwin on one side and Malthus on the other. The former, trusting to the increasing ability of science to make nature produce, believed that an age of abundance was dawning on mankind, and that the march of history was a march of progress toward human perfectibility. Malthus lacked trust. He was more impressed with the ability of fecund, improvident men and women to produce children than with the possibilities of technological advance. The only way he could see out of nature's trap was an ascetic "moral restraint," and sociological invention, and for this way he had scant hopes. Moreover, he was perhaps the first economist to foresee that depressions might be permanent. For him there was no question about perfectibility: man had his choice between late and frugal marriage, coupled with intensive work, and the various miseries from war to pestilence by which in the past the adult population was periodically aborted. His book on population was written as a reply to Godwin, Condorcet and the other utopians of his day.

Now it seems to me, though I may well be mistaken, that Godwin and Condorcet, though in their personal lives badly treated, were to a considerable extent in line with late eighteenth-century ideas: they might be vilified, but they did not stand alone. By contrast, Malthus, whose personal fortunes were much more secure, was heretical; and, indeed, his views on depressions remained so for many years. Trying to look at these thinkers in terms of their own day, I respect and admire both sides, and do not feel called upon to take a stand with one and against the other: each made a decisive and stimulating contribution to our understanding. However, when the argument shifts to our own day, my attitude shifts to some extent also. Moving in circles where Malthus is greatly esteemed, and Condorcet and Godwin, if regarded at all, sneered at as childish Enlightenment utopians possessed with *hubris*, my tendency in teaching and writing is, without derogating Malthus, to emphasize the courage which Condorcet and Godwin also had, and the importance today of faith that nature, including human nature, is not a trap, though we can make it one. On the other hand, where complacency still rules, there one would want to stress Malthus, and some of the neo-Malthusians are probably quite useful in this direction. But where, as in so many intellectual circles, there prevails an anti-Enlightenment temper which prides itself on its realism, its refusal to share any dreams of man's potentially fine future, there a reappraisal of Godwin and Condorcet is desirable—taking account, however, of all that Malthus and his followers have taught us.

IV. I must now confess—in an effort to communicate and to be relevant more than to be sincere—that what I have to say here has been guided in some part by a similar feeling for context. When I received this invitation, I assumed—perhaps unfairly—that the balance of opinion and assumption here would turn out not to be too radically different from the one that Lyman Bryson reported on for the Conference on Science, Philosophy and Religion; and I also assumed that I had myself been asked because the planners were themselves pluralists, at least to start with. So I felt it incumbent on me to stress that side of my thought which is skeptical about absolutes and, in a day when very few admit being relativists, to illustrate some of the possible advantages of a relative approach to values. By the same token, I would have done somewhat differently had I been asked to talk on scientific method before the American psychological or sociological societies; there, confronted with many who still believe in a value-free social science and a deceptively neutral operationalism, I might have stressed not only the importance of the study of values, but also the inescapable and creative role of values in the scientific process itself.

When I conduct myself in this way, a host of problems immediately arises, and in discussing them I may be able to clarify somewhat our elusive topic. In the first place, I may be mistaken about my audience: I may be hardening their prejudices when I am seeking to be liberating. I try to cope with this by insisting, when I discuss such matters, that there be an extended question period, or its sublimation in a panel like ours here; the question period may help correct my misapprehensions about the audience and simultaneously their misapprehensions about me. But it is not enough to know the audience; one must also know *their* context. They may be so buffeted by their adversaries that they need, at least temporarily, to have their prejudices confirmed rather than shaken. For instance, girl students at some of our liberal universities need occasionally to be told that they are not utterly damned if they discover within themselves anti-Negro or anti-Semitic reactions—else they may expiate their guilt by trying to solve the race question in marriage. But even that judgment has to be made in terms of the wider social context—in this case, a judgment that the lot of Negroes, let alone Jews, in America is not always so utterly desperate as to call for the ruthless sacrifice of protective prejudices. And, as I have indicated, each of these judgments of context, from the audience out in widening circles, may be mistaken.

In the second place, I may be mistaken about my own motives as a speaker. What may on the surface appear to me as my courageous choice of an unorthodox and unpopular position may turn out on closer examination to be a form of exhibitionism. Or I may be more conciliatory than is warranted because I want to be liked. More probably, I may be falling into the all-too-common academic pitfall of finding and clinging to a pet heresy, proud of my intransigence, while failing to realize that it has become, if not a popular orthodoxy, at least the vested heresy of an in-group. I must therefore try to keep up with myself, as-

I develop, as well as with my audience, and to watch for any symptoms showing that I prefer to shock or startle people rather than to enlighten them. At another level, I cannot help but be aware that a shifting position which takes a stand only against the need to take a stand on many exigently argued issues may have terrible moral pitfalls in convenient uncommitment—I say I cannot help this awareness because all my adult life I have been besieged by people who wanted to convert me to their loyalty and thought me cowardly for refusing to join. It has taken me a long time to recognize the possible values, including courage, behind such refusals. But still, this issue too has to be re-examined. To complicate matters further, I know that ambiguity is fashionable today in the literary world, so my plunging into it as a pedagogic device may not be entirely disinterested. Let me hasten to add, however, that I don't think I or anyone else need be faultless before opening his mouth, for the history of thought teaches us how many men were productive for the "wrong" or at least very neurotic motives, and vice versa.

Discussion may help somewhat, as I have said, to clarify an audience for me and me for an audience. Even so, someone is likely to ask me: "Don't you think so-and-so is true, irrespective of time and place? Isn't taking your audience into account a complicated form of lying?" A somewhat more subtle questioner may ask: "Don't you place yourself above your audience, and even above the ideas you deal with, by making yourself into a governor or thermostat for the society, trying to prevent its going to extremes? Can't 'extremes' be right? And doesn't this conduct make you, after all, a servo-mechanism, dependent for your own motion on that in the larger society?" All I can do now is to begin an answer to some of these questions—to deal with all of them would mean to discuss the function of intellectuals in our society; the possibilities of democratizing that function so that any number can play; and indeed a discussion of the play itself, of the play of the mind, of what Veblen termed "idle curiosity." But I can say right off what is perhaps already clear, that I do not take a relativist position on *all* issues—that would be another absolutism—

but only on some. Santayana said of James that he didn't think any questions were ever settled, whereas for me some questions are settled, some positions are indefensible. I cannot, for instance, agree that Plato, or anyone else, makes a tenable argument, in any context I can conceive of, for banishing poets. And while I can see that sadism when incorporated into certain personality types can be socially useful, for example if sublimated into a surgeon's work, I react negatively to the trait even in ameliorative contexts, and violently against it in destructive ones. In fact, destructiveness in its grosser and its subtler forms—when, for example, I see students' confidence that they can learn something being undermined by teachers or classmates or parents—so arouses my combativeness that, like Karl Popper in his book *The Open Society and Its Enemies,* I tend to become a fanatic crusading against fanaticism. The very position I have described to you here is taken partly because I want no possibly liberating voice in the thinkers of the past to be wholly lost by destruction of the psychological roots in us enabling us to sympathize with it.

Thus, there are issues on which I am a relativist and issues on which I am an absolutist and those on which I am in doubt as to what I am, or should be. Such moral experimentalism, while it has the perils I have already outlined and others I know not of, is essential if we are to meet life flexibly, listening to the ancestor within and the friend without, but not bound to obey either.

Let me add that I don't posit this as some sort of middle way: what *is* the middle is a contextual problem in itself, and extremes may be right. Nor would I quite define my role as that of a thermostat or other simple feed-back mechanism. For I define the context as including not only what is "really" there, as your self-styled realist would see it, but as including what is potentially there, given what my intervention may evoke in others and theirs in me. To find out this potential, one has to take risks, and one may be disappointed; but the only alternative is to condemn society to an endless regress in which each thermostat is reacting to each other thermostat or to a Generalized Thermostat of some sort.

To put this another way: I believe that the processes of communication are inherently ambiguous, since we understand other people's symbols in terms of our own character and the experience it has let us have. Therefore even those people who are sure they know what the truth is may not succeed in communicating it, but something quite the opposite, as the history of every reform movement testifies. Perhaps in America communication is especially ambiguous, for reasons already partly indicated. I think, for instance, that the wild exaggeration and tall tales so characteristic of American humor may reflect, among other things, the speaker's fear that unless his stretching of the truth is highly visible, he may run the risk of being believed. On the whole, to our loss, we have had few gentle satirists, and the *New Yorker's* development of some gentle cartoonists may signify the beginnings of a common culture among its readers.

Some will take this complexity of communication to American audiences as further evidence that we should seek lowered ambiguity through value-uniformity. But is it not better, while admitting that there are losses involved, to take heightened ambiguity as an indication of the great variety of experience available to Americans in the face of all standardizing tendencies? At any rate, I prefer to come to grips with this ambiguity directly, as the psychoanalyst uses his patient's resistance as a very central part of his cure, and to seek to develop values in the very process of discussing them. For I think we do well to take advantage of the fact that we live, as Albert Camus puts it, in *la civilisation du dialogue,* whence arises the problem of sincerity, and also the need upon occasion to interiorize and perhaps even to transcend the dialogue, in such recesses of privacy as we can make for ourselves, even at some cost in sincerity.

V. To return now to the beginning: I suggest that the anxiety manifested by so many intellectuals about values, especially other people's values, may be on the point of being overdone. Having watched what happened when the experimentalist progressive education of John Dewey, via the patronage networks of various teachers' colleges, was installed in many ill-equipped schoolhouses throughout the country, I am not attracted by the picture of a crusade to implant self-consciousness about values in all the pious and platitudinous teachers of America: I would rather have them teach languages and algebra and biochemistry. Movements of thought, it seems to me, do not so much reflect the society in which they arise as take account of what that society appears to have left out of account—to emphasize individualism when mercantilism reigned, or groupism when laissez-faire did. But as society becomes more highly differentiated, and as the audiences among whom intellectuals talk become more stratified, it becomes more and more difficult to know whether, let us say, a preoccupation with values is at fruitful odds with the times or a cruel addition to its excesses. In this, as in other cases, it may begin as the one and end as the other. I think that ways of observing our society with some detachment, such as literature and social science, offer us the chance to understand these dialectical relationships better than we now do, and to safeguard our judgment as to what intellectual tasks need doing; some tasks, of course, are hardy perennials. And then when we communicate what we have observed back to these audiences, we will find that the same pluralism which exists in the society exists in many of its individuals, and that we are talking to one part of a person and against another. For such a situation, I like the motto of William Blake: "When I tell any Truth," he wrote, "it is not for the sake of Convincing those who do not know it, but for the sake of defending those that do."

Individualism Reconsidered

Since such terms as "society" and "individual" tend to pose a false as well as a shifting dichotomy, I must anticipate misunderstanding; if I succeed in being suggestive to at least a few, I shall be satisfied. We live in a social climate in which, in many parts of the world and of the United States, the older brands of ruthless individualism are still a social danger, while in other parts of the world and of the United States, the newer varieties of what we may term "groupism" become increasingly menacing. Actually, we can distinguish conceptually between the needs of society (as a system of social organization) and those of the environing groups (as a system of psychological ties and expectations). As so defined, society, the larger territorial organization, often provides the mechanisms by which the individual can be protected against the group, both by such formal legal procedures as bills of rights, and by the fact that large-scale organization may permit the social mobility by which individuals can escape from any particular group. Prior to the rise of passports and totalitarianism, the modern Western city provided such an asylum and opportunity for many, while the existence of this safety-valve helped alleviate the pressure of "groupism" everywhere.

I. Just as a self-proclaimed "realist" is a different fellow in the Middle Ages, in the Enlightenment, and in modern America, so also the meaning of "individualism" depends on the historical setting. And it is worth tracing here the

"Individualism Reconsidered" was first published in Religious Faith and World Culture, *ed. by A. William Loos, Prentice-Hall, 1951. It was later reprinted in* City Lights, *Vol. 1, No. 3, 1953.*

paradoxical development which, in the course of the modern era, freed Western men progressively from many previous restraints while at the same time developing a seemingly individualistic character-type enclosed within new psychological restraints. Men of the emerging middle classes, after the Renaissance, were turned loose in an economic order freed from the supervision of mercantilism, in a political order freed from the supervision of an hereditary aristocracy, in a religious order freed from the supervision of ecclesiastical hierarchy. To many observers of this process, whether radical or reactionary, these men who were freed of external restraints under the slogans of laissez-faire economics, utilitarian philosophy, and so on, appeared fiercely and viciously individualistic and competitive.[1] But if we look at these new men from the inside, so to speak, we can see that it was precisely their internalization of a great deal of restraint that allowed them to become free of the group sanctions that might have been arrayed against their "individualism." They could disregard the religious anti-moneymaking attitudes that had survived from the medieval and early Reformation period only because (as Max Weber pointed out) their Puritan religious ethics provided them with stern justification and with a shell of protection against the shocked attitudes of their contemporaries.

Today, with some old evils behind us, we can admit that the hardy men who pioneered on the frontiers of production, exploration, and colonization in the last three hundred years were usually men who acted according to a code and who, though of course there were many pirates like Daniel Drew and the slave traders among them, were more likely to subscribe to high moral principles (e.g. the elder Rockefeller). These men were bound by a character orientation I have termed "inner-direction": they were guided by internalized goals and ideals which made them appear to be more individualistic than they actually were. Often, they

1. To Werner Sombart, these men appeared free of "scruples"—that is, free from such traditional obligations as those of guild morality. The fighting slogans were, of course, often blatantly individualistic.

were men who walked in the imagined footsteps of idealized parents—and this gave them their seven-league boots, and their feeling of having a personal destiny. And since the ideals that were internalized included many vestiges of older traditions, they were frequently paternalistic men, who, despite nominal belief in free enterprise, helped ameliorate the worst abuses brought about by their innovations. They shared, then, more than appears of the ethics of their anti-individualistic critics, from Owen and Marx to Karl Mannheim and Tawney. Evidence of this may be found in comparing these Western enterprisers with their counterparts in other countries, such as South America or China or the Soviet Union, where when traditional restraints on ruthlessness broke down, fewer internalized restraints were available to take their place. In sum, it proved possible in the West in early modern times to carry individualism to its limits of usefulness—and, in some cases, far beyond these limits—because a fair amount of social cohesiveness was taken for granted. . . .

Moreover, the same sort of moral compulsions which many of these "freedmen" carried within themselves, as the result of their socialization in a patriarchal family, were also turned loose upon the society at large. Individualistic "promoters" turned up not only in business and colonization, but in the many zealous reform movements of the last several hundred years. These movements fastened new restraints on a society that was shaking loose from old ones —how effectively, we can see by contrasting the attitudes towards law and society in India today, as the legacy of British rule, with the attitudes in neighboring countries which were not compelled to internalize the "white man's burden." In the West, the nineteenth century witnessed the triumph of the Victorian way: a triumph of legal and orderly justice, of honesty in business and government, of greater concern for women and children, and so on. (Inclined as we are today to patronize the Victorians, we generally see the seamy side of their attainments and emphasize their hypocrisy, failing to observe that this hypocrisy was itself some evidence of their success in driving corruption, vice, and social sadism underground.) In the eighteenth century it was impossible to walk unarmed in many English cities, let alone in the country; public and private violence abounded; corruption was taken for granted; the slave trade was thriving. By the middle of the nineteenth century, the lower orders had been freed, the lower impulses (as well as some higher ones) subdued. The development in America ran parallel, but was never, of course, as complete or as spectacular; as we all know, lawlessness reigns in many areas of American life today.

Nevertheless, anti-individualist writers such as Tawney, while they may have neglected the dangers of collectivism out of their disgust with their acquisitive society (and their failure to appreciate that medieval society was in some ways more acquisitive still), do express a very common mood of dislike for the cash nexus—a mood which appears in more astringent form in Veblen. It is hard for people to find satisfaction in a society whose best defense is that it is a lesser evil than some other social form. People can become greatly attached only to a society which takes account of their longings for connection with each other, and they may even opt for totalitarianism because it pretends to satisfy these longings and to get rid of the felt indecency of the cash nexus. To the degree that capitalist individualism has fostered an ethic of callousness, the result has been to undermine all forms of individualism, good and bad.

II. In the perspective of hindsight, we can see how Darwin's *Origin of Species* came to be so completely misinterpreted when it first appeared, as a brief for struggle to death *among individuals.* We can see, as the pendulum has swung towards groupism, that Darwin's book might just as well be interpreted as demonstrating the need for social solidarity or symbiosis within and among given species in order to achieve survival; thus (as Kropotkin pointed out) the book has much to say about cooperation as a technique of competition.

But the hardy Victorians, who had freed themselves from external restraints on economic competition and who were at the same time still sensitive, as I have indicated, to anti-moneymaking ethics, welcomed their interpretation of Darwin as a support in their continuing polemic against restraints—a polemic carried out also within themselves. One can, for instance, almost watch William Graham Sumner trying to stamp out, with the aid of Darwin, any softness and tenderness towards those who were pushed aside in the competitive struggle; he would have been less violent towards "do-gooders" if he had not feared their echo inside himself.

Today the argument against Sumner, and against this nineteenth-century variety of individualism, seems very dated. We have come to realize that men who compete primarily for wealth are relatively harmless as compared with men who compete primarily for power (though, to be sure, there are violent, even totalitarian, implications in the treatment of labor, at home and abroad, as a commodity). Nevertheless, we are still inclined to use the word "bourgeois" as an epithet; we are well aware of the vices of the money-grubber, and perhaps less sensitive to the meannesses of spirit that develop in a monastery or a university where wealth as a goal is minimized. Even so, the centuries-old campaign against the middle class should not have hidden from us the advantages of a social system in which some men seek wealth (including wealth through power), pretty much for its own sake, and others seek power (including power through wealth), pretty much for its own sake, thus establishing a dichotomy of drives which allows a protective separation of specifically political powers to grow and be maintained.

I recall Walter Duranty talking some twenty years ago about the Soviet abandonment of the "New Economic Policy," the policy by which, in the early twenties, a moderate capitalism had been encouraged in Russia. He spoke of the horror with which the ascetic Communists had reacted to the champagne parties and lovely ladies of the burgeoning NEP-men who were speculating in commodities, and making fortunes overnight by methods hard to distinguish from black-marketing. I felt then, and still feel, that if these Communists had been more historically minded and less morally indignant they might have seen that the

NEP policy offered the only chance of curbing the totalitarianism which sets in when only power, and not money, talks. (The Communists were like those farmers who, in their hatred of varmints, get rid of the very creatures on whom the whole ecological balance depends.) At the same time, we can see that if the Russian capitalists had not allowed moral restraint to be monopolized by the Communists, they might have aroused less of this sort of antagonism. (Today, it is the top Party functionaries—and occupation troops—who have access to champagne and ladies!) And we also see that economic control through the "impersonal" market mechanism (Adam Smith's "invisible hand"), where this is at all possible, is decidedly preferable to the all too visible and personal hand of the state or private monopolist.

III. In the epoch when "money talked," the conception of human nature underwent a series of changes quite as ironical as the social developments themselves. The view of man as naturally cooperative runs through the writings of a number of otherwise quite diverse nineteenth-century thinkers: St. Simon and Comte, Kingsley and Marx, Durkheim and Bellamy, Kropotkin and Ruskin. All these writers, more or less explicitly, reject competitive capitalism in favor of a medieval type of guild harmony and order, while differing in their attitudes towards the machine and in their remedies for the diseases of industrialization.

Likewise, the view of man as naturally antagonistic has given rise to a number of diverse solutions to the problem of the social order thus presented. Freud, for example, deeming men innately aggressive, thought that a strong elite, with a monopoly on the capacity for being reasonable, would have to compel the majority to cooperate in the tasks of civilization, at once demanding submission from the masses and providing them with consolation. In Elton Mayo and in other recent writers, one can find a similar elitism and a similar concern with the formation of group consensus through strong leadership.

All these writers thus arrive at positions in which they become advocates of what I have labelled "groupism," whether they start from reactionary or revolutionary political positions, or from Rousseauistic or Freudian and even Hobbesian views of human nature. That is, whether one begins with the assumption that cooperation is man's natural state, which he is prevented from attaining by a reactionary social order, or with the assumption that the "state of nature" is one of war of all against all, one can readily end by focussing on forcing or allowing men to define themselves entirely as social animals. (To be sure, in the early Marx, and even in Bellamy, one finds more anarchistic strains; and some thinkers of the last century and of this one, such as John Stuart Mill and Bertrand Russell, have worried less about order than about liberty.)

Obviously, the preoccupation with the desires and needs of men for group affiliation testifies, often enough, to the actual presence of disorder in the society. But it often testifies also to the obsessive feeling on the part of some intellectuals that disorder in itself is a terrible thing. Furthermore, one of the themes that unifies many of these writers is their attitude towards the disorderly trait of "selfishness"; in true medieval fashion, they denounce it and welcome, if not always altruism as such, then at least a class or national consciousness that submerges individual self-interest. The confidence in self-interest that ran from Mandeville through Smith to Sumner seems to have been almost utterly defeated among influential thinkers by the end of World War I; it is still assumed that self-interest is natural—and sometimes, indeed, that an "enlightened" self-interest is called for—but on the whole, reliance is placed on concern for the needs of the group.

This altruism might have worked during the 1900–1950 shift toward emphasis on the group, if those group needs had themselves been clear. In that case, people might have developed a pattern of obedience to the group in certain limited spheres (regarding the group demands as a kind of tax collection), while retaining individuality in other spheres. If this had happened, the shift from the preceding attitudes of subtly socialized individualism would hardly have been noticeable. But in fact, the group needs have not been clear; moreover, they have been constantly changing. There has developed today a great preoccupation, less with specific needs, than with group mood—a feeling on the part of individuals that they wanted or felt they had to spend their energies, first in making a group, and second in attending to and improving its morale.

This groupism, which rests not on obvious group emergencies but on the vague disquietude of lonely individuals, is probably strongest in America, where people appear to be most vocally concerned about the problems of group participation and belongingness. Americans have devoted less scientific attention to the measurement of group needs and potential wants through market research techniques (save in the most obvious commercial forms) than to what we might term "mood engineering" in work, play, and politics. Mood engineering leads not so much to specific "altruistic" behavior as to a general readiness to participate in the given group activities of the moment, even if their only purpose is to help other people pass the evening. As Margaret Mead has pointed out, Americans feel selfish if they stay at home when they might be amusing people who are "underprivileged" in the skills of self-amusement.

It would take us too far afield even to begin to try to explain the reasons for the psychological changes which have occurred at least as rapidly as those in social and political organization. For example, shifting patterns of child socialization are important: among other things, parents today face the responsibility of "making a group" with their children—are on the defensive vis-à-vis their children's moods—in a way quite different from the attitude of parents in an earlier day. Not all the developments towards groupism are to be deplored. Groupism rests in part on an increasing sensitivity to subtle states of feeling, and this is an advance. Only, as always, such advances bring with them a dialectical train of new perplexities and limitations. We must skeptically question the demands for greater social participation and belongingness among the group-minded while, on another front, opposing the claims of those who for outworn reasons cling to individualism as a (largely economic) shibboleth.

IV. It is not easy, for obvious reasons, to discover the actual state of this conflict in Soviet Russia today. We do not know, for instance, to what extent people have become cynical and apathetic as a way of resisting an enforced group belongingness. However, occasional arguments appear in the press which, by claiming that the issue is settled, show that it is not settled. Thus, in 1940 there was a discussion of a psychology textbook which was attacked, not only for its "objectivity," but for its failure to realize that the whole science had undergone a profound change in the Soviet Union. "The tragedy of the loneliness of the individual," it was asserted, "which characterizes a society founded on classes, has been liquidated. The conflict between the individual and the community has disappeared. The interests of the Soviet people are harmoniously identified with the interests of Soviet society." Furthermore, theories about "unchanging human nature" are damned as bourgeois (an issue not absent from American social science polemics)—it would seem that Lysenko-ism operates in the field of psychology too.[2]

2. A poignant newspaper story from Warsaw indicates that the Poles may be maintaining some resistance to the Stalinist extremes of groupism. A young Polish girl loosed a flood of abuse and correction on herself by writing a letter to the newspaper *Standard of Youth* declaring that "my private life does not concern anyone." She continued that the ideal member of the Union of Polish Youth was a "creature with wings . . . wearing a long and clean cloak of sackcloth. When it meets a pal it discusses only Marxism. It does not push in tramways nor spit on the floor and walks only on the right side of the street. . . . According to you we should wear only a spotless uniform of our organization, straight hair and, of course, no trace of makeup . . .—all, in order to discuss the development of education in the New China! . . . I am young and lucky enough to have survived the war and have a right to live as I like. Z.M.P. meetings, discussions and some artistic shows are not enough for me." For this display of "selfishness," the writer was termed demoralized by war and occupation, said to "almost sanction(s) debauchery," and informed that "exceeding the production target . . . is happiness. Work in the organization provides happiness certainly greater than that gotten out of dancing or making up."

To be sure, it is no adequate answer to Western advocates of groupism to show how the idea has fitted so well into the totalitarian pattern (which eventually serves to destroy all local groupings). In fact, the advocates of an anti-individualist position use the seeming success of the dictatorships to buttress their views (not seeing to what extent the dictatorships, beneath their ideology, are seeking to imitate *us*), pointing out that men welcome social solidarity even if they must pay, in the loss of freedom, a high and terrible price for it; and that actually they want demands made on them—a point to which war experience also testifies—rather than to be left alone and forced to direct their own efforts. Still other voices argue that, in order to defeat the USSR, we must evoke our own spirit of sacrifice and devotion to the group: our alleged anarchy will be our undoing in the war of the two worlds. And still other, though few, voices would like to see international anarchy put down by an all-powerful world state.

What strikes me in many of these proposals is an ascetic uninventiveness reminiscent of the discussions which bored the Polish letter-writer quoted in the footnote. We assume that all possible forms of human relatedness have already been experienced, so that if present forms are unsatisfying, then better ones must be looked for in our own past, in wartime comradeship, or in the grisly present of the Soviet Union. Ironically, the very people who extol groupism, whether as an inexorable necessity or as desirable in its own right, usually do not themselves lead parochial and "groupy" lives; they draw sustenance from all the continents and all of history; they have friends everywhere, just as their material needs, through the modern division of labor, are met from everywhere. But like Plato and many other unhappy intellectuals since, they believe that those others, the masses (obviously, the very term "masses" is heavily value-loaded), can be saved from a Durkheimian anomie only by an enforced groupism and its concomitant ideology.

We can see, moreover, other forces than a simple nostalgia, or even simple elitism, at work. Anti-urbanites, for example, argue among themselves, in the guise of instructing the "masses." Unable to stand alone, lacking the "nerve of failure," they tend to project onto others their own uneasiness and frequently their own contempt for intellectuality. I do not mean, of course, that there is no malaise in our great middle and working classes in urban life; but rather, on the one hand, that the intellectuals greatly underestimate the terror, misery, and disorder of the "status society" of the past which they so much admire, while underestimating, on the other hand, the tremendous achievements of modern men in making themselves comfortable in the face of the novelty of a fluid industrial society.

Americans of the more mobile classes have not only adapted themselves to a fluid society, but have also begun to adapt the society to their own needs. They have achieved an extraordinary ability to make judgments about, and friends with, a great variety of humankind. Whereas more traditional societies have an etiquette to govern the relation between people of different age, class, and sex groups, these Americans have abandoned etiquette for a more individualized and personalized approach. And while we are familiar with the negative aspects of this development—its enforced joviality of the "greeter" and glad-hander, its enforced politeness of the Helen Hokinson type —we may in our self-contempt be less ready to see its great adventurousness: the liberation of people and their movements from the chain mail of etiquette.

In the arts of consumption as well as in the arts of production, Americans have moved so fast that, in architecture and design, in moving pictures and in poetry and criticism, we are living in what I believe to be one of the great cultures of history. It is not fashionable to say this. Yet we may ask, as Crane Brinton does in *Ideas and Men:* What is there in Pericles' famous praise of Athens that does not apply to us, in some or even in extended measure?

Sensitive Americans—and they are more in number than each individually is apt to think—have become exceedingly allergic to anything that smacks of chauvinism; this very symposium is in part a testimony to this development. Vis-à-vis Europe, we have lost the defensive aggression of Mark Twain, though his was a needed corrective; vis-à-vis Asia, we were until recently taken in by the image of the peaceable, unaggressive, technologically-unseduced Chinese. It now seems likely that we shall fall for the idea that the Russians have more to offer the Far East than we; and that they have unequivocally convinced the peasants that this is so. While this attitude stems in part from our disenchantment with machine civilization and our failure to use machinery as a means to greater, more creative leisure, it would appear ludicrous to that part of the world which needs machines before it can realize the possibility of becoming disenchanted with them!

One of the interesting semantic expressions of our own disenchantment is that of bewailing our society as "impersonal." What would the member of the village group or small town not give at times for an impersonal setting where he was not constantly part of a web of gossip and surveillance? Furthermore, this use of the term "impersonal" is a way of deprecating our great human achievement of turning over productive routines to machinery and to formal organization. One result of this attitude is clear enough: the sphere of work tends to come increasingly under the supervision of the engineers whose concern is less to reduce the time and strain of the worker, than to render the workaday world "meaningful" in terms of shared emotions reminiscent of the guilds, or perhaps of our nostalgic image of the guilds.

A contrary attitude would assume that we should be grateful to find, in our work, areas of freedom from people, where the necessary minimum of productive activity could be accomplished without the strain and waste of time involved in continuous concern for the morale of the working group. If men were not compelled to be sociable at work, they could enjoy sociability in their leisure much more than they often do now. In fact, while men in the nineteenth century may have underestimated their satisfactions from solitary occupations, hobbies and other pursuits, we tend today to reverse these extremes and to forget that men can enjoy, let us say, the physical rhythms of work or the private fantasies of leisure even when they are for long periods deprived of social comradeship at work and play. What is necessary is some sort of balance which will find room for quite idiosyncratic individual desires to be, variously, alone and with others. The flexibility of modern industrial organization, no longer bound geographically to rail lines and power sites, the steady decrease of hours of compulsory work which our abundance allows, and our increasing sensitivity to the psychic as well as physical hazards of the different occupations—these developments permit us to move towards the reorganization of work so that it can offer a greater variety of physical and social challenges and stimulations. But work should never be allowed to become an end in itself simply out of a need to keep ourselves busy.

V. Apart from the everpresent threat of war—not seldom used as a rationalization to sop up our "excessive" comforts, leisures, and painfully-attained easy-goingnesses—most of our social critics cannot imagine a society being held together without putting organized work in the forefront of its goals and agendas. Their efforts to restore the participative significance of work, allegedly enjoyed in earlier social stages, show the same poverty of imagination as their belief in the inevitable need for the parochial group as the only conceivable building block of society. When we turn to formal politics, we see that the same fundamentally reactionary ideology leads to a demand for national unity and a distrust of the chaos of democratic politics and of the war among the so-called "special interests."

The notion that there must be "agreement on fundamentals" in order that democratic politics may go on is an illusion. Carl J. Friedrich, in *The New Image of the Common Man,* provides a discriminatory critique. While it is true that people must be prepared to accept the fact of a vote or election going against them, and to accept certain legal and juridical minima of the same sort, this is not what is meant when agreement on fundamentals is asked as the price of national unity and survival. What is meant is actually a surrender of special interest claims, whether these grow out of ethnic loyalties, church affiliation, regional, occupational, or other ties. What is meant is agreement that democracy itself (defined to mean more, much more, than the legal minimum) is a good thing; agreement on equality of races; agreement to put American needs ahead of any foreign loyalty. Yet the fact is that our democracy, like that of Switzerland, has survived without securing such agreements. In our country, this has been attained by a party system that serves as broker among the special interest groups: the parties do not ask for agreement on fundamentals—certainly, not on ideological fundamentals—but for much more mundane and workable concessions. At the same time, our expanding economy (and concomitantly expanding state services) has made these concessions possible without bankruptcy and, on the whole, with a steady reduction in hardship and injustice.

Those who would like to see the parties "stand for something," and those who have framed their own image of the future in terms of some Armaggedon of proletarian revolution or overthrow of the "interests," feel unhappy and misgoverned under such a system. To them it seems simply a lack of system. Thus, we are in part the victims of ideals of polity which turn our virtues into vices and which have confused the Western world since Plato's *Republic,* if not before. What we need are new ideals, framed with the future rather than the past in mind—ideals closer to the potentialities actually realizable under the impetus of industrialization.

One of the elements in such a new ideal would seem to be a relaxation of the demand for political dutifulness now made by many citizens who are worried about apathy. Apathy has many meanings. Its expression today may be one of the ways the individual—in the Soviet zone or Franco's Spain, no less than here—hides from ideological pressures, hides from "groupism." Lacking an active counterfaith in individualism, or any way of meeting up with others who share his resentments, he falls back on apathy as a mask behind which he can protect the remnants of his privacy. If it were widely recognized that not all people in a democracy need concern themselves continuously with public affairs (or with the union, or with the PTA, or what not), but that all should have a "right of veto" of which to make sparing, residual exercise, they might more readily agree to comply with the minimal demands for information and participation that such a veto would need for its effectiveness. And with politics no longer regarded as a continuous duty, people might feel less resistance to participation.

VI. If the international (and hence domestic) outlook continues to be as grim as during recent months [written in early 1950], readers may wonder whether this advocacy of "irresponsible" individualism is not sheer escapism. It would be insufficient to answer that "escape," like "compromise" or "appeasement," has become a bad word to the crusaders for political and group commitment. It would perhaps be a better answer to observe that if America is to be saved from destruction or self-destruction, it will be by preserving, as part of our armory of significant escapes, our humor and creativity and sense of perspective.

I recognize, of course, that many Americans feel guilty about their "luxuries" if others are forced to fight and suffer, and so would welcome a kind of edited hardship as an alleviation of their guilt. But though this is understandable and, in many ways, desirable, it provides the privileged countries and groups with much too limited and hence too easy a morality. The present international dangers menacing America (real enough in the view I hold of Stalinism) can obviously be used by many people in America to rationalize their partiality for the shared hardships of war against the solitary hardships of developing their individuality in time of peace.

Again, it should be obvious to the reader that I speak in a social context in which anarchy and "unbridled" individuality are much less likely prospects (except on the international scene) than the all-too-evident danger of the "garrison state." This danger must make us particularly sensitive to the fact that we depend for advance, in morals no less than in physical science, on individuals who have developed their individuality to a notable degree. We must give every encouragement to people to develop their private selves—to escape from groupism—while realizing that, in many cases, they will use their freedom in unattractive or "idle" ways. Our very abundance makes it possible for us, even in the midst of war, to take the minor risks and losses involved in such encouragement as against the absolutely certain risks involved in a total mobilization of intellect and imagination.

Yet in these remarks I find myself, as a final irony, addressing the defense of individualism to some presumed director of unselective service: I am using, Adam Smith style, group-survival arguments to justify the "selfish" living of an individual life. (Much of the same irony overtakes many devout people who "sell" religion as a variety of group therapy—because it is good for morale rather than for morals.) Possibly I am thereby revealing my own arguments against my own guilts. But I think more is involved. I am trying to answer Dostoevsky's Grand Inquisitor in terms that he would understand, as well as in the transcendent terms that his interlocutor, Jesus, understands. I am insisting that no ideology, however noble, can justify the sacrifice of an individual to the needs of the group. Whenever this occurs, it is the starkest tragedy, hardly less so if the individual consents (because he accepts the ideology) to the instrumental use of himself. . . .

Social science has helped us become more aware of the extent to which individuals, great and little, are the creatures of their cultural conditioning; and so we neither blame the little nor exalt the great. But the same wisdom has sometimes led us to the fallacy that, since all men have their being in culture and as the result of the culture, they owe a debt to that culture which even a lifetime of altruism could not repay. (One might as well argue, and in fact many societies in effect do, that since we are born of parents, we must feel guilt whenever we transcend their limitations!) Sometimes the point is pushed to the virtual denial of individuality: since we arise in society, it is assumed with a ferocious determinism that we can never transcend it. All such concepts are useful correctives of an earlier solipsism. But if they are extended to hold that conformity with society is not only a necessity but also a duty, they destroy that margin of freedom which gives life its savor and its endless possibility for advance.

The Ethics of We Happy Few

We Happy Few[1] is the ironic title of Helen Howe's novel of an academic community. The community happens to be Harvard, and the English Department. But both Miss Howe and her readers have insisted that this is merely coincidental, and that the same sort of self-centered behavior is to be found on other campuses and in other departments. It is a study of intellectuals, and my interest in it here is in the representative character of its ethical attitude towards them.

The central character of *We Happy Few* is Dorothea Natwick, accomplished daughter of a liberal New England family. In observing the Natwicks, Miss Howe has seen through the conventionalities of people who seek desperately to be unconventional. "To *épater* the bourgeois both of the faculty of St. Cuthbert's and the countryside around Constable was the crusade into which Mrs. Natwick was forever flinging herself, while from her tilted lance fluttered the pennant of the good, the true, the beautiful, and the 'interesting.' And the greatest of these was the 'interesting.'" When Mr. Natwick dies, Mrs. Natwick holds a service in her barn: "Isn't it too good to be true?" she announces gaily to Dorothea, "I've got the Gordon String Quartet to say they'll play. I thought the Mozart Clarinet Quintet would be just right. . . . Then there's a chapter from Fabre's *Life of the Fly* which your father was particularly fond of. . . ."

The picture of the Harvard faculty into which Dorothea

"The Ethics of We Happy Few" was first published in the University Observer, *Vol. 1, 1947.*

1. Helen Howe, *We Happy Few*, Simon & Schuster (1946).

marries is drawn in the same spirit. Everything is "interesting"; nothing is serious—nothing, that is, except the bitter rivalries for prestige and place. There is a terrible striving always to be *avant-garde:* to "discover" Henry James, T. S. Eliot, Melville or the more obscure modern English poets. There is a standing rule for admission to the happy few, who call themselves "The Little Group": *never to be taken in* by any person, idea or emotion.

So far, very good. Miss Howe has had the nerve to tackle not the easy targets of the Babbitts or the Hucksters, the Sammy Glicks, et al., but people who are far above the average, even among intellectuals and academes, in intelligence, sensitivity, and breadth of view. She has not been taken in by the self-deceptions of the elite of culture. She has their number with the wit of a Helen Hokinson, but with a mordancy of her own.

The main sin of The Little Group is pride, meaning self-centeredness. Dorothea symbolizes arrogant unconcern for ordinary people, ordinary emotions and ordinary events. The war news annoys her. She finds Basic English more interesting than the RAF. Miss Howe's criticism of these "selfish" attitudes and preoccupations becomes clearer by contrast with the brave, unselfish males in Dorothea's life. The males—Dorothea's suitor, husband, son, and father—are completely uninterested in themselves. The suitor is a gauche Idaho crusader who becomes a fighting liberal Senator. Uncultivated and inhospitable to the play of ideas, he is out of sorts in the Natwick atmosphere. He is a sterling democrat from the great open spaces. He gets things done. He finally rejects Dorothea because she is too snobbish, frivolous, and unworthy. The husband, John, is immersed in the study of seventeenth-century England as Dorothea's father had also been immersed in his teaching, his research, and his hobbies. John, despite Dorothea's pushing, refuses to angle for the mastership of "Bromfield House," one of the swank Harvard Houses. When war comes he enlists in the British Navy, quietly, without fuss or feathers. When Dorothea consoles herself with a lover, he is not jealous, but only concerned lest Dorothea be wounded. He dies at sea. Their son, Johnny, is exempt from service as a medical school student and is fascinated by his work. But he, too, is unselfish. Again quietly, without fuss or feathers, he seeks to enlist and finally gets Dorothea's permission to do so. Even Dorothea's lover, a wonderfully sketched portrait of the slick success-boy who makes women and money for the love of making, comes off at least no worse than The Little Group. Since he is uncomplicated and unintellectual his selfishness is undisguised. He debunks the academic airs, and is billed as a more intrepid and successful lover than any Harvard professor could possibly be. Except for him, then, the men close to Dorothea and thus contrasted with her and The Little Group, are models of unselfishness, devoted to their work, their cause, or both. They are not always looking out for number one.

THE ETHICS OF INDIVIDUALITY

If we look at The Little Group and Dorothea, we must grant the charge of selfishness. But we must grant it from a quite different critical position, namely in terms of Erich Fromm's distinction between selfishness and self-love.[2] Fromm points out that a "selfish" person has no real self, and no fondness for the self; therefore, he must continuously seek security in terms of conquests and power to compensate for his lack of "self-love." In other words, the selfish person is not interested in himself, but only in others' evaluation of himself. He shines in their reflected light—he is their satellite, even when he dominates them. On the other hand, the self-loving person is confident of his own self-evaluation. He does not need others for psychic security, but is capable of loving them as he loves himself. He has an erotic attitude towards the world, not a greedy one. Dorothea and all The Little Group were selfish and lacking in self-love as thus defined. Dorothea depended on the Group for admiration, and won it; the Group basked in its conviction of superiority over the less esoteric and ad-

2. See "Selfishness and Self-Love," *Psychiatry*, 2:507–523, 1939. I am also indebted to his *Man For Himself*.

vanced. Lacking any conviction of their individuality, they needed constantly to appear "original" and "interesting"; the war on banality was a major problem. Lacking ambition for personal quality and distinction, their aims were necessarily petty. Their fault was not an excess of pride but a deficiency of it.

"Moralists are constantly complaining," De Tocqueville observed in 1834, "that the ruling vice of the present time is pride. This is true in one sense, for indeed everybody thinks that he is better than his neighbor or refuses to obey his superior; but it is extremely false in another, for the same man who cannot endure subordination or equality has so contemptible an opinion of himself that he thinks he is born only to indulge in vulgar pleasures. He willingly takes up with low desires without daring to embark on lofty enterprises, of which he scarcely dreams.

"Thus, far from thinking that humility ought to be preached to our contemporaries, I would have endeavors made to give them a more enlarged idea of themselves and of their kind. Humility is unwholesome to them; what they want most is, in my opinion, pride."[3]

Pride in De Tocqueville's sense, like self-love as Fromm uses the term, is an essential ingredient of true individuality, which is based on an awareness of, and liking for, one's self in its particularity and uniqueness. The individuality of the members of The Little Group was factitious—a put-up job with differentness cultivated for its ability to create status. The Little Group is liberal-minded, but its method of achieving individuality resembles that of the reactionary Uncle Jules, in Sartre's "Portrait of the Anti-Semite," whose one claim to fame was that he could not stand the English. Thus true individuality goes together with pride, while a want of individuality frequently appears in our culture as selfishness.

3. *Democracy in America* (Phillips Bradley ed., 1945), Vol. II, p. 248.

THE ETHICS OF COLLECTIVISM

A selfish person, then, if he is to change, needs to cultivate above all else a feeling of pride, and an understanding fondness for his own individuality. As is evident, Miss Howe's therapy for Dorothea's selfishness is just the opposite. Dorothea finds in suffering and humility the cure for her Little-Groupish pride, and in the collective activities made available by the war the cure for her Little-Groupish individualism. With the war, Dorothea suffers a series of losses and defeats: husband, lover, son, and maid abandon her in one way or another; Bromfield House and Basic English also fall away. Then she is put through a number of "experiences" which bring her close, physically at least, to the troubles and pains of ordinary folk. Becoming a nurse's aid, she meets other nurse's aids socially; they are fine and dull. Traveling to Coeur d'Alene to be near her son in training, she "sees" America: in the stench of the ladies' room, the sadness of platform partings, the good-heartedness of Middle-Westerners. The townsfolk of Coeur d'Alene are another "experience"; they, too, are fine and dull. At the end, Dorothea returns to Cambridge a sadder and wiser woman: her pride is gone, and she has learned humbly to admire the great open spaces and the open sentiments usually associated with them in song and story.

Suffering and physical discomfort, however, do not always succeed in submerging one's individuality, though they are among the most useful weapons. Nor are feelings of identification with others, whether in Coeur d'Alene or elsewhere, adequate; such feelings are quite consistent with a strong feeling of individuality and personal value. So Dorothea, following the penances set out for her by Miss Howe, must further submerge her own self by the device of self-belittlement: in order to build up the common man, she must learn to run herself down. This lesson of submersion begins, rather mildly, when Dorothea discusses with her mother, Mrs. Natwick, the "original" arrangement for burying Mr. Natwick at the cheery barn funeral already described.

"Even Dorothea," Miss Howe writes, "found herself wondering if it might not have been 'simpler' to accept the common lot, and to take death with all the other trappings and the suits of woe decreed by the organized morticians, along with millions of other anonymous human beings who had never hoped to assert an individuality in life and certainly would not have the temerity to storm the ramparts of eternity on their own momentum." Is there any greater virtue in bowing to the pressure of the organized morticians than in bowing to the private need to be "original"? At least the Natwick style of life was an attempt at individuality, even if it failed as too external a "creation."

Dorothea has absorbed this anti-Natwick lesson of acceptance by the time her own husband dies. At the service "the beautiful words of the Burial of the Dead engulfed her. It was comforting to lose oneself in their blanketing anonymity. *The burden of being one's own arbiter of taste and feeling had been removed.* John was not narrowed into a gifted young man, with nice tastes and a knowledge of the seventeenth century. He had become enlarged, enfolded. He was simply one more 'man that is born of woman who hath but a short time to live.' . . . One must go with it, accept it, believe that some transubstantiation was wrought, beyond our power to understand."[4] Where have we heard before of loss of oneself in blanketing anonymity? Of the burden of taste and choice? Of one's duty to accept what one neither likes nor understands? Is not that the essence of the denigration of the individual in the reactionary ideology—none the less so because here put in the context of John's anti-fascism?

Dorothea continues learning the lesson of self-belittlement. After John's death, her lover deserts her. Dorothea is overwhelmed with shame for having slept with him, for having given way to her desires. "She had been dethroned by her own flesh." As a result, she feels she has no right to condemn Japanese atrocities; she had finally "made up (her) mind that (she) was not one bit better than the meanest of earth." She says to herself caustically: "What

4. Italics mine—D. R.

insufferable hypocrisy and arrogance that she should dare to hand out moral judgments. . . ."

Having been dethroned by the flesh, Dorothea must mortify it; hating illness and filth, she is taunted into becoming a nurse's aid by a fellow-traveling and wholesome member of The Little Group who has already joined. "Don't tell me the lady has an idea she's somebody!" is the friend's irrefutable comeback to Dorothea's protest that the work would not make use of her special gifts. Dorothea's education continues; she learns that: "What makes a good nurse is simply the power to forget yourself—completely." Staggering through the agonizing days at the hospital, she learns in her few off hours to enjoy Schumann as well as her beloved Bach and Mozart: "Her aesthetic as well as her human taste was stretching, too—cruder, possibly, but warmer and more inclusive." In other words, whatever makes for individualization and idiosyncracy in taste requires "stretching"; in compensation for this, she makes herself believe that "quintessential beauty is to be found at the very heart of human pain." How convenient! *Ad astra per aspera.*

The pain, submission, and self-belittlement which put an end to Dorothea's efforts to achieve individuality are symbolized by her change of attitude towards Harvard. No longer is it a subject for jokes, or for Natwick insouciance. Listening to Churchill's speech at Harvard in September 1943, she glows with thoughts of sacrifice: "Here, in this dark, mellow, sanctified hall was the distilled essence of values worth dying for." The institution, too, is sanctified: Dorothea concludes that "Harvard College—like any community of men dedicated to a goal higher than themselves—was greater than the sum of its parts."

At the end, in a touching scene, Dorothea shows that she is "cured," she has learned her lesson well. She is taking leave of her son Johnny at Coeur d'Alene; he is about to be shipped out. He is a gifted, sensitive lad, just eighteen. He is also Dorothea's one remaining human tie with life, and she is genuinely devoted to him. But now she sees him, "for the first time, as only part of the general whole—no longer anything special or remarkable or favored—just one more American gob." Again, how convenient! These are precisely the sentiments of passivity and resignation which make it possible for the underlying population to take the miseries of war with a minimum of fuss and feathers. But why should people not weep, protest? Why should they so easily be reconciled?

Dorothea's soul is "saved" by the most humble and uncritical surrender. Her surrender must be humble, in Miss Howe's ethics, because her claims at the beginning of her career were regarded as so proud. It is the very American morality of the higher they come the harder they fall.

THE ETHICS OF AFFIRMATION

Are "Little Groups" of intellectuals, then, more proud than most people, or more selfish? As Miss Howe is aware, frantic concern about status is to be found in almost all groups, little and big. The notion that sensitive and educated people are more conceited or more vicious than the average is a romantic fiction; and, like romantic fictions generally, serves a social function. That function is to justify attack on a weak and powerless minority: the intellectuals. They are, Miss Howe says, detached from America. But what does this mean, except to say that they are weak; otherwise, one might claim that America is detached from them, and that is too bad for America.

I do not, of course, intend to deny that the intellectual, like everyone else, faces a staggering problem of relating himself genuinely to other people and other problems than his own. How can he give up selfishness for self-love, in a culture which practices selfishness and preaches self-abasement? How can he maintain a feeling of belonging in the world, of having just claims on life, if the world ignores or rejects him? Miss Howe lets us and herself down into the one easy answer which we know to be false. That is also the judgment of Diana Trilling, whose brief, brilliant review of *We Happy Few* stimulated my own attempt at a more extensive analysis. "Miss Howe is scarcely alone among current novelists," Mrs. Trilling writes, "in regarding democracy—or the proletariat, or the fight against fascism, or a sweeping view of the multitudinousness of American life—as if it were a medicine especially prepared to cure the sick soul of the modern individual. One recalls, as an extreme instance, the novel of a few years ago in which a young woman was cured of neurosis by giving visas to refugees; or the more recent example in which the heroine was saved from nervous collapse by joining the movement for cooperatives. As a matter of fact, asked to name, on the evidence of the novels I read, the one dominant trend of our progressive literary culture, I would probably specify this mechanical notion that the individual finds himself by losing himself in some larger social manifestation."[5]

In fact, we can observe the same trend in writers of such different backgrounds from Miss Howe, of such tremendous power, and of such exceptional awareness of the issues, as Koestler and Silone. In *Arrival and Departure*, Koestler is frightened by his own mocking of contemporary liberal and democratic values, mocking which he puts into the mouths of Bernard the fascist and the woman psychoanalyst. He is unwilling to face his fear, and to take the responsibility for his mockery, for if he dealt with them in their own terms he might be defeated. His answer? A symbolic plunge into "affirmation." Peter, the hero, is parachuted into enemy territory, a dangerous war exploit; by his act, he seems to reject the mockery, which nevertheless remains verbally persuasive and unanswered. He drowns the self-doubts with which the analyst has filled him in violent, unreflective anti-fascism.

Silone's recent play *And He Hid Himself* is a good deal more ambivalent in its conclusions; yet it contains a similar lesson. Murica, a revolutionary student who has been living beyond his psychological means, under pressure betrays his comrades to the Fascist police. No one knew; no one would know; he is safe. But he finds it intolerable to be alone in the sense of being detached from the revolutionary movement, and also in the sense of having no one to submit to. He is tormented by remorse and confesses, first to his girl, then to Don Benedetto, a sympathetic cleric, and finally

5. *The Nation*, 163:50, 51, 1946.

to Pietro Spina, the socialist leader who has disguised himself as a priest. By these confessions he risks his life, for he knows the law of the underground: traitors are assassinated. However, Spina forgives him, permitting him to rejoin the movement; Murica remains unpunished until, at the end of the play, he is captured and tortured to death by the authorities. He dies without betrayal but instead with psychological solvency. Silone treats this final act of heroism as redeeming not only Murica but also the peasants whose revolutionary ardor and hope it stimulates after they had become cynical and apathetic.

The play throughout is framed in Christian imagery. The priestly robes in which Spina hides himself are more than make-up for a getaway: they represent an effort to combine Socialist and Catholic traditions. And though the allegory is not, for me, quite clear, it seems that Murica's sacrificial return to the illegal movement symbolically resembles that of Christ, who also took upon himself the guilt of the suffering poor. Thus, while Silone has wonderful things to say about the virtue of pride, he nevertheless is also, with part of himself, on the side of those who believe that man is redeemed from weakness and neurosis by "taking punishment" and by joining, through submission, the hierarchies of Church and Party.

THE NERVE OF FAILURE

None of these authors means to be popular. They do not intend to join the chorus, and they are certainly unaware of doing so. They believe themselves to be daring and heretical. What, then, is going on in them? Sidney Hook has referred to the contemporary "failure of nerve" among intellectuals.[6] The concept is significant and correct, but it is only part of the story. It assumes that, if there were no failure of nerve, the intellectuals might win battles, might save themselves from defeat, from the rout of democratic and liberal values. But such defeat, for the time being, seems inexorable. Hence, the other part of the story is the

6. *Partisan Review*, 10, 1943.

courage to accept the possibility of defeat, of failure, without being morally crushed. This courage I would call the "nerve of failure." The "failure of nerve" concept looks at the problem primarily from outside; it assumes there is no failure but that of nerve. The "nerve of failure" concept looks at the problem primarily from the inside; it assumes there is no nerve but that of failure. Plainly, little nerve is required on the winning side: nerve has no meaning except when we must face the possibility, today the probability, of failure.

What is feared as failure in American society is, above all, aloneness. And aloneness is terrifying because it means that there is no one, no group, no approved cause to submit to. Even success—the seeming opposite of failure—often becomes impossible to bear when it is not socially approved or even known. This is perhaps why successful criminals often feel the need to confess, that is, to submit to the community's judgment, represented in the person to whom the confession is made. They will confess, as Murica did, even under circumstances where this will probably, if not certainly, endanger their previous success: proof, I think, that aloneness is more intolerable than mere failure. For mere failure, provided it is found in company, can rather easily be borne; many ideologies have the function of making it possible for people to digest the worst miseries and even death. Under the sway of the ideology, they do not feel the impact of their failure; they are in the grip of an authority, even if it lets them down. On the other hand, one who is alone lacks this solace which can make even failure comfortable.

Of course, this problem of aloneness existed before democracy and before fascism. It is part of the problem of man's relation to the world and to other men which intellectuals today face with such specialized acuteness. The "nerve of failure" is needed to face the fact that the problem remains unsolved, and the possibility that it is insoluble. Thus we may experience defeat in our personal life-goals as well as in our social aims. Franz Kafka expressed these problems in his writing. He had the "nerve of failure"; he faced failure without illusion and without affirmation.

THE USES OF GUILT

Kafka was virtually alone. Most writers—writers of the sort we have been discussing—lose their nerve of failure by allowing themselves to succumb to feelings of guilt. Such feelings are accompanied by the need to submit to others and to affirm others' affirmations. An intellectual today, simply by virtue of being an intellectual, has perhaps a harder time than most people to escape such feelings of guilt. He is weak; he is despised; he has no assured social role and status; he is out of step. In a culture which values strength and power, the weak and powerless are easily made to feel that there is something wrong with them. What is taken to be wrong, of course, are all their individual defects which they share with other men. But beyond that material which is always available, the intellectual can focus on those very elements which differentiate him from the majority. Do I prefer Bach to Schumann? Do I prefer sensitive and cultivated people to squally brats on trains? Do I fail to thrill to mass ceremonials in Sanders Theatre? Then I must be guilty; I am impious. But this is only the beginning. What is really differentiating and most valuable in the intellectual is his gift of sharply and critically seeing through many conventional values, "democratic" as well as fascist, "wholesome" as well as treacherous. Since he cannot help, given his originality, having a critical attitude toward the dominant culture, he either represses those insights which detach him from that culture, or mixes them, as we have just now seen, with penances of "affirmation." What kind of authority has laid down the rule that it is wrong to be critical or negative if one cannot also be constructive? It is the same kind which favors the yes-man and yes-woman in business, politics, and domesticity. It is the same kind which, long ago, alleviated and manipulated guilt by inventing the confessional and coupling it with a system of penances.

In the conventional judgment, confession is regarded with approbation; it is good for the soul. We are invited so to regard it, although with qualifications, in Silone's play.

Yet confession is often more immoral than the original act which is confessed, because it means that the person is unwilling to bear the responsibility for his actions; by confession they become no longer *his,* but are shared. Penance serves to destroy the last vestige of aloneness. Had Murica, for instance, been a moral person, able to stand alone, he would have felt neither remorse nor the need to confess; he would have recognized his betrayal as *his,* not to be shifted, not to be wiped out in the bookkeeping of the heavenly authorities. He would have decided what he was, and wanted to become, on the basis of his potentialities for the future, rather than on the basis of the judgment of his past made by outsiders.

Of course, the intellectuals and the novelists who represent them and speak for them are not Muricas; they are not dissembling traitors. Yet they, or the characters with whom they identify, go in heavily for self-accusation. Dorothea becomes expert at accusing herself. Koestler luxuriates in the guilty self-doubts which assail Peter, through the words of Bernard and the psychoanalyst. Silone's *mea culpa* is more complicated and more ambiguous; it deserves greater respect. Yet it has led him from the wonderful irreverence and humor of *The School for Dictators* (1938) and the early novels to the sticky piety of some parts of *And He Hid Himself* (1945).

It is, I think, guilt which lies behind this sticky piety which is, in turn, the trade-mark of all these writers' "affirmations." Consequently, while talent and passion enliven their satire and criticism, their affirmations turn out to be "negative" and "unconstructive." *And He Hid Himself* ends lamely with the once-disillusioned and apathetic peasants uniting for new revolutionary action, although nothing in their character makes this turnabout convincing. Koestler concludes *Arrival and Departure* with a Hollywood trumped-up ending, also disguised as anti-fascist heroism. Such an ending shows a lack of respect for the previous seriousness of the book. In Miss Howe's book the ironic contradiction is even more striking, because so much of the book is devoted to Dorothea's discovery of American democracy, common or garden style. As Mrs. Trilling observes: "It is the lesson of democracy that finally cuts Dorothea down to size. The only flaw is that, with her, democracy itself also gets cut down to size—Miss Howe's firmest intentions to the contrary notwithstanding. *We Happy Few* ends with the wide American panorama presenting itself as little more than a series of small-spirited, harassed, and unhappy people who in their uneducated fashion are just as egotistical as the well-educated Dorothea. The commonalty of man, therapy for a poorly balanced emotional nature, shows itself to be largely a matter of helping make sandwiches with the other ladies or holding a neighbor's crying child. . . . It is as if the eye and ear that can catch the subtle nuances of the first section of *We Happy Few* cannot but go on to betray Miss Howe's formulation of conscience. While Miss Howe's program calls for Dorothea's regeneration through contemplation of some vast body of corporate virtue called the United States of Democracy, her literary senses feel out all the petty snobberies and prides that are bound to inform a nation of human beings. . . . Because draughts of solemnity taste so bad, we deceive ourselves that they are our eye openers instead of our newest opiates."

To answer serious questions with trivial "solutions" is deceptive. For it puts the weight of the writer's earnestness, ethical conviction, and insight into the business of telling the reader that *his* doubts, too, are "negative" and bad. The reader is only too ready to believe this, and to indulge in his own orgy of identification with the pride of a Dorothea and the fall that follows. He, too, convinces himself that he is guilty, and thus rationalizes climbing on the bandwagon and stifling his critical uniqueness. There results a failure to develop his potentialities and, in Fromm's terms, an "escape from freedom." Readers, like writers, need support of their "nerve of failure" not anaesthesia. The ethical convictions that they lack are the belief in their own values, and the belief that only in their differences from others will they find their identity with them.

I trust no one will misunderstand me as saying that anti-fascist or pro-democratic activity is worthless or immoral. My point is that many people engage in such activity without ever deciding whether it has real meaning for them, and without the realistic judgment as to the practical possibilities which cannot be made in the absence of the nerve of failure. Instead, collective activity appears affirmative, sustains illusions, assuages doubt, and finds guilt useful; these are some of its attractions for powerless and isolated intellectuals.

THE ETHICS OF EXPERIENCE

There is, however, another side to this powerlessness and isolation. The intellectual believes that he wishes to submerge his pride—i.e. his independence—in the fate of common humanity. In Silone's play where Murica offers himself up to almost certain death; in Koestler's novel where Peter returns to the wars despite conduct which should make him feel entitled, if anyone ever did, to a passage to America and relative peace; in Miss Howe's book where Dorothea gives up her intellectual life and shares the hardships of a hospital, of wartime travel, of the camp-followers of servicemen, the motives appear noble. To a large extent they are. But there are other aspects of this type of behavior which are not noble at all. In many cases, the attempt to share wider human burdens and situations is a disguise for the greedy cult of experience, an anxious fear of missing those experiences which others have had or claim that they have had. Dorothea doesn't want to let any pitch of life go by. But the "experience" is not given raw by nature; we really experience only what we as individuals can interpret and assimilate as our own. In the phoniness of "sharing" common experiences, there is masochism of two sorts, one obvious, one indirect. The obvious masochism is that the experience is usually painful and humiliating, as in Dorothea's case. (In an earlier generation of novelists who were less religious and less ideological, the experience was generally supposed to be pleasureful, e.g., sleeping around or getting drunk.) The more concealed masochism lies in submission to the experiences everyone is supposed to have. It is really easier to do this than to experience one's course of life directly, let us say as an intellectual; for this latter requires an individuality of interpretation: the interpretation is not given by the culture. Dorothea does not ask herself what she, as a unique person, can uniquely experience in the very process of living; rather she welcomes being overwhelmed by what might be called the collective experience. "The burden of being one's own arbiter of taste and feeling had been removed." Her son loses his poignant closeness to her to become "just one more American gob." . . .

THE ETHICAL ELITE

This submission to generally shared interpretations of experience is the most self-effacing form of the intellectual's response to his feelings of social weakness. Often, however, if not usually, his response disguises a strong desire for power and status. In joining the common man, the intellectual really wants to lead him; he feels called upon to save society. Apparent submission to the common lot and the common work—rather than the specialized work called for by his gifts—conceals delusions of grandeur. The intellectual is not willing to accept himself as he really is, with his unusual assets and their compensatory drawbacks, but he must be an "operator"; he must be "versatile"; he must be "practical." Coupled, therefore, with the masochism of pain and of rejection of the person's own talents and values, there is an even more concealed desire for domination, in which great claims are covertly staked out for leadership in the day-to-day social scene. Such a person privately feels that he has his finger in the dike against fascism, or whatever other evils threaten, and that if this finger were removed, but only then, the flood would overwhelm us. (Of course, situations can arise where this fantasy will be true; but where there is no "nerve of failure," judgments of social need and personal capacity cannot be realistic.) Thus the intellectual who professes to engage in the activities of ordinary folk only partially wants to lose his individuality in the collective whole; since he believes with Dorothea that the whole is greater than the sum of its parts, he wants the difference for himself. That is, he makes the secret stipulation that he is not really lost but will become one of the elite.

The form this stipulation takes in *We Happy Few* is subdued. Miss Howe demands of Dorothea, of her class, and perhaps of her sex, that they suffer more pain, become more unselfish, more humble, and in general lay claim to higher, more altruistic standards of behavior. Dorothea is harder on herself for sleeping with Gordon than she is on Gordon, or than she probably would be with one of the girls in Coeur d'Alene. This in itself may conceal pride—the arrogance of the member of the elite who must be a hero, or at the very least, an "example." Dorothea begins her mature life by rejecting marriage with the Idaho crusader. In this rejection there are some elements of snobbery: she laughs at his crudity and lack of sophistication. In her later encounter with him she feels herself inferior to him—this time he has rejected her. He is so much nobler and finer; his lack of aesthetic sensitivity, his simple moralistic sureness, become assets in her eyes. Dorothea, it is plain, has learned to value his differentness from her, but also to undervalue her differentness from him. If she does not belong among the happy few, he surely must. Our culture lives by these judgments of superiority and subordination, and differences among races, classes, and individual personalities are largely made use of to place oneself and others in the social hierarchy. In feeling unworthy, just as in feeling superior, Dorothea practices not the ethics of democratic equality but those of the collectivist discrimination between elite and mass.

This feeling of unworthiness, this need to rank herself, brings us back to the role of the romantic myth mentioned earlier: that intellectuals, that is, the self-conscious people, are more vicious than ordinary folk. Others are of course glad to hear this, for it means that demands are not to be made on them, but on the intellectuals who had the nerve to challenge them. And their envy is assuaged by learning that intellectuals are not only immoral but unhappy. More generally, this teaching means that people who are aware of the problem of choice are morally inferior to those whose choices are largely made for them by the culture. If this is so, a rational individualistic ethics becomes impossible. For where is new moral insight to come from, if not from the self-conscious few, from the morally perceptive Helen Howes and Koestlers and Silones? It is not likely to come from the "shared values" of some collective enterprise.

THE ETHICS OF SACRIFICE

Catholicism is older than the answers of the Koestlers and the Howes, and it is illuminating to compare the attitude of Miss Howe towards Dorothea with the virtually identical attitude of the Catholic nuns towards the heroine, Nanda, of Antonia White's novel *Frost in May*. This is a very moving story, plainly autobiographical, of a young girl growing up in a convent school. At the school, one finds precisely the same feeling as in *We Happy Few* that pride, in the form of self-love, is the most intolerable sin. When one of the schoolgirls really enjoys her excellent performance as Beatrice in *The Inferno,* she is removed from the role, lest she become vain. And Nanda is told by a nun: "It is a hundred times better to knit a pair of socks humbly for the glory of God than to write the finest poem or symphony for mere self-glorification."

Nanda is warned not to choose her friends "for such superficial attributes as cleverness and humour, and even for the still more unworthy and frivolous reasons of mere 'good looks' and a social position . . ." but instead for "solid piety" and a lower social status.

Beauty is, in fact, a great temptation: "A saint said it was dangerous to walk through a beautiful wood." For it means that things, and people, are looked at for their own sakes rather than as manifestations of collective purposes, in this case called God. When thirteen-year-old Nanda begins to write an adolescent novel, she is brutally expelled, and the head nun explains: "God asks very hard things from us, the sacrifice of what we love best and the sacrifice of our own wills. That is what it means to be a Christian. For years I have been watching you, Nanda. I have seen you growing up, intelligent, warmhearted, apparently everything a child should be. But I have watched something else growing in you too—a hard little core of self-will and self-love. I told you once before that every will must be broken completely and re-set before it can be at one with God's will. And there is no other way. That is what true education, as we understand it here at Lippington, means." In return for this sacrifice of self, the convent offered collective security. If one did penance for one's own individuality, one was deprived of "the burden of being one's own arbiter," and permitted to feel at one with God.

The nuns were especially severe with Nanda for two reasons: she was remarkably sensitive and gifted, and she was not of an old wealthy Catholic family. It is always the individually gifted and socially weak who are the first to be asked to give themselves up. The same point might even be put more strongly. It is a truism that certain qualities or behavior traits are differently valued, depending on the social position of their possessor. What is offensive arrogance in an underling is charming insouciance in a lord. What is squirming subservience in the lower middle class is lovable modesty in the upper. At Miss Howe's hands, Dorothea's pride comes off more shabbily than that of Mrs. Calcott, the "true" aristocrat into whose family Dorothea climbs by matrimony. Likewise, the galling pride and independence of the intellectual is impressive in a "temperamental" movie star or ball player. Conversely, Nanda had, from the nuns' viewpoint, too many stubborn intellectual gifts for her sex and station.

Nanda escapes the nuns, very probably because she was ejected for rebellion, which was scarcely conscious and not at all planned. And it is generally not too difficult to escape the nuns, for their Puritanism—the especially virulent Puritanism of the Counter-Reformation—is other-worldly and is out of fashion. But, as Max Weber pointed out, the western world has closed the monasteries and turned earth itself into a nunnery. It is very much harder to resist the diluted but pervasive Puritanism of sacrifice and subservience which takes modern and "progressive" forms. It is harder for Dorothea to resist the "education" given her by what her society calls "life"—as in the phrases "that's life," "that's how things are"—than for Nanda to resist the "education" of antiquated Lippington.

Intellectuals today do have a hard time resisting their education, resisting attack. They need to be defended not attacked, if they are to succor their "nerve of failure." Miss Howe, a member of the class, attacks the "Happy Few" for their selfishness and pride. As we have seen, the intellectuals turn against themselves because they are few, and because they are not happy enough; that is, they have not enough love for themselves, or pride in what they are. "We ought to have our own class-consciousness," William James declared in his 1907 speech *The Social Value of the College Bred.*[7] "'*Les Intellectuels!*' What prouder clubname could there be than this one, used ironically by the party of 'red-blood,' the party of every stupid prejudice and passion, during the anti-Dreyfus craze, to satirize the men in France who still retained some critical sense and judgment!"

7. *Memories and Studies* (1911) p. 323, quoted in Ralph Barton Perry, *The Thought and Character of William James* (1936) vol. 2, p. 299.

A Philosophy for "Minority" Living

The "nerve of failure" is the courage to face aloneness and the possibility of defeat in one's personal life or one's work without being morally destroyed. It is, in a larger sense, simply the nerve to be oneself when that self is not approved of by the dominant ethic of a society.

In America, "success" is central; we are provided with a catalogue of what is success and what is failure, and nothing matters except achieving the first and avoiding the second. Whoever accepts the prevailing social standards of our times is not alone, not morally isolated; even if he is a "failure" he remains related, if only in fantasy, to the dominant theme. Such a person has no more need of the "nerve of failure" than a gambler who has had a bad day at roulette: for him life is centered on the wheel, and he remains related, though anxious and miserable, so long as he can go on watching the others who are still in the game. The "nerve of failure" is needed only for really heretical conduct: when one renounces even the company of misery and takes the greater risk of isolation—that is, the risk of never rejoining the company.

The "nerve of failure" is akin to the traditional virtue of "courage in defeat," praised in a number of ethical systems. But it differs in this sense: it comes into play before defeat is actual, when it is only a possibility. To be sure, one may have a good deal of the "nerve to fail" and still be cowardly in extreme situations. But, on the other hand, while many can find courage in defeat only when others are defeated too, those endowed with the "nerve of failure" have the capacity to go it alone.

"A Philosophy for 'Minority' Living" was first published in Commentary, *Vol. 6, No. 5, 1948.*

A man may maintain a lonely course by other means. He may not realize that he is heretical—Rousseau, the "primitive" painter, seems to have thought he was painting just like everybody else. He may be more or less crazy, constructing an elaborate system to justify himself—as did Fourier and Comte. He may attach himself to nature and to imagined transcendental forces—as did William Blake. He may overestimate his personal influence and the extent to which others are listening to what seems to him self-evident and reasonable—as did Robert Owen, the English manufacturer and utopian socialist, whose later life was on the surface one long series of failures. He may convince himself that history, or science, is inevitably on his side—as did Karl Marx. He may protect himself from aloneness by remaining conventional in many spheres—as Darwin did. He may surround himself with a small body of ardent disciples and limit his contact with contemporaries—this also was Comte's way. Only very rarely will an individual with enough originality to disturb society be able, without such adventitious aids, to face his situation realistically and yet be unshaken by what the majority considers "failure."

These moral attitudes in the face of frustration and defeat become even more complicated, enormously more so, in the life of groups lacking material power, whether domestic "minorities" or small nations. Negroes, Jews, intellectuals, and women as domestic "minorities"; Poles, Irishmen, Italians as small nations coping with big powers—all feel the need of protecting themselves in one way or another from the moral impact of power. In different historical periods they develop different means and modes of coping with this problem. If I discuss the fate and problems of the Jews here, it is because, despite all differences, they still provide one of the most suggestive paradigms of the relatively powerless group.

I. For the last two thousand years the Jews have been a minority; before that, it may be suggested, they were a "small power," a buffer state.[1] But until recent times, many

1. I am indebted to Dr. Erich Fromm for calling my attention to the relations between Jewish power and ethics

Jews did not have what we might today regard as a typical minority outlook. Their ethical regime was quite defiantly Ptolemaic, revolving about the small group of Jews, not the larger Gentile group—and, accordingly, they learned to remain unimpressed by Gentile temporal power. Being unimpressed did not mean being unafraid—material power might beat or starve one to death; it did mean refusing to surrender moral hegemony to the majority merely because it had power. Instead, the Jews saw through power by observing its blindness in comparison with the vision possible to the weak. A saying of Nahman of Bratzlav exemplifies this outlook: "Victory cannot tolerate truth, and if that which is true is spread before your very eyes, you will reject it, because you are a victor. Whoever would have truth itself, must drive hence the spirit of victory; only then may he prepare to behold the truth."

In other words, since the Jews' ethical scheme placed no great premium on material power, on material success, the majority was not looked up to with envy and admiration; hence its verdicts, both as to the ends of life and as to the value of the minority itself, did not echo in the Jews' self-consciousness.

A related attitude was expressed in the belief—which kept the Jews Jews and not Christians—that the Messiah was still to come. To be sure, many Jews during the dark periods between the eleventh and seventeenth centuries were deceived at times into believing that the Messiah had indeed come. But these aberrations were limited in scope and time: Jews in general continued to have faith in the continuance into the future of the process of revelation and to be unimpressed by contemporary events and the would-be Messiahs who, consciously or unconsciously, exploited these events. If we do not take this belief, that the Messiah will yet come, too literally, we can see that one of its meanings is an attack on the powers that be, and an emphatic statement that justice and peace shall some day

in their historical changes. The reader will recognize, of course, how difficult it is to generalize about Jewish ethics, as about anything else concerning "Jews"—or indeed any group.

—as they do not today—prevail everywhere among men.[2]

Jewish ethics, though not devoid of authoritarian strains, is, like Greek ethics, based primarily on reason, although reason has sometimes descended to casuistry. It is an ethics of reason both in its ends, which are human and earthly, and in its means, which are argumentative rather than dogmatic. Even the casuistry seems often to have been turned to the humanizing of authoritative texts, as a lawyer might "interpret" a statute or decision in order to reach a more humane and reasonable result.

Such an ethical pattern as the one just described would seem admirably fitted to the psychic situation of a powerless minority which—unlike, let us say, the Republican party during recent years—has no chance of soon becoming a majority. But, as we know, ethical systems are not developed in the abstract; though they have a momentum of their own, Jewish ethical patterns arose in connection with given social and economic conditions; and they were embroidered by complex, demanding rituals and racial myths.

Occasionally, the group's "nerve of failure" was supported by the notion that its very powerlessness proved the Jews to be in fact the Chosen of God. In this way, defeat itself could strengthen the faith of the "saving remnant" of Jews. On the other hand, we should recognize that the spiritual forces that gave the Jews their immense moral resistence in the ghetto rested on a material base that, though often precarious, had considerable solidity. The Jews were part of the medieval order, which gave them, like everyone else, a relatively fixed psychic place, even though theirs was that of pariah. (See Daniel Bell, "A Parable of Alienation," *Jewish Frontier,* November 1946.) Within the medieval order, moreover, the Jews developed a near monopoly of certain skills, in artisanship as well as in trade,

2. There are many Messianic, or as we should say, utopian elements in Christianity, of course; but the established institutionalized churches have always tended to play down these disturbing notions and to treat revelation as a completed or at least a centralized process. Dissenting sects have tended to restore the Messianic faith.

which were handed down, as in the guilds, from father to son.

Thus, the ghetto walls buttressed the Jewish ethical walls.

II. The rise of modern capitalist society and the levelling of ghetto walls may be said to have started an uneven dialectic of change in the spiritual and material bases of Jewish life. Many Jews in the main Western countries surrendered their inherited ethical system in return for a chance to participate in the wider world, thus losing their special sources of spiritual strength. Sometimes this was done out of opportunism; more often than not this drive was mixed with more idealistic motives. For among the forces that broke down ghetto barriers from the outside was the Enlightenment. Liberty, Equality, and Fraternity were a set of values with great moral appeal—as well as with many parallels in Jewish ethics.

The Enlightenment was impious towards authority, utopian about the future, and hospitable to reason. What then could have been more attractive to many of the most ethically sensitive Jews, especially at a time when the ghetto tradition itself seems to have become somewhat impoverished in Western Europe? Such Jews could move from a religious to a political minority position with hardly any change in ethical attitude.

The great Jewish intellectual and political leaders of this period represented, in highly individual ways, mergers of Jewish and Enlightenment ethics, and the retention of the "nerve of failure." At the same time, certain skills and attitudes nurtured by ghetto life became useful and rewarding assets in the modern world. In the expanding era of international finance and international markets, the developed financial and commercial skills of a Rothschild, as later of a Rosenwald, were important: some Jews, that is, had a head-start. Jewish cultivation of a particular type of intelligence, moreover, could be turned to account in modern managerial, professional, and intellectual capacities; while the Jewish view of an open future (the Messiah still to come) was well adapted to leaders of progressive political or labor movements. In sum, many Jews gained personal power and self-confidence during the free capitalism that lasted until the close of the nineteenth century.

In those days, Jewish self-contempt did not exist in its characteristic contemporary forms. While rising Jews often shared the attitudes common to parvenus, they had confidence in their ultimate social acceptance, or that of their progeny; consciously or unconsciously, they felt they had something of particular value to offer. Likewise, those Jews who took a direct share in the struggles of the Enlightenment felt no insecurity or self-belittlement as Jews; they could be wholeheartedly indignant at discrimination since they had confidence in the ultimate triumph of the ideals of the Enlightenment. They, too, felt that they had something to offer—namely, a social program that the majority needed and would learn to want.

During this period, therefore, the consequences of Jewish acceptance of a largely Gentile ethics were positive: both because that ethics was rational and progressive and because the role and material power of Jews were on the increase.

III. However, historical developments soon began to undermine the material position of the Jews and give a different meaning to their new ethical position. As heavy industry grew in importance, it gradually freed itself from the free market. Jewish family and group "trade secrets" soon became common property. "Fair trade" acts and similar autarchic limitations on the free market came to restrict Jewish merchandising talents (while permitting, however, the marginal survival of many small Jewish shopkeepers). Though Jews shared in the growing managerial and professional openings of the "new" middle class, they began to be faced with increasing competition.

This lessening of the Jew's sense of economic value, and of his self-confidence in the possession of a special skill, helped lessen his feeling of ethical security, and made him increasingly a psychological victim of the dominant social and economic systems of the modern world.

But this is also a fate that, both in its economic and its

psychological aspects, has overtaken vast numbers of the less "successful" classes in our new society, and condemned them to "alienation." For them, as for Jews, the relative security of a social role fixed by skill, family, age, and sex has vanished. One must now "show one's stuff" in a competitive market, and one's stuff is one's "personality," an externalized part of the self, and not primarily one's matter-of-fact skill. (See Erich Fromm, *Man For Himself*, pp. 67–82.) In other words, it is not the genuine self that is put on the market in the race for success, or even economic survival, but the "cosmetic" self, which is free of any aroma of personal, non-marketable idiosyncracy as it is free of "B.O." or last year's waistline. If this artificial self succeeds, then doubts may be temporarily quieted. However, since self-evaluation has been surrendered to the market, failure in the market, or even fear of failure, is translated into self-contempt. (The market in this sense includes all spheres of life—business, politics, art, love, friendship.)

For the dominant groups—those that, by birth or temperament or luck, have been able to make the grade—the subjection of all values to the test of the market is convenient. It justifies their own existence in what amounts to moral rather than merely power-political terms. In a market situation pervaded by what Karl Polanyi has termed the "market mentality" (*Commentary*, February 1947), control of the economy will carry with it, to an unusual degree, control of the ethical regime. And the market, we must remember, has had perhaps a more complete sway in America than elsewhere.

Now, add to this the fact that America happens to have colonials—Negroes and other ethnic minorities—within its borders, and that we have developed a racialism not to be found in Europe. Upon the Jewish minority, this situation operates with special force, as can be seen in the encounter between Jewish traditions and the melting pot.

The melting pot had, especially in its early days, valuable elements: a kind of Whitmanesque equalitarian vigor and a seeming hospitality to cultural diversity—but it increasingly became a form of internal imperialism in the interest of the earlier arrivals. Its aim was narrowed to producing "Americans all" of a starched uniformity, freed of all cultural coloring, maladjustment, or deviation. The main burden was on the minorities, while fewer demands were made by the ethical system upon the Protestant majority. (Protestantism and modern capitalism, having grown up together, have always been congenial.)

Even today, the typical Protestant businessman still makes money as a by-product of his devotion to his work and his organization; the money, as Max Weber pointed out, serves as a proof of fulfilment of ethical duty, of having found one's "calling," one's proper—and therefore prosperous—social niche. But there is no such compatibility between non-Protestant ethics and modern capitalism; hence the moral disorientation worked by the latter among Mexicans and South Americans generally, Eastern and Southern Europeans, and Treaty-Port Chinese. The same moral disorientation was produced among these people when they emigrated to America, affecting not only Jews from pre-capitalist Eastern Europe, but also Italians, Greeks, Mexicans. For these non-Protestants, business was not originally the expression of their religion, but a by-product of the need for money, status, or family security. For the dominant groups, the Protestant—or, more accurately, the Puritan—strain in our culture permitted a development of a kind of ethics intertwined with business. "Mere" money-making, for example, was open to criticism when not accompanied by an ethos of business as "calling" or as service. The non-Protestant, on the other hand, was often led, both by the special pressures of modern capitalism upon him and the strangeness of the Protestant market ethic to his own, to discard his own values without assimilating prevailing values. As a result he often became a caricature of the American careerist.

In this process, certain elements in Jewish ethics—the attitude towards power, towards the future, and towards reason—often tend to become distorted. The irreverent attitude towards power becomes contempt for what remains of the Puritan ethics of business and professional enterprise, which is interpreted as softness or hypocrisy. Irreverence towards authority degenerates into an indiscriminate disrespect for convention, whether that convention is an exploitative device or a crystallization of decent standards of personal intercourse. This Jewish irreverence may also appear as a cynicism that seeks money and power without the conviction that they represent the fruits of virtue or that they are genuinely important ends—or even the means to such ends.

Similarly, the Jewish attitude towards the future, with its Messianic devaluation of present reality, can be fitted, by distortion, all too nicely into the American success tradition, where—as the Lynds have remarked—people live "at" the future, eternally "on the make," either awaiting a lucky break for themselves, or planning for one for their offspring.

Finally, the Jewish attitude towards reason can also suffer a change. "Pure" reason for its own sake, what we might call Talmudic intelligence, is at a discount in America: it is not "practical." On the other hand, manipulative intelligence is exceedingly useful; in fact, the entire Jewish constellation of intelligence, humor, and charm is often humiliatingly exploited—for instance, by so many Jewish comedians—as entertainment and self-ingratiation.

Jews in America, like other Americans, go in for hero-worship; and it is possible to trace, in the types they frequently select for admiration, patterns of compromise between the American Protestant tradition and their own. Though they can afford to admire the "impractical" Einstein because he has been such a world-famous success, they tend more to bestow their medals on intelligent operators like Brandeis and Baruch. Though these men have the ear of presidents, they are not mere "court Jews": they are quite outspoken; moreover, they are old and white-haired, appropriate to the Jewish reverence for aged wisdom—yet they are also energetic and eupeptic, in keeping with the American worship of dynamic youth.

It goes without saying that—like Jewish ethics—American Protestant ethics contains many divergent themes, and that the Enlightenment still lives in its best representatives. However, the Jew emerging from the European ghetto was not met at Ellis Island by the representatives of Enlightenment. At most, he was given a choice between accepting the melting pot and the ethics of success—as interpreted by earlier immigrants often bent on exploiting him economically or psychically—or trying to retain his traditions as a transient in a voluntary ghetto. If he took the latter course, he was seldom stimulated towards any effort to reinterpret the meaning of his ethical background in terms of the American context; rather he tended to freeze defensively in his memories and rituals. If he took the former—perhaps more typical—course, he altered his ethical and intellectual inheritance so that it could be turned to account in the struggle for success, just as a neurotic makes use of his illness, or a cripple his misery, for fragmentary advantages.

However, the same recent social and economic changes that have weakened the material position of Jews have also tended to alter the meaning of success as such. The mere matter-of-fact achievement of high economic or even political position no longer satisfies. Since we market our personalities, it is imperative that we be popular, accepted; and handicapped ethnic minorities are not popular. The Jew who plays the power and success game can hardly help viewing himself through the eyes of the more successful players.

Bernard Marx, a character in Aldous Huxley's *Brave New World,* despises himself because he is short. The majority, stunted lower-caste people, are also short, but he compares himself with the tall top-caste to which in other respects he "belongs," and to which, though with some ambivalence, he surrenders his ethical judgment. That is, he accepts from them the same cultural emphasis on height that sells Adler Elevator Shoes (the sexual reward being, as so often, a symbol for the reward of status). Since his society puts a high value on science, Bernard Marx's shortness is explained in seemingly rational terms by the rumor that some alcohol accidentally got into his feeding solution when he was a bottled embryo (alcohol being intentionally used only to stunt the lower castes). In any rational ethics, of course, there would be no correlation between height and human value. Yet Bernard does not quite dare look behind the "scientific" social judgment, and so must turn the blame upon himself. Among Jews, this relation between physical appearance and ethical valuation is seldom quite so obvious (there is more of this among Negroes, who tend to rate each other according to lightness of skin and other white characteristics); nevertheless, the Jewish devaluation of Jewish physiognomy is not confined to Hollywood, as the flourishing state of plastic surgery in Manhattan would testify.

IV. If a minority accepts the majority's definition of good looks, we would expect that the majority's definition of good conduct would be likewise accepted. And so it turns out. But is the Jew who sharply criticizes the behavior of his fellow-Jews accepting the majority's standards, or is he not simply exercising his human privilege—from which it would be anti-Semitic to exclude him—of disliking certain kinds of behavior? We cannot tell at first glance, though we may wonder why, amid all the evil in the world and all the examples of vicious and mean conduct, he fastens on the Jews. Moreover, even when the traits he selects for attention are not so obviously differentiated according to race—where, for instance, a Jew claims to despise Italian and Greek as well as Jewish manners—we may ask the same sort of question: why is he preoccupied with differences in manners and not, let us say, with differences in coldness and warmth, gloominess and wit? Has he not accepted the majority's judgments as to what is important and the majority's criteria of good and evil?[3]

However, the Jew whose focus of criticism is the poor behavior of his fellow-Jews may urge that, far from accepting the majority's standards, he feels merely threatened by them: he is worried by the menace of anti-Semitism if Jews do not conform, and is being "realistic." Here we may

3. I don't mean to enter here upon complicated questions of national character and to examine whether Jewish manners are characteristically undignified, or British behavior is really lacking in warmth; I am raising the problem rather of the way in which majority ethics gives rise to a process of stereotyping and selection in which certain traits are valued, others devalued, still others ignored.

ask why, among the many "causes" of anti-Semitism, he selects primarily those over which Jews themselves seem to have some control. Perhaps better manners on the subway would mitigate anti-Jewish feeling; perhaps if Jews did not appear in public at all—no Frankfurter on the Supreme Court, no Dubinsky in the labor movement—they would not be noticed. But in advocating such things, has this timorous Jew done anything more than accept the majority's anti-Semitic stereotype, as well as their rationalizations for refusing to accept Jews as individuals on their own merits? Is this Jew really concerned about the daily quality of direct personal contacts between Jews and non-Jews, which might, in the long run, have some marginal effect on anti-Semitism?

But ordinarily I think it can be shown that the threat such a Jew feels is that of being himself caught, in his own deeper consciousness, in the majority stereotype of "the Jew." This involves not only contempt for "the other Jews," but his own self-belittlement. The real cause of his concern with the behavior of his fellow Jews is the moral retreat he has made in servilely accepting the majority's ethics, not the so-called undesirable Jewish traits that provoked his anxiety. And if he wanted to do something about anti-Semitism—and if he understood what in the face of fear is difficult to understand—he might begin with his own moral subservience, where he has at least a real chance to change things, instead of trying to reform the manners or career choices of his fellow-Jews.

If we confined our attention to such instances of the acceptance of majority judgments as these (and of course we are selecting a particular segment of majority opinion and not the entire spectrum), we might underestimate the extent of present-day Jewish ethical bondage. However, since many Jews, especially in recent years, have tried to repress their tendencies towards group-belittlement of themselves, evidence of this self-belittlement—where not covertly released in gibe or gesture—is less obvious since it issues in reactions that are seldom fully conscious.

Apologetics as a reaction to attack hardly needs discussion in these pages. It surrenders the ethical initiative, for it permits the anti-Semite to frame the issue of debate and the norms of criticism. Denials that Jews are rich, radical, or rude concede to the anti-Semites that it is a crime to be rich, radical, or rude.

Another reaction is self-denial, in which Jews deny as Jews that there are such things as Jews. Sometimes this self-denial is a "liberal" reaction, an insistence that there are no anthropological (racial) differences, out of a fear that such differences would be exploited. Sometimes this self-denial is rationalized as a "radical" reaction, by the insistence that there is no "Jewish question" whatsoever, but only some other question, such as the question of capitalism. Jews who take this latter course do at least identify themselves with a submerged group larger than their own, but they run the risk of carrying the position to extremes in believing that the Jewish problem, despite cultural and historical differences, is in all respects similar to—let us say—the Negro problem, or the problem of the working class as a whole. In this way, the specifically Jewish overtones are lost; but indeed this is precisely what the self-denier wants.

Still a third reaction occurs as a revulsion against all traits associated with the majority stereotype of "the Jew." Are Jews pushing? Very well, we will be retiring. Are Jews over-critical? Very well, we will swallow our protest.[4] The minority group actually expects more from itself than from the rest of the population; that is, it applies the majority ethics but with a double standard.

4. Some Jews indulge in what looks on the surface like just the opposite reaction. They aggressively play up what they accept as Jewish traits; sometimes they select the very ones that are detested in the majority stereotype; sometimes they indiscriminately fasten their affection on those traits, good or bad. Are Jews pushing? Very well, pushing is nice, and we will push. Are Jews critical? Very well, let us exploit this fine cultural resource. Some young Negroes, too, play this pathetic game, accepting the whites' judgments in the very act of using them to make an issue with them. Likewise, many middle-class intellectuals spend their lives reacting against middle-class standards and values, for instance in bohemianism, as if this were the only ethical contrast to what they conceive as the middle class.

It is evident that this timid double standard is very different from the feeling of *noblesse oblige* of certain ruling classes. These classes have no doubts of their right to rule, even when they are far from perfect; in contrast, the "double-standard" Jews seem to say that Jewish claims for full equality are invalid if Jews are merely human.

In all these instances Jews try to cope with American anti-Semitism in terms of majority stereotypes, which by their very irrationality prevent both minority and majority from making any fresh approaches to reality.

V. Recent events have brought still another aspect of Jewish self-doubt to light. I think that exaggeration of the uniqueness of the crime committed by the Nazis against the Jews may sometimes be read as betraying an unconscious doubt as to the ethical justification of the Jewish case. When some Jews claim that no injustice was ever so great, nor any dictator the peer of Hitler, they are not always simply venting an understandable grief. They are afraid that the very enormity, the irretrievable quality, of the killing of the Jews must prove something about them, something in fact against them. For there is no way that a success ethics can cope with unavenged material defeat. Some may try to still the doubt—whether, after all, Hitler was not right—by racist vindictiveness against the German people. What seems to be lingering in the minds of so many is the notion that Hitler somehow won a victory over the Jews.

On the other hand, a Jew who has found his way to an independent ethics would say with Rabbi Johanan: "All distress that Israel and the world bear in common is distress; the distress confined to Israel alone is not distress" (From *In Time and Eternity*). On the ethical side, he would find little to choose between the Nazi murder of Jews and of Poles, or between the concentration camps of Hitler and Stalin; on the political side, he would be free to perceive that the slaughter of the European Jews was to some extent a historical accident in which they happened to become material game and spiritual symbol for a congeries of reactionary forces.

Victory and defeat, success and failure, are facts. But they are facts in the world of power, subject to an evaluative judgment in which defeat may become victory and victory defeat. Who "really" won in the war between Athens and Sparta? It is conventional today to decide in favor of Athens. What, for example, about Weimar Germany? Are many of its critics, who attack its experimentalism, its pacifism, its artistic and intellectual "irresponsibility" and lack of consensus only disapproving of these tendencies because they did not ward off political defeat? Many generations hence, may not people look back with admiration on the cultural and even some of the political and social achievements of that brief period between 1919 and 1933, and pay little attention to all our elaborate explanations for its "failure," explanations which, as in the case of the slaughtered Jews, consciously or unconsciously subordinate ourselves to an ethics of success pure and simple, and overemphasize what was wrong with the victim?

Even such devastating defeats as those of the last decade the truly moral man must find the courage and the capacity to face with the nerve of failure.

VI. Of course, it would be applying a double standard to expect Jews to have the nerve of failure when other groups do not. Moreover, it would be as unfair to blame Jews for losing their traditional ethics in the melting pot, as to blame them for not emerging from it as Anglo-Saxon gentlemen. But the opposite error, which tolerantly understands all minority behavior as the inevitable consequence of persecution, is not helpful either. The real question is, what choices do the Jews now have?

There is no want of proposed solutions, many of which seem to me to repeat or exacerbate the circular problems in which a minority is so often caught. One is a plea for a return to the ritual and religious elements historically linked to the ethical resources of Jewish life. It is not surprising that this same plea for what amounts to a medieval revival is also being made at this time by many non-Jews as a general therapy for modern alienation.

The usual criticism of such efforts to restore psychic security and dignity is that they are impractical, since the change from medieval to modern times cannot be reversed. But another criticism can be made from the standpoint of the very Jewish ethics which one wants to recapture. That ethics contains a fervent claim for a more decent future, a claim that takes the form of Messianic hope. Though the glories of Biblical Palestine are looked back upon with pride and sorrow, utopia lies in the future, not in the nostalgic past. To seek restoration of an earlier time is to confess intellectual and ethical impoverishment. The nerve of failure implies the ability to face the *possibility* of failure, but it is rooted in the assumption that past and present failures need not mark the limits of human powers. To be satisfied with something no better than that which medieval Jewry had—assuming, in defiance of all reason, that this could be attained—is a surrender of that demand typical for Jews (though of course not exclusively theirs) for a more decent future for Jews and non-Jews alike.

The surrender of utopian claims is one of the most revealing symptoms of the current state of minority ethics. Despite differences in shading, such claims are a part of Judaic, Christian, and Enlightenment ethical systems. But they are very much at a discount today. The powerful do not need visions; they either fear or scorn them. Their response to such claims is: "If you don't like it here, why don't you go back where you came from?" Some minority representatives aggressively propose to do just that, to go back —in time. Whereas the older success game permitted many minorities to be easily satisfied with petty gains in the American scene, the newer religious revival would satisfy them with petty dreams from the past.

Political Zionism is another suggestion proposed as a means of obtaining psychic as well as physical security for Jews. Jewish nationalists seem to be even more impressed by worldly power than Jews who urge a religious revival; they have given up the success game on the domestic scene only to transfer it to the international sphere; this entails a complete acceptance of majority attitudes towards force and *raison d'état*. Thus they abandon the critical attitude which subjects to principle and to reason all claims of power and all demands for loyalty—an attitude which I believe to be among the significant contributions of Jewish ethics to the general problem of the powerless minority and the small nation.

If Jews are to avoid self-defeating courses of action, it would seem necessary to clarify the themes in their ethical tradition that fit the problem of the powerless, and then to separate these from their cultist and ritualistic trappings. The way food is prepared or the style of beards are locally various and ethically quite indifferent matters—questions of taste and not of value. To attach one's love and admiration to them is to risk putting the superficial or parochial aspects of Jewish culture in the center of affection, rather than its ethically significant elements. And it is this sort of love that so easily runs over into fondness for, or defensiveness about, even the weaker sides of Jewish life in America. This sort of chauvinism is particularly easy to rationalize today, just because the Jews seem at the moment a defeated people on the world's stage. It would be well, however, to recall Nietzsche's advice not to love a defeated nation. (Nietzsche seems to have meant that an honorable person finds it harder in defeat than in victory to detach himself from his nation—witness German nationalism after the First World War.)

The concept of minority ethics suggested here is not meant as an invitation to minority fanaticism or as a condemnation of all majority ethics as such; the minority position in itself is no guarantee of ethical superiority. Rather, it points out that the Jewish minority in America must discover what are the ethically significant themes relevant to its present situation, which in turn requires reinterpretation of Jewish tradition.

Such a reinterpretation of tradition would in itself do something to overcome Jewish self-belittlement by giving the past meaning without mystery. But the more direct function of this reinterpretation would be to foster a Jewish self-image counterposed to the majority ethics. Adherence to majority ethics may be a help in social climbing, or in rationalizing one's acceptance of the values of the culture that happens to be dominant. But the experience of many Jews in America must be that this adherence is emotionally precarious, and that it easily becomes self-destructive once things do not go well for oneself or one's group. There are more ways of acquiring a feeling of "belonging" in the American scene than the alternatives of melting pot or parochial separation.

Yet is it not merely wishful to ask that Jews today, of all people, be reasonable men looking for guidance in their personal and political lives to a rational, and therefore experimental and tentative, ethics? No matter how ethically inadequate the ritualist, racialist, and nationalist therapies may be, does not their very existence prove that the vast bulk of Jews cannot be expected to defend themselves morally against power without the encompassing support of daily ritual observances, or without the *ersatz* program of Palestinian terrorism? Is not one of my own arguments—that Jewish ethics has been closely related to Jewish material circumstance—proof of the impracticality of any therapy that begins with ethics and not with environment? I would answer that movements of thought among a people are never entirely determined by the material setting. On the contrary, an ethical and intellectual feature—such, for instance, as an eloquent tradition of utopian thought—may itself become one of the institutional forces of the environment. In the case of the Diaspora history of the Jews, utopian thought was even a decisive force. Of course, such a program does not pretend to "save" the Jews; its goal is moral independence from the majority, not physical survival or a solution of "the Jewish problem." Its gains would largely be in the happier lives of Jews and other powerless folk. Nevertheless, a reduction of Jewish self-contempt and an increase in the Jewish "nerve of failure" is bound to make for more realistic, as well as attractive, behavior by individual Jews and Jewish agencies, and so reduce those minor, pointless tensions and self-defeating patterns that Jews themselves may create.

Specific groups of Jews in America are meeting widely different problems and experiences. There is room for research into the intricate relations between their ethics and their attitudes toward themselves, research that would test and refine such hypotheses as those suggested here. Such work has meaning for minority groups in general. At the same time American Jews have much to learn from other minority experiences and traditions—from Negroes in America and South Africa; from anti-fascists in Mussolini's Italy, Hitler's Germany, Franco's Spain, Perón's Argentina; from intellectual and cultural dissenters from modern capitalism and Stalinist Communism; and so on. Moreover, the utopian traditions of Christian sects, of the Enlightenment, of America itself—these have contributions to make to the development of a minority ethics. In fact, is not such development enjoined on almost all of us by our human situation? For who does not face at some time—at least as a child—a conflict between his own values and those of a stronger and oppressive power? Until a time when power is no longer used oppressively, minorities will have a compelling need of the nerve of failure to defend an independent view of the self and of what life holds.

Some Observations on Community Plans and Utopia

A revival of the tradition of utopian thinking seems to me one of the important intellectual tasks of today. Since we live in a time of disenchantment, such thinking, where it is rational in aim and method and not mere escapism, is not easy; it is easier to concentrate on programs for choosing among lesser evils, even to the point where these evils can scarcely be distinguished, one from the other. For there is always a market for lesser-evil thinking which poses immediate alternatives; the need for thinking which confronts us with great hopes and great plans is not so evident. Yet without great plans, it is hard, and often self-defeating, to make little ones. Such utopian thinking requires what I have termed the "nerve of failure," that is, the ability to face the possibility of defeat without feeling morally crushed. Without this sort of courage, any failure implies a personal defect, and brings feelings of intolerable isolation; to avoid this fate, people tend to repress their claims for a decent world to a "practical" point, and to avoid any goals, personal or social, that seem out of step with common sense.

Curiously enough, however, in a dynamic political context, it is the modest, common-sensical goals which are often unattainable—therefore utopian in the derogatory sense. I do not mean, of course, that "anything can happen"; I do mean that the self-styled realist tends to underestimate the strength of latent forces because he is too impressed by what he "sees." To take only one example, it often seems that the retention of a given status quo is a

"Some Observations on Community Plans and Utopia" was first published in The Yale Law Journal, *Vol. 57, December 1947.*

modest hope; many lawyers, political scientists and economists occupy themselves by suggesting the minimal changes which are necessary to stand still; yet today this hope is almost invariably disappointed; the status quo proves the most illusory of goals. To aim at this goal requires little nerve, for many people share the same hope; so long as things appear to go well, anxiety is stilled; and even when things go badly, many people will join in providing rationalizations for the failure: misery will have company.

The problem of how individuals can fortify themselves, without insanity, to the point at which they will believe their own, isolated imaginations, is of course a very old one. It is this problem that Spinoza deals with when he discusses how the Biblical prophets attempted to assure themselves of certainty:

"For instance, Jeremiah's prophecy of the destruction of Jerusalem was confirmed by the prophecies of other prophets, and by the threats in the law, and therefore it needed no sign; whereas Hananiah, who, contrary to all the prophets, foretold the speedy restoration of the state, stood in need of a sign, or he would have been in doubt as to the truth of his prophecy, until it was confirmed by facts. 'The prophet which prophesieth of peace, when the word of the prophet shall come to pass, then shall the prophet be known that the Lord hath truly sent him.'"[1]

Today in America, at least in intellectual circles, the Jeremiahs share a widespread, and in that sense comforting, defeatism; there are few Hananiahs who prophesy restoration and peace. The recent book *Communitas: Means of Livelihood and Ways of Life*,[2] by Percival and Paul Goodman, is therefore particularly welcome; it is avowedly utopian, both in its critique of earlier community plans and in its presentation of new ones. I propose in this article to indicate some of the Goodmans' contributions to utopian

1. *The Philosophy of Spinoza* edited by Joseph Ratner, Modern Library, 1927. p. 51.
2. University of Chicago Press (1947). All quotations are from this source unless otherwise indicated.

thinking; but first to place these in perspective by a review, necessarily sketchy, of the present state of such thinking in America.

I. A hundred years ago, in the *Communist Manifesto,* Marx and Engels welcomed the criticisms which their so-called utopian predecessors, such as St. Simon, Fourier, and Owen, had made of capitalist society, but they rejected the peaceable methods of these men for achieving socialism. Their label "utopian" (expanded in Engels' *Socialism: Utopian and Scientific*) stuck as a derogatory term. Moreover, having taken their polemical position, they were themselves bound by it, and carefully avoided setting forth more than fragmentary views on what the classless society might look like: this refusal became a mark of realism and orthodoxy—and a great convenience to left-wing politicians and writers. While some Europeans, such as William Morris and Theodor Hertzka,[3] continued to work in the older utopian tradition as late as the '90's, the masses were soon recruited either for Marxist "scientific," i.e., hard-headed socialism, or for Fabian and Social-Democratic versions of practical, unmessianic politics.

In the rough and ready America of the last century, a serious interest in utopian thought found other obstacles than Marxism. However, the country itself seemed to be a functioning utopia to peoples elsewhere, and it was the scene of most of the utopian experiments of the period, as in Oneida and New Harmony. Immense enthusiasm greeted Bellamy's *Looking Backward* (1888); during the same period, huge audiences in the Midwest were inspired by the utopian prophecies of Ignatius Donnelly.[4] All this ferment has vanished. The appeal of such writers as Bellamy appears to have declined just about the time that the socialism of Debs and DeLeon began to make some headway in America. But since this type of socialism, too, has died

3. For discussion and bibliography see Lewis Mumford, *The Story of Utopias,* 1922.

4. The early chapters of Dorfman, *Thorstein Veblen and His America* (1934) evoke and document this atmosphere.

out (of course, economic determinism has always been influential in America, from the Founding Fathers on down), we must look for deeper causes at work.

The idea of a dialectical opposition between "ideology" and "utopia" is suggested by Karl Mannheim's book, though I use the words here in a somewhat different sense from his.[5] A "utopia" I define as a rational belief which is in the long-run interest of the holder; it is a belief, not in existing reality, but in a potential reality; it must not violate what we know of nature, including human nature, though it may extrapolate our present technology and must transcend our present social organization.[6] An "ideology" I define as an irrational system of belief, not in the interest of the holder. It is sold to him by a group which has an interest in swindling him; he accepts it because of his own irrational needs, including his desire to submit to the power of the vendor group. An ideology may contain elements of truth; these serve to lend plausibility, rather than to open the eyes and increase the awareness of the recipient. Contrariwise, a utopia may contain elements of error, initially less significant than its truth, which assist its later conversion into an ideology: in this way, the utopias of one age tend to harden in a distorted form into the ideologies of the next, taken on faith rather than rationally rediscovered.

The America of the last century, I suggest, made room for a limited amount of utopian thought and experiment

5. Mannheim, *Ideology and Utopia* (translated from the German by Wirth and Shils, 1936). See also Mannheim, "Utopia," in *Encyc. Soc. Sci.*, 15:200.

6. These features distinguish utopian thinking from, on the one hand, a mere dream, and on the other hand, a mere description of existing facts. In other words, "utopia" is a place—in contemporary terms, a plan—that now is nowhere, save maybe for pilot models, but that may someday be somewhere, so far as science can say; thus, heaven is not a utopia in my sense, while the Boston of *Looking Backward* is one. An element of ambiguity remains in these, as in Mannheim's definitions, perhaps reflecting the complexity of the topics themselves. For a thoughtful discussion, see Kenneth Burke, "Ideology and Myth," *Accent*, 7:195, 1947.

because, among many other factors, the capitalism of that period was singularly unconcerned about propagandizing itself as an ideological system. Perhaps this is because it was so much taken for granted that it did not need verbal defense, though Southern writers continued to attack its Northern version. The system was written into the landscape, so to speak; it did not need to be written into books. After the Civil War, a dominant capitalism got brutal, but it did not get especially articulate; its critics, from Mark Twain to Veblen, treated it with an impiety and irreverence which we seldom find today. A few preachers continued to mumble grace over the economic system, but their combination of theology and economics was on the wane, while the new one of Social Darwinism coupled with laissez faire seems to have made little impression before William Graham Sumner started writing such essays as "The Absurd Effort to Make the World Over."[7] Throughout the period, to be sure, Eastern capitalists met resistance from the Populists, and perhaps the gold standard should be called an ideology; but on the whole dissent could be bought off without too much debate, *e.g.*, by homestead rights, or by subventions to the appropriate political rings.

By the turn of the century, however, many developments, including tremors of socialism, put the capitalists on the defensive; they could no longer quite so freely use Pinkertons; they began to talk, to bargain collectively "through instruments of their own choosing." Then, a whole new class of university-trained demi-intellectuals began to find jobs and status in doing the talking: personnel men, trade-association men, organization-chart men, lawyers, economists, house-organ men, advertising men, etc. Meanwhile the school system had taught almost everyone to read. Thus both the quantity of and the receptivity for capitalist ideology grew enormously, most of it paid for—as Veblen pointed out in his article on "The Breadline and

7. *Forum*, 17:92, 1894, reprinted in *Sumner Today*, edited by Davie, 1940.

the Movies"[8]—by the underlying population, which subscribes to the mass media.

Business enterprise in America has, however, always tended to disguise its ideological pressures under a coating of apparently utopian aims, such as the promise of a chicken in every pot or a car in every garage. These promises, when made in the United States, can scarcely be called utopian. First, given our resources, it is not difficult to fulfil them; they are, in very fact, just around the corner. Second, attainment of these goals would not make the great mass of well-fed Americans noticeably happier. The fulfilment of utopian aims, on the other hand, is a revolutionary affair; it makes substantial demands on the community, and promises substantial gains in human happiness. While in the Age of Liberalism, capitalism was associated with just such great human aims, it has become distanced from them in its later phases of complacency, ideology, or reaction. But the utopian coating referred to has tended to satisfy masses of people with spurious social goals, while many thoughtful folk rebelled by doubting the whole Enlightenment concept of gradual progress towards a liberal utopia.

With minor exceptions, moreover, the large-scale anti-business movements in America have tended more and more to copy business methods in covering an essentially ideological approach with a few utopian trimmings. Populism, for example, was ambivalent: it included not only ancient rural hatred for city slicker "usury" but the scarcely veiled "me too" cry of the farmers, unions, small businessmen and small debtors to be cut in on the big money. The New Deal added to these Populist aims (expressed in the Holding Company Act and other anti-Wall Street measures) the goal of achieving the Social Democratic attainments of the Continent, such as social insurance, a minimum wage, and public assistance in housing; none of these measures promised a fundamental change in the quality of American life. The T.V.A., some F.S.A. projects, and a few housing ventures such as Arthurdale and Greenbelt—these

8. An editorial in *The Dial,* reprinted in *Essays in Our Changing Order* (1934), p. 450.

pushed beyond relatively easy attainment towards utopian goals; the T.V.A. particularly serves as a pilot model for a new way of life, a new community plan. But the general poverty of aim of the New Deal is shown by the fact that, by 1937, it had reached its own limits, a point obscured by its continuing ideological competition with "The Interests." The war provided a welcome agenda for avoiding insight into this impasse; the government ideologists sold war bonds (or "unity") by the same sort of specious arguments as had sold N.R.A.'s blue eagle.

The more recent political developments which have tended to engender disillusion with all systematic thinking —ideological and utopian alike—hardly need review. The positive goals of both world wars were oversold; peace movements have seemed so futile, and have been in such bad company, as to be discredited among all but the most courageous and independent (or religiously-supported) thinkers. Marxian Socialism, once a branch of bourgeois Enlightenment utopianism despite its founders' assertions to the contrary, has tended, like capitalism, to degenerate into an ideology, notably, of course, in Communist hands. In fact, the Stalinist bureaucracy has brought Russia under the sway of the most leaden and impenetrable of ideologies; its propagandists continue to make utopian claims which conceal from the faithful the actual abandonment of those utopian advances, as in the treatment of women, which the Old Bolsheviks had fought for. As hypocrisy is the tribute vice pays to virtue, so ideology pays tribute to utopian thought. But as hypocrisy revealed discredits the very possibility of virtue, so people who are disillusioned find it hard not to reject the utopian aspirations as well as the ideological pretense.

While these disillusionments are general, the fear of being intellectually out of step, of belonging to a political party with no chance of immediate power, seems to be considerably greater here than in Europe; this was true even in the nineteenth century, as Tocqueville and Bryce observed. In the absence of a tradition of respect for independent thinking, many Americans have found only one workable defense against the pressure of their ideological environment, namely apathy, often touched with humor, or a self-protecting cynicism. This attitude resembles the way in which many adolescents cope with the ideological authority of their parents: they brush it off as the mouthings of the "old man" or the "old lady," and largely disregard it in practice, without ever taking the genuine risks of commitment to an untried and independent ethics. This is the way soldiers dealt with the ideological output of the Information and Education branch of the Army; and it is the way in which many civilians cope with the public-relations staffs of business, government, and labor.

However, these amiable defensive aspects are not the whole story: apathy and cynicism—and a kind of self-deprecating humor which is often attractive—also serve the function of gaining status through toughness or slickness, or through the smoother type of indifference to enthusiasm of the well-bred. These attitudes are so strong in America that decent, constructive people, too, come to fear being taken for suckers, or enthusiasts; from childhood on, boys especially have been made ashamed of their own impulses towards warmth, commitment, generosity. Among intellectual groups, one fears to be accused of the "bourgeois" virtues; or more fashionably today, fears lest some humane reaction escape one which might be translated in the Freudian dictionary, where, *e.g.*, "justice" may be read simply as "envy." It is a characteristic of utopian thinking, however, that it springs from humane enthusiasm; those whose greatest fear is to be gullible, serious, or "soft" are immune. But, as we know, those who fear most to be taken in, while they will escape utopia, are in fact among the easiest prey for ideology. Astrologers, anti-Semites, editors of the *Daily News*, and other confidence men make their living from the very cynics who will fall for the craziest story or ideology, if only it appears sophisticated, brutal, illegal or mysterious.

These seem to me to be among the many factors which have contributed to destroying the market for utopian thinking in America. The increasing division of labor characteristic of an industrial society has meantime played a part in inhibiting the production of such thinking which by its very nature requires a broad approach to the problems of the society as a whole. Specialists shrink from this task; being "in the know" as to a particular set of details, they are suspicious of the injudicious who make large plans without such knowledge. Indeed, a whole theoretical analysis, typified by Von Hayek, holds that large-scale planning is a human impossibility without a compulsory limiting of choices, on the ground that no planner can know enough to do the job if choice remains free. Where scholars and men of superior intellectual training fear to tread, cranks and charlatans—*e.g.*, Howard Scott of Technocracy—fill what market there is for big, bold, bad plans.[9] More sedate is the work of men like Ralph Borsodi, and the Southern Agrarians; while seemingly just the opposite of the Technocrats, these nostalgic writers are quite as insouciant in prescribing for the power-relations of modern industrial society.

These writers, moreover, can hardly be called utopian, in the sense in which I use the word. For utopia is time-located in the future: it is a social order which has not yet been tried, though it is a realistic possibility, not a mere idle dream. But the agrarians and anti-industrialists generally seek to restore something—their picture of the earlier age is usually distorted by convenient historical amnesias—without too much serious attention to limiting technological factors. Thus their writings have often an uneasy similarity to dream-work on a more popular level, like the cults of California.

If we turn to the universities, we shall not completely escape such literary restoration movements. However,

9. Of course, such writers often make slashing, though hardly original, criticisms of contemporary society, but what they would substitute for it is left vague. For instance, a recent issue of *Technocracy Briefs* has the running-head: "Technocracy Engineers Have Designed a Blue Print for A 'New America,'" which appears in the repeated injunction to "Think North American!" and in such statements as: "Not 'Dictatorship of the Proletariat,' but Dictums of Technology; Not 'Equality of Birth,' but Equality of Opportunity; Not 'Geopolitics,' but Geotechnics; Not 'Sovereign States' but Mechanics of Area Operations."

American social science has in general sought escape from ideological pressures—where this is not guaranteed by specialization—by means of ethical relativism, a value-free attitude which might be thought of as the academic counterpart of popular cynicism. (Curiously enough, Sumner represents both tendencies: the hardening of capitalist ideology and the beginning of a relativism which would have revolutionary implications vis-à-vis capitalist as well as other mores and ethnocentric prejudices.) In recent years, under the influence of thinkers such as Dewey and the Lynds, this sort of relativism has been under attack, and properly so. However, the insistence on an immediate plan-for-action and a somewhat Puritan distrust of "idle" curiosity and "irresponsibly" speculative scholars have tended to bring utopian as well as relativist-descriptive thinking under condemnation.[10] Both academic movements—value-free and action-oriented schools—are reinforced by a stereotyped notion as to what constitutes research. Research is organized either about the methodological framework of the existing disciplines or about "problems." But the problems are those things which we know bother us, such as poor administration, too much employment or too little, race and international tensions, etc. Researchers do not go looking for other problems which we ought to have, and indeed do have; in any case, the problems we are aware of are so urgent that they are felt to provide not only a necessary, but also a sufficient agenda.

By and large, the people whose function it is to think, under the division of labor, are over-impressed by what they think about. That is, they are over-receptive to their data, which they take at face value; even where they are not ethical relativists, they are terribly concerned with "what is." On the other hand a few intrepid heirs of an

10. In view of the reactionary onslaughts against Dewey today, I wish to make plain that I speak here only of a tendency in his thought (something of the same sort can be said of Lynd's *Knowledge for What?*), which is not actually central to it. In fact, Dewey is not nearly so narrowly "pragmatic" as his enemies often assume; on the whole, he is certainly a "utopian thinker."

older tradition try to impress themselves on their data, without too much respect for "what is," *e.g.*, Spengler, Sorokin. These latter, therefore, come closer to the cranks and poets already mentioned for whom "what is" is to be found inside their heads; the aggressiveness of such thinkers towards the facts, the enormous empirical material they deal with, may perhaps be related to the reactionary *content* of their approaches to questions of social reorganization. Few scholars achieve the kind of sensitive and friendly relation to reality which is necessary for utopian creation —a relation in which one respects "what is" but includes in it also "what might be" and "what ought to be."

One small group in our society, the architectural fraternity, has continued to produce and to stimulate thinking in the utopian tradition—thinking which at its best combines respect for material fact with ability, even enthusiasm, for transcending the given. (Perhaps the architects are in a good position to do this since they have had so little building to do!) Veblen was mistaken in hoping for great things from the engineers; the unideological matter-of-factness which he thought their work-a-day tasks would encourage usually succumbs to a pedestrian acceptance of the prevailing ideologies—a more uncritical acceptance, often enough, than that of their businessmen or governmental bosses. Architects, however, are engineers with a difference: their profession would have no future if there were no difference. Architects, that is, are paid to dream—paid even to waste, Veblen would say—but they must not ignore engineering requirements if they wish their structures to stand. Of course, most architects do not dream; they are simply businessmen, and their "waste" is of a most prudent kind, since their customers buy just the right amount of it to qualify for the social status they want. There remains a minority: *e.g.*, Wright and Le Corbusier; Behrendt and the Bauhaus group; the young editors of *Task* magazine; also there are community planners, such as Lewis Mumford, Charles Ascher and Catherine Bauer, who have worked with architects and have learned to relate their social thinking to this form of technological experience. This minority, despite the fundamentally reactionary character of Wright's and Le

Corbusier's types of planning,[11] has helped to keep alive the utopian tradition both in the drawing of plans and in the experimental demonstration of new possibilities for living.

However, the architectural utopians have generally remained isolated from other forms of technological experience and analytical tools (classical economics and social psychology, for example); they have indulged, like most isolated men, in fanaticism and wars of sectarian annihilation, as in Wright's assault on Le Corbusier; we might even suggest that such eccentricities and blindnesses were necessary to preserve their "nerve of failure," their courage to be different and to stand alone.[12] The book *Communitas* is one attempt to break down this intellectual isolation. One author, Percival Goodman, is an architect and city planner; the other, Paul Goodman, a novelist and social critic. They have studied, not only the physical plans of some predecessor architects, but the intellectual constructions of some predecessor utopians. Their effort is ambitious to see what man is and may become, what society is and may become.

11. For Wright see, e.g., *The Disappearing City* (1932); *When Democracy Builds* (1945); and the remarkable interchanges between Wright and a group of English architects in *An Organic Architecture* (1939). For Le Corbusier see, e.g., *When the Cathedrals Were White* (1947).

12. Since writing the foregoing, I have read the brilliant review by Meyer Schapiro of *Architecture and Modern Life* by Baker Brownell and Frank Lloyd Wright. "Architect's Utopia," *Partisan Review*, 4:42–7 (1938). Mr. Schapiro argues that the utopias of such contemporary architects as Wright serve no constructive function but rather operate as reactionary middle-class ideologies, glossing over class relations by the use of words like "organic," "construction," "framework," which mix metaphors taken from architecture and from social thought. He sees the architects, especially of the depression period, as just another underemployed profession with delusions of its central role; these men, contemplating architecture as the mirror of society, fail to grasp those social realities which cannot be read directly from the physical forms. I am persuaded by Mr. Schapiro that there is less difference between architects of this stripe and engineers than I had supposed.

II. As utopians, the authors' ethical and moral platform rests on a scientific psychology only hints of which are given in the text. It is a psychology which sees man as fundamentally good, capable under proper social and physical arrangements of enjoying work, family life, nature, privacy and cooperation—and alternating, temperamentally varied, rhythms between them. They see their fellow-Americans as, by and large, an unhappy folk, trapped in their competitive production and competitive consumption, strenuously passive, sourly emulative. They believe them, even now, to be capable of more spontaneous pleasures and more democratic cooperation. Thus, they have not fallen into the contemporary mood of a gloomy, Niebuhrian view of man, but have remained attached to more optimistic Enlightenment traditions, as represented in such various men as Godwin, Owen, Kropotkin and Dewey; like these thinkers, they see "what external conditions have grown inordinately large and are obstructing the harmony of society and the internal freedom of the people"; like them, they look for counterforces, for unmanipulative leverage, especially education. To hold this view today takes, I think, a certain amount of courage, more so, paradoxically, than to confess defeat at the outset. For the person who has the "nerve of failure" takes the risks of failure but also the risks of an improbable success; he dares to look at life in all its contingency. It is easier, and also more fashionable, to play the Cassandra role, and thus to reap from each new atrocity and impasse in world affairs new moral assurance and confirmation for one's position—like Prince Bagration in Tolstoy's *War and Peace* who gave the appearance of calm mastery by looking wise at each bit of catastrophic news from the battle as if he had not only foreseen but planned it just that way.

In one way or another, the Goodmans feel, most contemporary city planners avoid any responsibility for the ultimate values which their plans will freeze, destroy or serve. Believing that planning only makes sense on the assumption of peace, with its economic surplus and political choices, they are critical of those planners who are concerned simply with finding methods to minimize atomic destruction though this might become the easiest kind of planning to sell.[13] They are also critical of those more modest plans which aim at no positive good, but merely at the minimizing of lesser evils than atomic war: for instance, the relief of traffic congestion, or of unemployment (community development subordinated to make-work and pump-priming). For they feel that the planner, by virtue of his position and skill, has a responsibility to see, not only what people think they want, or have been persuaded to want, but what they might want, if they knew of its possibility. Unlike many utopian radicals, however, they sympathize with those planners who limit themselves to what can be realized at any given time, provided that the choice of evils, or of small gains, is informed by larger aims, and a full realization of the social consequences of amelioration.

It is also clear that the Goodmans do not think of utopian planning as a kind of exercise in legislation, in which the planners fit people to their theory; rather, it is an exploration of alternative possibilities. It is, therefore, a piecemeal approach: there is no one plan, no philosopher's stone. Technologies of scarcity, such as the Orient, pose entirely different alternatives than technologies of surplus, such as the United States. Each geographic region, each cultural constellation, each stage of industrial development presents material for exploiting quite different optima. This sounds like relativism or eclecticism, but it is not; among the utopias they sketch, the authors have reasoned preferences which are grounded in a systematic ethics; the same ethics leads them to dismiss as immoral still other alternatives—such as an improved Garrison State—which are conceivable, even probable.

13. Lewis Mumford writes of an earlier city planner, who faced somewhat similar problems: "Leonardo da Vinci . . . dealt in his notebooks with the city proper, suggested the separation of pedestrian ways from heavy traffic arteries, and went so far as to urge upon the Duke of Milan the standardized mass production of workers' houses. But despite these pregnant suggestions, his contributions to the art of city building remain poor and meager compared with his extraordinary zeal in improving the art of fortification and assault." *The Culture of Cities* (1938), p. 86.

The Goodman brothers evaluate those great city and community plans of the recent past which, on the basis of the attitudes just indicated, they feel to be of continuing importance. They ask of each plan: what does this tell us about the architect's underlying assumptions as to the ends of life? How, for instance, does he feel about modern industrial work—is it something to be belted off from the wives and children? In the design of the suburb, what are his implicit attitudes towards cultural variety—is he freezing in his plan the one-class, one-race, one-outlook ghettos which, as Catherine Bauer has observed,[14] are increasingly fostered by government and philanthropic planners and builders today? In the location and design of the factory, is his only value the goal of more commodities—and even within the limits of this goal, has he been taken in by current conventions, technologically outdated, as to the efficiency of mass production and the limits of machine-analysis of parts and subcontracted assemblies? In the design of the home, and landscaping, how does he feel towards children—is it, for instance, more important for them to have a workshop and climbable trees than, since choices must be made, for their parents to have standard plumbing and a white picket fence? In this fashion, by looking at the plans—the book is full of drawings and sketches—the Goodmans read off from them the implicit social values of the planners and those for whom they worked: in their hands the recent history of architecture becomes a record of evaluations and ideas. It is also a dialectical process in which the avoidance of some evils has brought others, usually unanticipated, and in which the commitment of social resources in physical form has its own logic, opening some possibilities and foreclosing others.

We may compare the Goodmans' method to that of a psychoanalyst who examines the unconscious choices, and values which have crystallized in the posture, the gestures and the character structure of a given individual. His task is to help the individual bring these values into conscious

14. Bauer, "Good Neighborhoods," *Annals*, 242:104 (1945).

awareness and then to see what other structures can be built from the materials already given. This type of study owes much, in my opinion, to Mumford's writings; he has seen the interconnectedness of city shape, city movement, and city values;[15] the Goodmans, however, do not deal either with his analyses or with his own plans, such as those for Honolulu or post-war England.

The Goodmans feel that the central problems for the modern planner are posed by the Industrial Revolution. Is the planner revolting against its coal and iron slums, like the creators of Garden Cities and Greenbelts (*e.g.*, Ebenezer Howard,[16] Unwin, Stein)? Is he concerned with its economic insecurity, its Frankenstein qualities, like Frank Lloyd Wright? Or is he, on the contrary, fascinated with capitalist technology, anxious to speed the Industrial Revolution and plunge us all at once into a World's Fair kind of city, like Le Corbusier? Does he think primarily of consumption values, like Buckminster Fuller, or of production values, like the planners of the Soviet state farms, or is he concerned with restoring the relation between consumption and production which preceded the Revolution, like Borsodi? Or does he have his eye primarily on the possibilities of economic surplus given by the Revolution, and on the alternatives in production and consumption offered by these in turn, like the planners of the T.V.A.? To illustrate the Goodmans' analyses, I shall select their treatment of Buckminster Fuller and of the T.V.A.

Most readers will remember Fuller's Dymaxion House as a prefabricated mushroom—a mobile hexagonal house on

15. See especially *The Culture of Cities* (1938) and *City Development* (1945). I am indebted to Mr. Mumford for a number of helpful references and suggestions.

16. The Goodmans view the work of Howard too narrowly. Like them, he made plans not to divorce, but to reunite, work and residence. Far from espousing bigger and better suburbias, he insisted on the integration of industry, agriculture, and dormitory along regional lines which took account of local resources and cultural patterns. Significantly, he was inspired by Bellamy. See Giedion, *Space, Time and Architecture* (1941), p. 509.

a mast, one of the absurd technocratic dreams of the depression days. Fuller (who was trained not as an architect but as an engineer) called it a machine for realizing the "Eternal Now," without commitment to site, cities, or tradition. Fuller also roams all fields, untroubled by the division of labor. His "economics" rests on "automatic minimum existence credits selectively contractable . . . based on foot-pounds per hour of physical effort, with time study credits for labor-saving contributions of individual activity . . . plus sex-segregated maintenance of anti-social laggards," combined with a system of mass speculation in 10¢ industrial shares. His "politics" is abbreviated by securing, through patents and city services (though what role these would play in the self-contained Dymaxion House is not clear), world control for the Universal Architects, a self-effacing elite "after the manner of the Ford planning department." His "religion" is a new phase of Christianity where, through mass-production and divorce from material concerns, especially landed property, men will again become (rather curiously isolated) brothers. His "psychology," starting from the child's fear of noise and falling, analogizes the structure of the House to the structure of the human body (however, in the World War II version of the House, the functions of "fueling" and "refusing," *i.e.* elimination, are put on one side rather than in the central shaft).

One might dismiss all this as a mad pot-pourri, including Fourierist, money-crank, and possibly fascist bits. The Goodmans, however, take Fuller seriously both for what he says and what he symbolizes. They note the importance of the Dymaxion House's freedom from ground rent and public utilities (this is an as yet unimplemented aim: Fuller's proposed machine for using sun-power has not yet been invented; perhaps a little atomic pile will do instead). And the Goodmans see in the utter convenience of the House, its drive for complete consumer's effortlessness—no furnace to fix, no garden to putter in, no screens to hang—a symbol of the current craze for photoelectric doors, button-lowered car windows, and other magic-carpet fantasies. I find this search a very puzzling phenomenon, since the effort which is saved, for instance of cranking a car window, is not actually unpleasant; on the surface it appears to be a pathological laziness, but the people who go in for it probably play golf or go bowling. The Goodmans do not try to give a complete explanation, but they observe that the consumer, by the proliferation of these magic, foolproof devices, becomes progressively enslaved and helpless in the hands of the "Universal Architects" who, in Fuller's scheme, monopolize all creative and decisive steps in the productive process.

In some respects, the T.V.A. may be thought of as a complete contrast to Fuller's work, though the Goodmans call attention to the Dymaxion-like section-trailers developed by the Authority for its mobile construction workers. For the T.V.A. does not divorce production from consumption; in its efforts at grass-roots democracy, as in its use of electric power, the two are brought into novel and multiple relations. The T.V.A.'s success rests on the adaptation of its plan to the logic of the man-nature pattern in the Valley: to keep the dams from silting up, it is necessary to prevent erosion, the land must be fertilized, and some restored to grass; to get these grass-roots, it is necessary to teach good land-use practice and to make possible more intensive cultivation of the plowland; this requires encouragement of the cooperative movement, the sale of cheap fertilizer, and the easing of the farmer's tasks by cheap power and cheap appliances; and so on. People are freed from their primary, archaic relationship to the land; but are then enabled to relate themselves to the land and their neighbors on it in a more abundant, though more complicated, way. The authors, in their brief treatment, do no more than hint at the full meaning of the T.V.A. experience; they say little that is concrete; they move altogether too quickly from T.V.A.'s achievements to the issues it has not so far touched: "the problems of surplus and leisure, of the relation of culture and work, the role of great cities." For the solution of these, they turn to their own model plans.

III. The authors present three such models. Each chooses to solve one problem to the exclusion of the others. The first model aims to increase leisure and the consumable surplus; the second, to reintegrate culture and work; the third, to reduce to a minimum both economic regulation and economic insecurity while maintaining large urban concentrations. The authors believe that the great plans of their predecessors expressed mixed aims; and they realize that any conceivable plan would likewise blend patterns from each of their three separated goals. In their logical abstractness, the plans are "ideal types" in Max Weber's sense; but they are also ideal types in the vernacular sense of something to be striven for, something utopian. Thus, the models, or, as the authors call them, paradigms, may be thought of as tools for analyzing any existing plan; but in their statement, they are also efforts at analyzing the conflict of aims in contemporary America.

The latter purpose comes out most clearly in the first plan, which rather sardonically assumes that there is to be no change in dominant American cultural values and socio-economic organization and raises the question: how can such values be unequivocally represented in the plan? Here the authors present a paradox in Veblen's thought: Veblen wanted to remove the archaic and pecuniary fetters on production by applying the matter-of-fact logic of the engineer; however, having stepped up production, he also wanted to step down consumption by getting rid of leisured waste and emulative luxury; would not the result be still greater mass insecurity through "overproduction"?[17] The Goodmans feel that this paradox is not solved by Keynesian methods, both because, short of building pyramids, there are not sufficient objects of public spending to sop up the excess production, and because such public works do not give sufficient incentive, including psychological incentive, to profit. Their "solution" in this case is therefore an advertising man's dream: *city planning for efficient consumption of luxury goods.*

This requires the following physical arrangements: (1) Metropolises, large enough to permit mass production of

17. The authors realize that Veblen did not live to see the present potentialities for abundance in America.

luxuries, and to encourage the sway of emulation and thereby the insatiability of desire. Buildings will be crowded together to lower distributive costs, so that even more resources may be devoted to production, shopping, and consumption. (2) The center of the city becomes a huge shell of a department store; the shell also provides room for offices, entertainment and other light industry, and hotels; the corridors of the department store are the streets, so that no one may walk without being tempted to buy; and of course people are forced to walk—they need not and cannot drive their cars in these corridors. By thus merging streets and corridors (Bellamy suggested enclosable streets in *Looking Backward*), and building a cylindrical 21-story skyscraper one mile in diameter, the authors calculate that they could include all the non-residential facilities for the population of Manhattan—and New York of course comes closest as it is to their model. A tremendous gain in servicing and construction efficiency would ensue. But the most important gain would be in the opportunities for display and advertising—a world's fair every day and everywhere. (3) In their irony, the planners naturally fear lest the poetry of the great writers compete with the poetry of advertising. Hence the universities, museums, and other great institutions of non-popular culture are zoned—like any nuisance—outside the central cylinder; however, by visits there, people weary of the fashion-show at the City Center, weariness which would be economically disastrous, may renew themselves for further bursts of consumption. (4) A somewhat similar renewing function is served by planning a zone of open country, a real "escape," quite near, perhaps five miles from the concentrated Center, beyond which would lie a further zone of state parks and adult camps. (5) Since the authors believe that the true alternative to the city is country, not suburbs, the residence zone is not a satellite town of free-standing homes, but an encircling ring of apartment houses. The apartments, however, are merely service shells, permitting the individual occupants to partition and decorate their space to taste—and emulation.

At the time of spring inventory, by a revival of carnival practices, there would be a season of immense idleness, with bonfires of outmoded furniture, a crescendo of waste—in preparation for the next organized spurt of highly efficient consumption.

The reader of this abstract, as of the text, may not always be sure here what is sexy but serious satire (as in Huxley's *Brave New World*), what plain silliness, and at what point the authors are stating their own genuine goals. In general, however, the moral of the plan comes through without ambiguity: it is a criticism of popular culture, with its drive for less work, more pay and more play; it is also an effort to reveal certain hidden elements of moral worth in modern capitalism. The criticism—the air-conditioned nightmare theme—is familiar enough among radical writers, who sometimes tend to attack with equal fervor the worst abuses, such as lynching, and the most venial foibles, such as radio commercials. But the implicit ethical defense of capitalism on the ground of its provision of bounteous consumption is seldom found outside Chamber of Commerce circles. Sophisticated people who defend capitalism do so either on lesser-evil grounds, or as an interim system, or as a support for political and intellectual freedom; they tend to be apologetic about its encouragement of consumer self-indulgence, if not about consumer values generally.

This general attitude springs, it seems to me, from a growing intellectual hostility to the values of consumer free choice.[18] It is not simply a question of poverty, for many people do not even enjoy window shopping. The left-wingers feel the choice is immoral, because unequally distributed; many, Puritan at heart, would prefer to distribute scarcity. Social hygienists feel it is bad for people: they eat too much rich food (a feeling often rationalized by reference to starving people elsewhere in the world), go to too many movies, etc. Snobs, especially in the older Seaboard cities, react against popular emulative consumption—and the growing cult of effortlessness referred to above

18. For discussion of the percolation of consumer attitudes into all spheres of life and the overreaction against those attitudes, see my article, "The Cash Customer," *Common Sense,* 11:183 (1942).

—by cultivating an indifference to material things; driving Fords, for instance, until they, too, became designed for comfort, rather than more plushy "petit bourgeois" cars such as Oldsmobiles. Those influenced by Veblen or theorists of functionalism in design are hostile to "waste," to conspicuous consumption, and to competition in sale and display. And many people seek to assert their individuality, not by enjoying choice among available consumption products, but by making an issue of resistance to all salesmanship and advertising. Indeed, it has become fashionable even for advertising men to attack advertising.

These attacks are indiscriminate: the joys of consumption, of free consumer choice, of "waste" and frivolity and excess, are thrown out along with the obvious evils of inequality and of anxious emulation. Yet while we are waiting for a better social order, or more meaningful job-opportunities, it would be a mistake to overlook this freedom and the available chances for making it still more free.

This, if I understand them, is one of the points the Goodmans have in mind in their "City of Efficient Consumption." The efficiency they seek is of two sorts. On the side of production, they follow Veblen in seeking to eliminate waste, for instance excessive distribution costs, in order to increase, while lowering hours, the total annual consumable product of goods and services. But on the side of consumption, the "efficiency" is of a different order: it is an effort to heighten waste and emulation in order to make sure that everything produced is consumed, lest the economy be choked by its own superlative productiveness; the pump to be psychologically primed is that of the individual spender. Perhaps, too, the Goodmans seriously feel that by enhancing the efficiency of consumption of the population as a whole, it might be possible to avoid the economic, maybe even political need for periodic creation of an enlarged class of professionally-efficient consumers, namely the armed services. If by consuming luxuries, we could avoid "consuming" armaments, most of us would settle for their City, any day. But it is intended rather as a caricature than as the best of their possible worlds.

In their second model or paradigm, the Goodmans present their own values explicitly. There they try to deal with the divorce of production from consumption in modern industrial society, and to recreate forms of work which will be meaningful without a futile attempt at full retreat to handicraft production. But unlike most of the writers from Marx on who discuss this problem, often in terms of modern man's "alienation," they are fully aware that the impersonality of work today has certain advantages, even if these advantages are analogous to the "secondary gains" of a neurotic illness. They see, for example, that punctuality on the job, which seems to enslave man to the clock, "makes the work itself much more tolerable; for it establishes it in an impersonal, secondary environment where—once one has gotten out of bed early in the morning—the self has already resigned all claims." At work, one is "relieved" of one's family; by the same token, after hours one is "free" of work. Nevertheless, it is, humanly speaking, a crazy divorce, which is simply made smoother by those planners of suburbs who shield the residential area from any contact with the productive economy. The Goodmans try to see what utopian reunions are possible.

To reunite workshop and home, they advocate restoring some work to the home, as domestic industry or subsistence farming, while taking out of the home, and into the larger economy, some domestic services. As to the former, they point to the decentralization made possible by electricity and the new types of small machine tools; as to the latter, they rearrange the home itself, and the role of children.

What the Goodmans are suggesting here is a program which, by increasing the self-sufficiency of the home, the city, and the region, will both lend variety and meaning to work and provide the economic basis for freedom. In this, they follow Frank Lloyd Wright on the physical side and Kropotkin on the social and political; they insist that each producer must have a say in the distribution of "his" product. They believe that the solution of the problem of political power in an industrial economy lies in planning for farm-factory units on a regional basis, where each unit will have enough self-sufficiency to defend itself in bargaining against other like units. This involves "the close integration of factory and farm workers—the factory hands taking over in the fields at peak seasons; farmers doing factory work in winter; town people, especially children, living in the country; farmers making small parts for the factories." But the self-sufficiency must not go too far; each farm, each unit, each region will be integrated into the national and international market as to some of its dealings; there is to be none of the "wilful provincialism that is so nauseating in movements of regional literature and art." Education on and off the job, and frequent changes of job, are to give the producers the knowledge to support their control of distribution, and the world-minded outlook which will guide trading of their regional surpluses for surpluses from elsewhere.

The Goodmans say nothing as to how such a redistribution of resources is to be set up, nor how it will differ in operation from certain patterns of bargaining we have at present, when, let us say, Montana trades its copper for Pennsylvania's coal. In their effort to create a kind of internal balance of economic power, they are up against the same sort of problem which is faced in the Acheson-Lilienthal report on atomic energy: namely, how to find the leverage to distribute economic (or war) potential in such a fashion as to prevent either raids or autarchy. Those who now have the potential (in the atomic case, the United States) hesitate to surrender it, even for the hope of peace; those who lack it (in the atomic case, the U.S.S.R.) hesitate to surrender the chance of getting it, even for the fear of war.

The authors are more instructive in their psychological analysis of the problem of bringing productive work back into human scale. They see the problem as even more difficult, since they see man as even more complex, than many of the industrial psychologists who have been influenced by Elton Mayo. To illustrate: they do not insist, as the Mayo group does, that most workmen want always to work in teams, but rather that men want both group and individual work, both city and country work, both supervision and apprenticeship. Now, since it is undeniable that many factory workers today do not seem to want such diversity, but prefer their accustomed routines and their cluster of associates, we would have to say that this is not what they might want under a different social structure and a different educational system. While many industrial psychologists attempt to adjust workers as they find them to their malaise, as by seeing that they have "recognition" from management and agreeable team-mates, the Goodmans, being utopian, are more interested in adjusting the factory-system to their vision of what man is "really" like. For instance, adolescents would spend five months in general education, two in study-travel, and four in productive work, divided between farm and factory; older workers would shift around less, but would still work on a rhythmic basis with some time devoted either to supervision or to work at their highest technical skill. The jobs themselves would be reanalyzed, not with an eye to technical efficiency, either for production or consumption, but with an eye primarily to joy in work and the assurance of freedom: "Any end is prima facie suspicious if its means, too, do not give satisfaction."

"Supposing one of the masters, away on his two months of individual work, drafting designs for furniture, should decide—having studied the furniture of the Japanese—to dispense with chairs!

"It is problems like this that would create a bitter struggle in the national economy."

It is important to observe, in this otherwise idyllic passage, that the Goodmans do anticipate "bitter struggle" even in Utopia. This is an advance on the work of Bellamy as well as earlier utopians (including Marx) who, focussed on the sordid struggles which spring from capitalist relations, were not sufficiently attentive to clashes of temperament and interest which would spur the making of new utopias even when theirs had been achieved.

The Goodmans illustrate their plan—which they term "The New Commune: the Elimination of the Difference between Production and Consumption"—with drawings of the farmhouses in which families with children will be living. The farms are to be diversified, and zoned quite near to the smallish (200,000) urban nuclei. All children will do farm chores and thus enter "the economy" at a point where it is most comprehensible; the family-sized farms, aided by cooperative marketing and mechanization, will develop a cultural tone which can compete with, rather than submit to, the metropolitan culture.

The metropolitan milieu itself is to recapture something of the quality of leisureliness and sociability of the medieval city square. In their illustrative plan for "Printers' Square," for example, there would be a place for causerie among the gathering workmen, more typical of the French cafe than of the American tavern or coke-bar. Fronting on the Square is the printing factory, with its attached technical school of printing and engraving; a library with terrace-tables for drinks and snacks; some shops; an apartment for urban (childless) dwellers, whose meals are home-cooked after the dirty-work of vegetable washing and peeling, etc., has been communally done. The concept of the Square is, however, rather artificial. Printing happens to be a noisy industry, though not perhaps inevitably so; its relation to the rest of the activities that front on the Square seems tenuous: mere ecological proximity will not produce the kind of local color and culture which the Goodmans seek. Any utopian planning faces the problem of visualizing the intangibles that would give social meaning to physical form and layout. The problem is symbolized by the authors' puzzle as to what kind of public monument they should locate in the Square. A church? Hardly, though Frank Lloyd Wright, despite the idiosyncratic character of his own religion, plunks one down in his plan for Broadacre City. The Goodmans half ironically suggest a Sir Patrick Geddes Regional Museum as the focal point of their Square.

Bellamy's *Looking Backward,* published 60 years earlier, gives us, I think, a more imaginative glimpse of the social and domestic life of a utopian city which in spaciousness and cultivation resembles the more fragmentary picture of the "New Commune"; however, Bellamy's handling of the problems of work and economic life generally is about as different as can be from the Goodmans'. Unlike so many of his contemporary utopians, Bellamy did not turn his back on the Industrial Revolution; he welcomed the increasing pace of mass production and trustification; under his plan, industry was to be "efficiently" run on a national scale, under the direction of the generals of the Industrial Army. All youth were to serve a three-year term at common labor in the Army (rather like a compulsory C.C.C.); those who lacked the ability or desire to specialize would stay on in its lower ranks. The political leaders were to be chosen from among the top administrators who had risen in the Army; in fact, politics was to be largely the process of industrial administration. In some senses, then, Bellamy was a precursor of the theorists of the "managerial revolution."

Since consumption goods and services were to be equally distributed, without regard to rank in the Army (invalids, too, would receive an equal share), Bellamy was particularly concerned to meet the charge of capitalist critics that there would be no "incentive" either to work or to rise—this old, but ever renewed charge based on man's alleged innate laziness. He met this argument partly as the Goodmans do, by an effort to make work meaningful and pleasureful in itself and by encouraging feelings of benevolence and human fellowship in work, but also by reluctant though heavy reliance on the love of praise and the fear of censure. Men were to be educated to seek glory through their industrial ardor, and to avoid being held in contempt for ducking their social responsibilities; officers would rise on the basis of the zealous performance of their underlings.

It seems plain today that production can all too easily be organized on such an emulative and centralized system (compare the "socialist competition" of the Russians); in fact, the motives of hunger and gain which are supposed to operate our market economy have been very largely dispensed with even there.[19] Bellamy, it seems, was not quite

19. Karl Polanyi's *The Great Transformation* (1944) raises the question whether hunger and gain were actual motives as well as approved ones to any large extent, even in the heyday of the market.

utopian enough. One reason is that, though he foresaw the possibility of abundance, if the nationalized industries were properly organized and competitive and distributive wastes abolished, he did not foresee—who could have?—the possibilities of overabundance, the bountiful surplusage of means of production. Equality, and a comfortable, unostentatious standard of living had therefore to be his principal goal, not joy and freedom in work.

Moreover, as we have just observed, the earlier socialists and utopians, including Bellamy, believed that politics would disappear, once the community owned the means of production; and that universal peace would reign, once people were no longer educated to meanness and fear by the ruthlessness of the capitalism of their day. Today, an Industrial Army would give us nightmares; our awareness of totalitarian dangers leads the Goodmans to turn to regionalist and syndicalist writers as against the authoritarian-nationalist Bellamy for suggestions on how to limit the power of the managerial bureaucracy. But as indicated above, their suggestions do not meet the issues.

On the side of the manner of living, however, life has not caught up with Bellamy to the same degree; if we judge by the Goodmans' work, he is still utopian here. The city pictured in *Looking Backward* has about as much sociability and amenity as the Goodmans' "New Commune."[20] There is ample leisure; there are goods enough to satisfy all "genuine" needs (Bellamy even foresaw the radio); domestic life is urbane, with the lot of women improved by communal services. A citizen who is willing to settle for a somewhat lower standard of living is permitted after a time to avoid industrial service, and to devote himself to study, the arts, or whatever he pleases—a suggestion which is also made in the Goodmans' book. Above all, human relations are to be friendly and unexploitative; women are the companions and equals of men (though organized for work in a separate hierarchy); and the individuality of

20. In his sequel, *Equality,* Bellamy dealt more fully with decentralization; Manhattan was to have 250,000 people.

children is respected; in fact from early years on, children are encouraged to develop their taste and their vocational bent. What is similar here to the quality of the Goodmans' Commune is the emphasis on quiet happiness, as against excitement, as the aim of life. There is to be neither war nor economic competition; the excitement of the chase, of sadism, of exploitation will be disapproved; the city plan calls for contemplative, easy-going, and cultivated joys.

The Goodmans do not really hope that we could move directly to such a utopia, when our values are so very largely the excitement-values of the "City of Efficient Consumption." They offer, therefore, a third plan which they term an interim measure: its purpose is to minimize economic regulation, and thus to permit once more a choice of economic goals.

Over-regulation in our surplus economy arises, the Goodmans argue, because "overproduction" jeopardizes the jobs of the poor and the profits of the rich; the government is forced to interfere to assure full employment, thus making employment itself—in all its modern meaninglessness—the very end and aim of the community's political activity. Then the free market, one of the few remaining freedoms, becomes entangled in regulation (private, of course, as well as governmental) and taxes (private, of course, as well as governmental) to raise funds to subsidize, insure, and otherwise shore up the economy. The authors propose: that the problem of subsistence be divided off from the problem of luxury; the subsistence market, occupying a small fraction of the country's resources, would be government-controlled, with some scheme akin to rationing providing everyone with his basic needs; while the luxury market would be free of control and entitled, since no one would starve in any case, to its privilege of boom and bust.

"The retrenchment might go very far, relaxing kinds of governmental regulation that are now indispensable; for, where the prospective wage earner has a subsistence independently earned, the conditions under which he agrees to work can be allowed to depend on his own education rather than on the government's coercion of the employer."[21]

The industrialist would then lose the subsistence market and its labor force; the worker, unless in post-adolescence he could afford a paid substitute, would be coerced for the fraction of his time (recall again Bellamy's conscription) needed to produce the subsistence goods and services.

The authors believe that such a pattern (its economic details, obviously complex, are barely sketched) would commit the community to less irreversible change, in architecture and layout, than is demanded by the present type of Keynesian-New Deal methods for insuring full employment. They fully realize, however, that the basic question "what is subsistence?" is a cultural, not a medical problem, and that its solution requires a decision as to how much in consumers' emulative goods (the "standard of living") we are willing to give up in order to gain a greater measure of freedom from regulation. The Goodmans assume that much of our expenditure on clothing, cars, etc., is really forced on us by a competitive race, failure in which threatens even the minimum of self-support. The subsistence economy will, accordingly, provide food, clothing, and prefabricated shelter which is adequate but not varied or stylish. On the other hand, since people are to be freed for such work in the luxury economy as they want, they must be assured, as part of their subsistence, more physical and psychological mobility than at present; hence, full transportation (and medical service) are handled as subsistence items also.

The most difficult political and economic questions arise in attempting to relate the two economies, the free one and

21. By giving those who want to pursue wealth an entire economy to themselves, insulated from the subsistence economy, the plan retains one of the chief advantages of nineteenth-century capitalism, where power was divided because some men sought it directly in the political sphere while others went primarily after money. Thus, unlike the modern managerial state, politics and economics were not entirely overlapping spheres; the result was some freedom in the interstices and a lessening of ideological pressures.

the subsistence one. (It is here, as the authors point out, that similar attempts—Robert Owen's plan for New Lanark, Louis Blanc's Workshops, the FSA and the WPA—have failed.) To keep the subsistence economy non-competitive, its standards cannot be permitted to rise; to keep the private, free economy from oppressing it, for instance by control of facilities such as transport that both would use, the government might have to use its power over the labor supply. In times of prosperity, demand for subsistence products such as clothing and shelter will diminish, since almost everyone will be able to afford the greater variety of offerings on the private, free economy; in times of crisis, the subsistence demands will rise—but this very pattern will tend to mitigate the business cycle. By the (admittedly) very roughest of calculations based on national income and production figures, the authors guess that no more than one-seventh of the available resources (in labor-time or money) would be required to produce subsistence for all Americans; and that this figure is less than that to which the country, in pursuit of the same security goals, is already committed. Obviously, these calculations, financial and political, would need refinement before one could be pretty sure that the plan of the Goodmans would be any less fragile than the Keynesian approach which they attack.

Most interesting on the architectural side are the elevations and layouts for the residences of the subsistence workers. The Goodmans, unlike Mumford, have faith that prefabrication can produce really cheap mass housing. Many of their trailer-type houses would not need public utilities; others would operate with community kitchens and showers; families could combine their allotments to secure more commodious quarters. The subsistence houses are not meant to be especially inviting—though, as drawn, they look better than millions of rural and urban slum dwellings —for if one wants better housing, one must work in the free economy to pay for it: the subsistence economy's purpose is freedom, not luxury.

Once the obligations to the subsistence economy have been met, one would not have to work at all; whatever one needed, within the subsistence limits, would be free (again compare *Looking Backward*). But do we really want freedom?

"Suddenly, the Americans would find themselves rescued from the physical necessity and social pressure which alone, perhaps, had been driving them to their habitual satisfactions; they might suddenly find the commercial pleasures flat and unpalatable, but they would not therefore suddenly find any other resources within themselves.

"Like that little girl in the progressive school, longing for the security of the grownup's making her decisions for her, who asks: 'Teacher, today again do we have to do what we want to do?' "[22]

Escape from bored freedom into compulsive activity and excitement might become a powerful political movement, until education had been able to nourish the instinct of workmanship, of spontaneous creativity, the capacity for happiness as against excitement, which the Goodmans, along with their utopian teachers, believe to exist in everyone. Perhaps, they suggest, there would be a revival of small business ventures (in fact, we have actually seen this among the veterans, who today come closest to having a subsistence claim devoid of moral strictures); "for the risk of fundamental insecurity of life has been removed, and why should one not work to amass a little capital and then risk it in an enterprise that was always close to one's heart?" In any case, there would be renewed emphasis on the problem of one's "calling," one's true vocation, when all have behind them the security and experience of the subsistence economy and can take their time, as only the rich can now do, before choosing one's work in the free enterprise economy. (Again, a theme from Bellamy.) Or, one might choose not to choose, but to travel or study, a modern (and therefore quite different) Thoreau.

The Goodmans, however, share values with Thoreau

22. Bellamy had observed: "The fact that all the world goes after money saves a man the necessity of anxiously debating what his life is for." From the unpublished papers of Bellamy, quoted in Arthur E. Morgan, *Nowhere Was Somewhere* (1946).

(and Frank Lloyd Wright) but also with Marx, who spoke of the "idiocy of rural life"; they do not want to dismantle the metropolis. But trailers will not work in a large city; even a city slum will be too dear for the subsistence economy—as, indeed, the poor today cannot afford big city housing where there is no direct or indirect subsidy. So, then, a man must pay for his metropolitan advantages by work in the private economy, without thereby securing exemption from his subsistence duties. Thus many might desert the metropolis for the subsistence centers, and the Goodmans realize that this problem is not fully solved in their theoretical structure. But, since the purpose of their plan is security with minimum regulation, it cannot be said to leave most big city dwellers worse off than today. Especially if they want freedom.

IV. It has not been my purpose in these pages to criticize the Goodmans' own models, nor their discussion of earlier community plans. The real value of their book lies not in this or that detail but in their explicit attachment to the now-languishing tradition of utopian thought. Their text, like a physical plan, does not render up all its meaning at first glance: an innocent-looking phrase may conceal a whole philosophy; I hope that they and others who are qualified will proceed with the necessary follow-up. The sort of imaginative courage, the sort of detail-work, which is required to plan today even for the development of a single city or region, is no news to the readers of this Law Journal, since the Yale Law School was one of the first institutions to recognize that community planning demands both a policy goal and a novel integration of the sciences.[23]

23. See Lasswell and McDougal, "Legal Education and Public Policy: Professional Training in the Public Interest," *Yale Law J.*, 52:217–32 (1943); Directive Committee on Regional Planning, Yale University, *The Case for Regional Planning* (1947). On the diversity of interests and skills required of the community planner, see Martin Meyerson, "What a Planner Has to Know" in *Proceedings, Annual Conference on Planning* (1946), p. 167. I am indebted to Mr. Meyerson for helpful suggestions.

But it may be news to the many community planners, at least of the older generation, who view their work as just another specialty. This problem of interdisciplinary cooperation may be illuminated by a brief comparison with a bold contemporary plan which is [1947] being put into effect, the Plan for the community of Warsaw. What follows is based on a conversation in the spring of 1946 with Szymon and Helen Syrkus, the former being one of the principal architects (now a director of the National Ministry of Reconstruction) and the latter an executive of the Plan.

Long before 1939, a small group of architects, city planners, social scientists and social workers had begun, in isolation from the dominant soddenness of the Polish government, to develop rather utopian conceptions of community planning. To a large extent, they seem to have been inspired by Robert Owen. They had an opportunity to build a "pilot model," a spacious though inexpensive cooperative in Racasiewicz, a Warsaw suburb; then the War came. After the bombing and capture of the city, members of the group continued to meet secretly to make plans for the rebuilding of the capital after the War. As they proceeded, they drew into their circle additional scientific collaborators. They discovered, for instance, that proper residential layout required an analysis of how far children could comfortably walk alone—for this they went to the child psychologists and social workers. From the economists, they secured data as to the cost to the community if private automobiles had to be provided for. From the data of the engineers, the group concluded what factories still had to be treated as nuisances under modern conditions, and what other factories due, for instance, to the type of skill employed, might add to the culture and amenity of the city; they proceeded with zoning on this basis. Architects and landscape architects worked on the problem: what sort of vistas, what sort of décor, create what sort of social and psychological attitudes in people; they wanted the walls and roofs and other shapes to say to people: "what's your hurry?" (The subtlety of this problem is such that it seems hardly to have been touched scientifically; the Rorschach test provides certain clues to its investigation, as Schachtel's work has shown.)[24]

On the basis of these and other studies, the cooperating architects then began to draw the detail plans for post-war Warsaw. Most of the group were eventually killed by the Nazis; the Syrkuses were among the few who managed to survive the wounds they suffered in concentration camps; many of the plans also survived. But after the isolation of the War, the survivors felt the need to see what had been learned elsewhere in their field; they journeyed to Sweden, to Russia, to the United States to find out.

It is my impression that they discovered little (save a few technical points such as new types of building materials) which their interdisciplinary group had not already explored. Reading *Communitas* fifteen months later, it was striking to see the resemblances between the Warsaw plans and those of the Goodmans' favorite utopia, the "New Commune," both with respect to some of the social values implicit in the plans and with respect to their physical features. The Warsaw residences are to be formed in super-blocks, but without the monotonous regularity of most of our own urban redevelopments; rather, with an eye to vistas, the paths will wind; the walk-up apartments will be variously grouped. At the calculated radii there will be: trees and play-yards for small fry; schools and libraries and meeting halls for the older folk; shopping centers will be on the through highways no further away than a mother can easily walk with a small child. Since the women are to be freed as much as possible from domestic drudgery, laundries, crèches, cooking will be communal; there are rooms where they can park their children at night to attend political meetings or go to the library with their husbands. But since women also enjoy cooking, when they are not compelled to it, and gain a feeling of status from the quality of a particular soup or casserole, the Polish

24. Ernest Schachtel, "The Dynamic Perception and the Symbolism of Form: With Special Reference to the Rorschach Test," *Psychiatry*, 4:79 (1941); "On Memory and Childhood Amnesia," *Psychiatry*, 10:1 (1947).

planners insisted that each apartment have a private kitchen too, even though they were trying desperately to save on plumbing and all dispensable expense. In this decision, they expressed their own values, and also, they felt, those of the people.

Interdisciplinary cooperation and scientific surveys, however, will not solve the problems which arise when the planners' values diverge from those of the general community. This point was raised by my question: suppose a family prefers the amenity of an automobile to the amenity of a kitchen, or would even sacrifice for it the minimum standards as to square feet of space per person that the planners had fixed upon; how could the family exercise consumer free choice and make its preference felt? The Syrkuses replied that, apart from obvious economic obstacles in present-day Poland, the example of America had convinced them that the automobile will spoil the best of urban residential plans; moreover, the factories and even open country will be within easy walking or bicycling distance from the homes; there will be a rapid transit system and a highway net along the River outside the City (I suppose, for common carrier and military traffic). They also added that the appropriate legislative bodies had enthusiastically approved the Plan. I was not entirely satisfied with this explanation.[25] Abstract as the question was in 1946, I had the impression that the planners might be freezing the shape of the City against private cars, perhaps without fully acquainting their constituents with the meaning of the choice being made in their behalf. Yet since health and the general welfare are clearly involved in minimum housing standards, I asked myself if the question really differed

25. Before the reader becomes too skeptical of the Polish dictatorship—on *this* score—let him recall that rent subsidies, multiple dwelling laws, etc., compel the renter in American cities to buy space and fixtures where he might prefer to spend his share of the social income on something else. A group of American architects and city planners, visiting Warsaw, recently commented on the "extremely humanistic" and undoctrinaire quality of the Poles' physical planning. N. Y. Times, Sept. 13, 1947, p. 6, col. 3.

from the forcible vaccination of individual recalcitrants by public health authorities. Anyhow, the car question came to symbolize for me the whole issue of coercion in utopian community planning.

The very gap that separates the thinking of the advanced planner from that of his clients tends to lead him to dictatorial measures. For his work teaches him that he can do little to achieve his goals by verbal persuasion: if the walls and streets and vistas, the cars and subways, the kitchens and showers—if these say "hurry, hurry," how can his message of communal quiet and calm possibly be heard, or, if heard, emotionally understood? If people are drugged with excitement, will they not crave more of the same, like any addict, especially when the whole economy would flounder if they failed to respond? Must not the planner at least jazz up his plans and elevations? I suggest that the true utopian errs if he allows himself to be seduced by such arguments. The moment he begins to manipulate (let alone use physical coercion)—even if the manipulation only consists in the use of reasoning which does not convince *him* but which he feels may "sell" his audience—he leaves the realm of utopia for that of ideology. Thereby he demonstrates, in many cases, his lack of the "nerve of failure." For it is not always his benevolence which leads him to force or manipulate people to do what is in their objective interest. It is his doubt as to his own correctness, which can be assuaged only by securing confirmation in plans and behavior he will live to see—these are his prophet's "sign."

The Goodmans quote Daniel Burnham who lived at a time (the turn of the century) when, or so it appears to us, faith was a less difficult virtue:

> "Make no little plans; they have no magic to stir men's blood and probably themselves will not be realized. Make big plans: aim high in hope and work, remembering that a noble, logical diagram, once recorded, will never die, but long after we are gone will be a living thing, asserting itself with ever growing insistency."

So might the Warsaw underground planners have thought, who later perished in the concentration camps, or in the city's battles of liberation. Their diagrams did survive. But this strikes us as somewhat accidental, a rather insubstantial ground for faith. The real question is one about people, not plans: are they really hopeless addicts or can they, enough of them, appreciate what a good community plan would be like even when they have grown up under a bad plan? The utopian's faith is that the answer is affirmative, though its timing—here he can learn from Marx and Engels—depends on a congeries of social forces. That faith is supported by the very tradition of utopian thinking in which the planner works, and which is a record of just such human ability to transcend the ideologies provided by the culture and to add something new to the small precious stock of social ideas.

Some Observations on Intellectual Freedom

> And if the ice was really to be broken, laughter and jest must be introduced into the consideration of the matter. In politics or business it would be obvious enough that one could not achieve a realistic view of what was happening if one was debarred from discussing principles or acts save in terms of respectful solemnity. Fun and ridicule must be allowed to play their part in the analysis of the motives or characters or doings of the principal actors; otherwise political discussion would remain at an unrealistic level, and those who discussed them would have a sense of servitude.
>
> —R. F. Harrod, *The Life of John Maynard Keynes*

Vague and hortatory articles and speeches about the crisis of our age are a sign of the "respectful solemnity" we ethnocentrically reserve for *our* problems. I myself have sinned by entitling a monograph "Civil Liberties in a Period of Transition," falling too uncritically in with the comfortably disquieting supposition that the time in which I happen to be alive is by definition such a period! Such rhetorical grandiosity may illustrate Tocqueville's observation that, as a result of living in a democracy, the American's "ideas are all either extremely minute and clear, or extremely general and vague; what lies between is an open void."

This article is an effort to enter, in a somewhat dialectical fashion, into the open void, and to do so without the sense of servitude that characterizes much contemporary talk and writing about the fate of the intellectuals. I shall discuss

"Some Observations on Intellectual Freedom" was first published in The American Scholar, *Vol. 23, No. 1, 1953.*

some new-found conformities that seem to be emerging among many people who claim, often with good right, the mantle of liberalism; I am also curious about general tendencies influencing the position and self-confidence of intellectuals. Archibald MacLeish's article on "Loyalty and Freedom" (*American Scholar*, Autumn 1953) is therefore the occasion compelling me to set down observations long accumulating. If, in what follows, I sometimes refer to his piece, I do so because it provides a ready illustration; many others could be found. I want to make it clear that I respect Mr. MacLeish's integrity and generosity; his motives recall Yeats' lines: "All things can tempt me from this craft of verse. . . . The seeming needs of my fool-driven land. . . ." If, to a person of my trade and training, certain poets and other artists appear at times politically naive when they make proclamations (while I must appear naive in another sense to them), this naivete doesn't bother me and doesn't require an "answer"; I will fight with any censor for the right of such people to go on being naive and "irresponsible." At best, my article is intended not to engender a debate, but to qualify a tone and thereby the better to represent the pluralism which is one of the glories of liberalism.

I. Intellectuals try to cope with their anxiety by telling each other atrocity stories about America. When this is done in science fiction, as in *Galaxy's* serial "Gravy Planet" (recently republished in a pocket book as *The Space Merchants*), it can be witty and even revealing. But when it is done with seriousness and portentousness, the consequences can only be anti-intellectual, can only stultify thought in the listener who, bemused at once by guilt and by self-righteousness, murmurs "Amen," "how true."

Other than as the expression of a current mood of a priori despair, the tales about America currently in circulation are often not entirely true. When, for instance, America's justly criticizable follies and excesses are compared with the systematic and calculated terror of the Soviet Union and the Nazis, the double standard applied misleads us in our estimation of events on both sides of the Iron Curtain. Totalitarianism, though it draws on attitudes and on techniques of organization available in the Western, and perhaps the whole world, becomes in its totality something new as soon as it seizes power; as Hannah Arendt has observed, we quite fail to understand totalitarianism when we simply extrapolate from (or back to) societies where the party system and its ideological competition still function, however badly. In my opinion totalitarian societies, once in power, dispense to a large extent with group or national loyalty (which involves danger of overadherence to principle), much as they dispense with ideological propaganda for internal consumption (replacing it with instructions in what the "line" now is, and who has hold of it). If many writers appear to overestimate the loyalty engendered under totalitarianism, they also fail to count their blessings when they attack the apathy, that is, the lack of loyalty to ideals, of many Americans. For this very apathy has its positive side as a safeguard against the overpoliticization of the country: the apathetic ones, often not so much fearful or faithless as bored, may be as immunized against political appeals, good or bad, as against much commercial advertising. Though, of course, there is much pressure for an undiscriminating chauvinistic loyalty and belongingness to a wide variety of groups, including the nation, I am impressed by the fact that among GIs there is far less nationalism than in the first World War—indeed, the pressure for loyalty may be, among other things, one, often unconscious, form of the battle between older and younger generations.

Moreover, the conflict between loyalty and freedom may be quite absent from the minds of many politically apathetic people who appear to be "followers" of Senator McCarthy: they see him in terms of the drama of his career: has he found a gimmick that will get him ahead? The meaning they see in him resembles what they find in figures of the entertainment world or the underworld who have risen to the top without gentility, without connections, and apparently without education. Some of those who have this dramatic view of what on the surface operates as an "anti-Communist crusade" are quite prepared to continue to befriend neighbors who have been called, as ex-Communists, before congressional committees; because for them the salient issue is not one of loyalty, or politics at all, they may even be a bit proud to know somebody who got into the papers. I don't know how widespread this apolitical reaction is, but I do know it is terribly difficult to interpret what Mr. MacLeish refers to as "our silence as a people"—European intellectuals can make very little of it either, perhaps because American cynicism and European cynicism exist in very different contexts. When we try to deal with so big and stratified a country as ours—so big it often cannot hear the talk of the articulate—we ought not begin by reading into others our own fears and idealisms.

Something of a double standard is also employed in many conventional comparisons of the American present with the American past. If, despite the Know-Nothings, a rough toleration has at times been maintained within our country, fears and hatreds have found outlets against Indians, Mexicans, Spaniards—and Japanese (wars often fought, or prolonged, for social-psychological reasons after the enemy had virtually capitulated). Moreover, to exalt the Founding Fathers as having faith in man, as Mr. MacLeish does, would certainly come as a surprise to crusty John Adams, and to Madison; Jefferson might be willing, periodically, to accept the accolade. The Constitution exists, and is the magnificent job it is, in large part because the Fathers had so very limited a faith in man that they sought to protect us from our own and each other's weaknesses wherever possible. The more we know about American 18th-century thought the more complex it appears: strands of religious pessimism persisted from the Great Awakening; the Enlightenment itself was no single-voiced adventure in optimism (recall Diderot's *Rameau's Nephew*); much talk of Reason took account not of all men but only of the educated; and so on. I am inclined to think we have, with a few exceptions, much more faith in man than the Fathers had, and I think this is in some respects a sign of our progress.

Very likely, however, we do not have as much faith as our parents did: we know a bit more, we have seen a lot more, and our aspirations are hardly less. The New Deal and World War II gave many intellectuals and academic people a pleasant feeling of being close to the seats of power, of being in on big doings. To some extent, this feeling was delusive—an aspect of the amiable come-on Franklin Roosevelt practiced with many different groups, from Groton graduates to Hollywood stars. Correspondingly, for all too many intellectuals it drew a connection between being influential and having self-confidence, a connection any even temporary fall in the "market" might sever; in the process, enjoyment of study and intellectual functioning for their own sakes became too much devalued. The post-War inflation which has raised the level of living for organized workers, many small businessmen, and other groups has relatively squeezed our financial security at the same time that, still prominent but no longer so politically protected, the intellectuals have faced a new (but I am hopeful to think presently receding) wave of loyalty oaths, investigations, and other marks of special suspicion and special attention.

Even so, I am inclined to think that many intellectuals today, so far as I can judge their views, overestimate the monolithic power of Reaction. Peter Viereck once remarked that anti-Catholicism is the anti-Semitism of the intellectuals. Certainly in many strata people like to exaggerate the Church's power as in less educated circles they enjoy exaggerating the power of the Jews; very seldom can one hear or read much discussion about the cleavages within American Catholicism or read analyses of the great reservoirs of decency there, analyses which show understanding of the role of the Orders, of missionary parishes, etc.

Likewise, gloomy talk about the "fascist menace" in America overlooks the fact that all efforts of fascist groups to join forces have in the past come to nought because the very suspiciousness and paranoia which are the fascist leader's stock in trade make it well-nigh impossible for him to cooperate with other salesmen on his side of the street—splinter movements seem endemic to "true believers." Moreover, our ethnic diversity, our regional and religious pluralism, our vested corruptions, all tend to confine a fanatical leader to "his" people and section. While only the smug would assert "it can't happen here," it does seem reasonable to assert that it is unlikely, and that the Nazi parallels that undoubtedly exist can be overdrawn. We are neither a small, nor a defeated country.

The naming of evils, intended as a magical warding-off, can have the opposite effect. It is easy to imagine a group of academic people or civil servants, sitting about in the hot summer of 1953, and swapping stories about who got fired from the Voice of America because he subscribed to *The Nation,* and how so-and-so was not rehired at Benton College because his wife had once joined the League of Women Shoppers—each capping the other's whopper of the reactionary menace. What is the consequence? A stiffening of spines? A clearing of the mind and will for action? I doubt it.

I often suspect [if I may quote an earlier article of mine[1]] that the people who tell such stories are, unconsciously, seeking to create a climate which will justify in their own minds the concessions they are making—or, sometimes, a climate which, being worse in those they have spoken to and convinced, is better "inside" than "out." That is, the person who tells such stories (and, as I've indicated, it doesn't matter that they are true stories, one must distinguish between the weight and purpose of different truths) can feel he is bowing to strong pressures when he himself for instance drops a friend who might be suspected of an undue interest in racial equality. . . .

In short, intellectuals who, for whatever reason, choose to regard themselves as being victimized contribute to the very pressures they deplore. These pressures are not so strong as alleged; thinking them strong helps make them so.

II. In a way, the attention that intellectuals are getting these days, though much of it is venomous and indecent, testifies to the great improvement in our status over that of an earlier day. What might not Henry Adams have given

1. "Some Observations on the Limits of Totalitarian Power," *Antioch Review,* 12:156 (1952). Reprinted in *Individualism Reconsidered,* The Free Press, 1954.

for such signs of recognition! In his day the intellectual was no threat to anybody: whether clergyman or scholar, he had to defer to the "practical" men, the men of business and affairs. It is almost inconceivable today that a father should say: "Where Vanderbilt sits, there is the head of the table. I teach my son to be rich." In the much more fluid and amorphous America of our time, the writer, the artist, the scientist, have become figures of glamour, if not of power. It is harder to say where the head of the table is. The practical, non-intellectual man feels uneasy with these changes; he resents the fact that his own importance, as well as his own understanding of the world, are threatened by the intellectual and the intellectual's ability to change ideas. There is a tendency for the older class struggles, rooted in clear hierarchical antagonisms, to be replaced by a new status warfare: one between the groups which, by reason of rural or small-town location, ethnicity, or other parochialism, feel threatened by ideas and the better educated upper-middle-class people (though often less wealthy and politically powerful) who follow or create the modern movements in science, art, literature, and opinion generally.[2] In other words, anti-intellectualism has increased in this country in proportion to (though not only because of) the growth of intellectualism. City slickers are no longer only bankers, lawyers, and drummers—they are drummers of ideas, that is, professors, teachers, writers, and artists.[3]

The reaction of many intellectuals to Stevenson's defeat may be taken as an illustration of my point about their real strength despite their professed weakness. They acted

2. Cf. Eric Larrabee's discussion of the Gathings Committee majority and minority reports in "Obscenity and Morality," address to the American Library Association, Los Angeles, June 1953.

3. Many of the humanists are in a paradoxical position, for they suffer the vulnerabilities without attaining the glamour and glory of other academics—one reason, possibly, for their frequent very great resentment of their colleagues who lay claim, justified or not, to the mantle of Science.

throughout the campaign as if *they* were up for election: they identified themselves with Stevenson's pathos as well as with his lovely wit. They saw the campaign through his eyes as an Oxford Union debate in which the opposition mulishly refused to answer "points" or explain contradictions. The same over-ideological outlook allowed them to be bemused by the notion, so strenuously promulgated by F. D. R., that the Democrats were the party of virtue and progress, the Republicans of reaction. Surprised, as I hardly think they should have been, that Ike swept the country, they felt they had been rejected. In their despair, they neglected the impressive fact that their man, their identity, had garnered over 27,000,000 votes against one of the most appealing candidates ever put up, and in spite of all the inherited handicaps of the Democrats. Perhaps, like any rising class, we do not feel we are rising quite fast enough, and momentary setbacks unduly dismay us.

III. As one move toward greater differentiation, we should review some case-histories of people who have refused to make concessions urged upon them, and consider whether and to what extent they have suffered for it. I think that such a study would show how, for instance, a professor can call and be called names and survive unscathed. An account of the detailed reasons why Harvard, Sarah Lawrence, Chicago, and many other places have not succumbed to the first trumpet blasts of investigating committees would seem to me both more illuminating and more important than to add to the well-rehearsed choruses of academic degradation. Without doubt, liberals as well as fellow-travelers are under attack in many parts of this country. But are these places where they were formerly secure?

I do not overlook the fact that liberals teaching in small colleges in fundamentalist or reactionary communities are still less secure now.[4] And such people do need succor and

4. A balanced estimate would have to take account of shifts in the issues, manifest and covert, to which the community is sensitive. In 1890, Veblen was refused a post at St. Olaf's College because he "does not see the difference between science and religion," and "would treat the his-

defense. Articles in Mr. MacLeish's tone may give such people succor through recognition, if not clarification, of their plight: through giving labels to their mood. But by and large I would assume that the *American Scholar* circulates, not in these areas, but in the larger centers where, in sizeable groups, views such as Mr. MacLeish has expressed are not news. In these latter groups, there seems to exist a blind fright and frenzy about "witch-hunts," all committees and their membership being lumped together in a composite caricature.

From the Hiss[5] case we may perhaps date the beginning not only of the excessive power and renown of many Johnny-come-lately anti-Communists but also, on the other side, of what might be thought of as a new united front in some liberal colleges and universities, admission to which is gained by denouncing "witch-hunts" and refusing to cooperate with them. Much as the Communists were forgiven their earlier treacheries when they joined in the Resistance against the Nazis in occupied Europe, and indeed fought their way to leadership, so in the new American front the menace of McCarthy helps bring about a similar factitious solidarity among those who are sympathetic to, or apologetic about, or opposed to Communism. In some colleges,

torical content of the Bible as he would handle an old document that one might find in China." (See *Scandinavian-American Studies and Records*, 15:128–29 (1949). Neither such views nor sexual irregularities would cause a professor similar trouble today. In our time, professors may have become conformists in many respects—there may be fewer "characters" among us—but I am struck with how many, provided they are anti-Communist, have held on to Marxist views without being vilified or pressured.

5. I believe Hiss, in his arrogant treatment of Chambers and the Congressional Committee, was doing the country a far more serious disservice than in his earlier, very likely inconsequential espionage and other efforts to influence foreign policy. If he had told the Committee, as less publicized witnesses have done since, how it happened that a more or less idealistic and successful young lawyer could get involved with the Communist Party, he would have contributed to clarification instead of mystification, and perhaps partially disentangled the knots of identification

professors who testify before the Velde or Jenner committees with dignity and restraint (often educating committee members in the process, as Hiss so notably failed to do) are slandered as appeasers. To the extent that Communists, by such tactics, can get non-Communists to claim the Fifth Amendment, they too can pass off their men as martyrs to principle. This is the general confusion that let Odysseus out of the giant's cave; and in the scramble, the chief ethical problem—to what extent one should tell the committee not about oneself but about others—is obscured. The very term "witch-hunt" is obscurantist.

It may be true that, as this new-found front gains momentum, in AAUP chapters and elsewhere, it will shift the context into which such articles as Mr. MacLeish's fall. While the view of America they bespeak is so dispiriting that in some circles a kind of internal neutralism may be encouraged—why defend freedom if it is already beaten?—in united front circles these writings may well stiffen resistance to loyalty investigations, and thus in some degree serve to strengthen academic freedom. But this might turn out to be an ambiguous dividend, won only because many professors will have become afraid of being thought scared, and because many who share Mr. MacLeish's premises will have concluded that any intra-academic dissension is treachery. However, in my opinion achievement of this airless conformism under the banner of non-conformity would be a confession of academic defeat and vulnerability.

Even critics of articles like Mr. MacLeish's may fall in with this kind of "don't wash dirty linen" clannishness: they may fear that his attitude would encourage European and Asian neutralism. Doubtless, many Europeans are already

binding so many decent people to him and hence to the view that he was being victimized. It might have been revealed that his case had special elements (special guilts, special arrogances, special impatiences) and that therefore, despite appearances, it was not a generation on trial but a fringe. Perhaps Hiss thought he could brazen it out. As the square-jawed, clean-cut hero of the two he would have a comic-strip advantage. Perhaps he was ashamed to disillusion his non-Communist friends and preferred to drag them down with him.

too inclined to accept some American intellectuals' estimate of their own situation. (In our tradition, what is critical often seems more plausible than what is approbatory.) And since the Soviet Union, Red China, their satellites and mass parties remain the chief threat to freedom, such writers as Mr. MacLeish may be criticized for giving indirect aid and comfort to the foreign foe. But at this point, I would come to their defense and say that we are not so weak as to need a unity chorus at home to persuade intellectuals abroad to love and admire us! Since I share Mr. MacLeish's enthusiasm for freedom of thought and expression, I gladly take the risks of Europeans or Indians overhearing our conversation, and drawing their own conclusions—not the ones, I feel sure, that Mr. MacLeish would expect them to draw.

IV. It is characteristic of our times that we raise public relations considerations, if only to reject them. I agree with the implication of Mr. MacLeish's article that we are not the men our ancestors were—we tend to be less rigid, more agreeable, more cooperative and conciliatory. In an earlier, less "other-directed" age, polemics could be carried on, as they still are among Europeans, with fewer restraints based on one's resonance with the other, one's awareness and sympathy and misgiving. Such "weaknesses," when judged by an older standard of intransigent self-righteousness, are among those that Mr. MacLeish would perhaps like to see expunged in favor of the Spartan virtues he attributes to an earlier America. In Lionel Trilling's novel, *The Middle of the Journey,* we can see the power of such virtues, in Mrs. Croom or in Maxim, as against the hesitant and conciliatory Laskell in whom all voices echo.

Yet if we are to find our way out of the tricky personal and social perils peculiar to our day, as well as out of those that afflict any given day, it does not profit us to strive for the moral athleticism and heroism that not even a William James could drill into us. We must work with the psychological tools available to us, and not waste time bemoaning the loss of those blunter ones our forefathers possessed. We know today, for example, that all communication is problematic, a trap of serried ambiguities and obscure consequences. One must always bear in mind—can hardly help bearing in mind—for whom one is writing, even if one violently disagrees with Sartre's theory of "engagement." (I am aware that I am writing this for the *American Scholar*, not *Life*, the new *American Mercury*, or even *The New Leader*.)

However, a writer may make mistakes both about his audience and the pressures they are under: in aiming to challenge complacency wherever he finds it, he may instead strengthen it, or he may further harass people too wounded to listen.[6] I have often been in just this dilemma, as a result of the domestic repercussions of the cold war, in my relations with students and audiences. For instance, when I speak, usually on non-political topics, in the Midwest or in smaller communities in the East, someone is almost sure to ask out of the blue what about Owen Lattimore or don't I think America is going fascist or something of the sort. Often, he turns out to be a *Nation* reader, isolated and bereft, decent and dogmatic, frozen in middle life into what may earlier have been a less spiky carapace of liberalism. He has been waiting eagerly for the coming of light and learning from the University of Chicago to help lift the siege he has been laboring under among his townsfolk: he wants to be told that he isn't crazy, but that the others are. What am I to do when I share his associates' opinions of his opinions, if not of his character and motives? Am I to add one more blow to his self-esteem? To deny my own principles to support his? The mixture of therapy with education is characteristic of our time, and we have no easy answer for a problem that would not have bothered the Victorians.

With students, similar problems arise. Before World War II, I had moderate good luck in getting totalitarian-minded students to chuck some of their stereotypes about America, even if they did not accept mine. When very little penalty, and often even kudos, befell the members of the Party-dominated student groups, I could attack their criti-

6. For fuller discussion of this problem see earlier chapter, "Values in Context."

cisms without seeming to attack them as individuals; one can do this with the young—their ideas are not affixed to them but are part of a diffuse process of development and discovery; individually, I could encourage them not to be intimidated by the fear of being thought bourgeois. They would not suspect me of worrying about the reputation of my university. Now, as I need hardly say, all that is changed. Radical-minded students have learned in high school or even earlier to be wary of adults; afraid of being seduced by expediency, they have put a kind of intellectual chastity belt around their views. Since some of the nobler-spirited young still want risk and emancipation from parents, the educator who offers them a less clear and less violent set of ideas tends to be fanatically resisted.

Another curious kind of situation arises when the question of the books one uses in teaching comes under the scrutiny of an investigating committee. One of the general education courses in the College at Chicago was criticized by the Broyles Committee of the Illinois legislature because it assigned the *Communist Manifesto* and other writings of Marx and Engels. Before that, some of us had felt these works to be inappropriate for the particular course—for one thing, because the students had not yet had any historical background to understand the portrait of English industrial misery in the 1840's; for another, because we felt the course already too overweighted on the side of the "great books" as against more empirical or experimental materials. But ever since the investigation, the *Manifesto* has been frozen into the course: to replace it now would be regarded as a symbol of knuckling under to egregious, ill-meant criticism; and we and our students have become to that extent a captive audience.

While perhaps a majority of students in this course find Marx dull—in a way, they feel they know all that, and it's irrelevant—a minority feels called upon to speak up for or about Marx, lest they conclude they have betrayed themselves. I hesitate to put students into a position where they must make such a choice (our course is required), but would prefer to have them select their Armageddons at their own time and place. And this is one reason among many why I am opposed to most teaching of social studies in the high schools or earlier, for neither students nor teachers can be protected there against at least some kind of inquisition; the result will either be mushy piety or muddled bravado: in neither case will it be critical understanding. The schools, I think, would do better to teach subjects less vague and less inviting to censorship, leaving the social studies until later or for independent student exploration.[7] But again, the context makes it difficult to say this, or for the schools to do anything about their curricula, without being put in the position of seeming to bow to reaction, or to the intemperate attacks on John Dewey and progressive education. Thus, captive audiences spring up all around, precisely in the most advanced sections of the intellectual community.

I recall in this connection a conversation with the energetic editor of a liberal periodical who had suggested in one of his articles that there was something to be said for the investigating committees: they were not all vicious, and after all Communist conspiracies had existed. As a result, he was bombarded by letters charging that now he, too, was betraying the cause, was giving in to hysteria, was leaving his loyal readers in the lurch. He *did* give in to hysteria—to his readers'—and decided to publish no more such articles. Who can blame him, for where will he find another audience if he alienates his present one?[8]

In sum, the current atmosphere tends to inhibit thought

7. It is an ironic symptom of the vulnerability of the school system that even Mr. MacLeish, in search of an explanation for our "escape from freedom," turns at the end to attacking education! "The underlying failure," he writes, "is a failure of education." Educators are fond of this kind of boasting, which so greatly over-estimates our role in the total culture.

8. In her otherwise admirable article, "The Menace to Free Journalism in America," in *The Listener*, May 14, 1953, p. 791, Mary McCarthy goes too far, in my judgment, in seeing such instances of editorial subservience as typical. It has even become the formula of many magazines to provoke or needle their readers; and certainly many seek to stay ahead of them.

in ways other than those generally recognized. United fronts for political action are one thing: intellectuals need lobbies and pressure groups just as other minorities do who in that way contribute to the pulling and hauling of American politics; but united fronts for intellectual understanding are as impotent as for artistic creation. In that area, each of us must go it alone, and, on occasion, even muster the courage not to take a stand.

V. But I would also maintain at the same time and in the same connection, that the effort to rid ourselves utterly of cowardice is inhuman (it is analogous to the effort to rid the country utterly of corruption, Communism, or McCarthyism). We must learn to fight battles while admitting our fear of the enemy, as the American soldier has increasingly learned to do. Otherwise, we encourage a needless martyrdom in some, and an excessive self-contempt in those many valuable people who cannot live up to the courage and stern morality our ancestors represent for us. A friend who recently visited some members of the New Deal government-in-exile in Washington wrote me that his own high spirits were taken as a kind of physiological affront. To be gay or glad about anything in these days is considered by many who share Mr. MacLeish's views to be a sign of idiocy, ill-will, or both.

To be sure, the guilt for being well-off (or well-to-do) is a notable and not wholly negative feature of the American educated classes—we feel it vis-à-vis our own poor and vis-à-vis the ill-nourished of the rest of the world. Likewise, those of us who are reasonably safe from attack by school boards or investigating committees because, out of good luck, timidity, good judgment, or whatnot, we never flirted with Communism, and because the hatred with which we have regarded Communism is now widespread—we, too, do not feel quite happy in our security, even if we do not share the widespread conviction that liberals as well as Communists and their fellow-travelers in general are being victimized. As intellectuals, we the "Pollyannas" inevitably and properly ask ourselves if we can be right, when the country is in some rough measure with us—and so many respected intellectuals are against us. In any case, we cannot but be sympathetic with the many decent people who are anguished, even if their anguish appears to us frequently self-defeating and the source for a monotonous style of talking about America.

But I regret that they do not see that we in America now live in what in many ways is a great age. Terrible things are happening but wonderful things too, and the former do not cancel out the latter any more than they do in one's personal life. The sudden rise to relative affluence of millions of people has intensified the struggle—no new thing in America—between the "old," Eastern-oriented merchant and professional middle classes and the "new," half-educated small business and small-town-manufacturing middle classes. In this confrontation, an astonishing number of the latter seek culture or worldliness in a benevolently energetic way—the heroine of *South Pacific,* for an exotic instance. But another group, as I have indicated, feels put upon and dominated by the intellectuals who seem to control or at least understand the respectable and influential people, media, and opinions; the very ferocity with which these anti-intellectuals sometimes try to outlaw the worldly and the educated is a sign of their resentment of their inferior status in the traditional hierarchies of prestige and comprehension. We are witnessing, not only a tremendous increase in the number of intellectuals in the occupational structure, but an anxious resurgence of some aspects of Populism. This springs not merely from rural areas, so greatly diminished, but also from the half-urbanized and far from urbane city folk for whom nationalism provides an identity of sorts when all else shifts.

And not only nationalism but other narrower groupings. The Pole in Cicero who has helped build a family, a parish, a neighborhood which Negroes threaten to invade, evicting him (and where shall he begin over again?), may find in a crusade against intellectuals some surcease for his own guilt for his inability to sacrifice much of the status he has precariously erected to the values of tolerance and charity the respectable teachers, media, and pastors urge upon him. The violence of his response makes him at least momentary prey for politicians who refuse to abide by the orderly rules of their body, just as he wants to smash the orderly rules of property and mobility which permit anyone with the money to buy a house, and hence school his children, anywhere. Increasingly, Congress and our state legislatures have become more democratic, more representative and less corrupt; they often speak for these previously under-privileged millions, and less often for the "wise, the good, and the [very] rich." By continuing to think of our country as banker-ridden or boss-ridden, we have sought not to recognize these sometimes tenuous changes in the sources of social and personal control of violence and impulse, or to find scapegoats in "demagogues" who whip up "the people," otherwise innocuous. Doubtless, demagogues play a part in "legitimizing" frictions within and among Americans—and how should there not be frictions with vast new populations entering the market for goods and ideas in little more than a decade?

These large-scale and scarcely understood changes and resistances to change in the bases of American life and allegiance are likely to have far greater long-run effects on the climate of freedom in America than the tendencies to conformism within liberalism to which this article has mostly been devoted. We should not allow short-run rises or falls in temperature, even while we suffer from them or oppose them, to obscure these climatic changes. But by the same token, we cannot predict the outcome of the complex, sometimes silent, sometimes vocal struggle against the influence and prestige of intellect and education, nor is there any course we can take which will guarantee victory to the scholar. However, in personal or political life I think there are limits to the usefulness of speculation on ultimate outcomes for oneself, one's group, one's nation, the white race, the Western world, or even the planet. Defeat is not the worst fate. The Athenians were "defeated." So were many other great civilizations. We must recognize the tragedy of every loss, every defeat, without banking too much on the quantifiable measure of longevity as proof of value. To become too fascinated by eventualities of destruction is not only not the way to ward them off but a way to distract ourselves from equally important questions about America: Why, for instance, are Americans often so anxious and unhappy, when Europeans, who live much closer to military or economic disaster are so sanguine in their personal lives, often expressing philosophies of despair with exuberant arrogance? Why are American young people so frequently aimless, lacking private passions and pursuits, when a greater variety of skilled careers are open to them than ever before? Why in intellectual circles is there so much malice, when there are jobs and prestige and tasks enough for everybody and to spare? The American culture, high, low, and middle, nearly always lacks the gamut of qualities our best and most creative spirits have evoked and represented, and the list of reasons for our not having become the promised land is endless—not to be dealt with by such general terms as "loss of faith" or "growth of reaction." Since small actions can have large consequences, the future of America is as bewilderingly open as the present is opaque. Nevertheless, it seems to me that individuals in America have still an undiminished potential for good and great, rich and fortunate lives. In living up to this potential, we express our freedom.

POSTSCRIPT

As the foregoing article implies, it represents one side of a debate staged in the pages of *The American Scholar* (the official organ of Phi Beta Kappa) between Archibald MacLeish and me. I had, as a member of the *Scholar's* editorial board, opposed our running an address by Mr. MacLeish entitled "Loyalty and Freedom," for I felt that the views expressed in it were not news to our readers, did not illuminate the issues, and—whatever value these views might have in magazines not read by people like ourselves—would, in the context of other articles previously published in the *Scholar*, only contribute to an atmosphere of resignation, depression, and misunderstanding of the intellectuals' plight. The article was, however, accepted, and I was encouraged to write a reply (something I would have refused to do in any more public forum not only because Mr. Mac-

Leish has suffered greatly from patrioteers but also because our differences, as far as the great anti-intellectual world goes, are marginal and intra-academic). Mr. MacLeish in turn wrote a brief reply to me, chiding me for lack of passionate concern for intellectual freedom and for a social scientist's presumed preference for cold analysis over eloquence and rhetoric.

Very much the same argument arose between me and Professor Laurence Sears of Mills College when I drew on this article in giving a lecture there. This argument attracted the attention of local papers and was reported in a distorted fashion, especially by the Hearst press: the argument itself could scarcely be understood from the reports, but the pleasure outsiders always take in seeing insiders fighting each other was evident enough. I had been trying to talk to liberal intellectuals and thoughtful college students, but was overheard by reactionary editors to whom I was not talking, to whom I would have said something very different. But of course one irony inside this irony is that it is very difficult to get across to people outside the academic world any such complex intention: such people want to know whether something is so or isn't so, and can't see any harm in broadcasting a debate especially if it encourages them to feel superior about professors! At the same time, as my article declares, I have never been willing to accept the "don't wash dirty linen" position, which implies that a group under attack must stop talking unless all exits are sealed. If we are not to succumb to overwhelming "inside" pressures, we have to take a good many chances.

Even so, I must add that when I wrote this article (in the spring and early summer of 1953), I did so with a good deal of misgiving lest it comfort those intellectuals, rather rare in my own circles but no doubt plentiful, who might take it as an excuse not to worry. At times, even the most intrepid among us may secretly long for excuses for inaction, and I was aware that, in criticizing the panic doctrine that America is on the road to fascism (my opinion in part based on the none too hopeful ground that we have always had illegality and violence in this country), I might leave some readers even more smug than before. I now think that

I did not pay sufficient heed to my own misgivings, for some reactions favorable to my article have had this smug quality; on rereading what I wrote, I feel I should have emphasized more some of the impalpable erosions of intellectual freedom that are related both to the general pressures hostile to individualism and to the specific tensions and irritabilities of the cold war.

Certainly, since my article was written, I have encountered painfully little evidence of the willingness of American intellectuals, let alone businessmen, lawyers, broadcasters, and government officials, to come out swinging in the old free-hand way, not only against McCarthy but against the careful, excessively fine-spun arguments of many of those whom McCarthy has attacked: the latter, if innocent of Communist ties, are often deferential and conciliatory, expressing neither firmness and conviction nor making use of the traditional American pattern of political vilification for one's own protection. What is involved here is perhaps not so much the rational fear of people for their careers; rather, people fear public embroilment with a bully, which can become an unbelievably harassing and time-consuming job. Many of us can recall, or prefer not to recall, our dismal encounters with bullies in high school or earlier; being Americans, unprotected by arrogance of class or family, we could not be sure we were in the right if we lost or ran away from such a fight. Thus, in dealing with a demagogue, we often lack assurance and are unprepared for virulence and bad faith; at times, we fall back on argumentative weapons deemed weak by a sports-loving public. And this weakness would seem especially grave when one is dealing with Senator McCarthy, whose sales appeal to the newly well-paid but socially uneasy strata in his constituency is as much his outspoken contempt for all symbols (such as Harvard, England, the State Department, or Army brass) of older and better educated strata, as is his opportunistic and picayune domestic anti-Communism.

Moreover, I sense among many members of the intellectual community an understandable tendency to establish our patriotism, our incontrovertible loyalty and anti-Communism, as a kind of public-relations gesture. And we are likely to argue that we are better fighters against Communism at home and abroad than McCarthy or *Counter-Attack*. These declarations are true, yet they have an air of enforced piety about them, like the declarations of some comic-book and pocket-book publishers who, instead of ridiculing the Gathings Committee's hypocrisy and denouncing its unfairness and mistrust of freedom, proclaim their own desire to avoid "obscenity" in cover and content. The fact that we feel such politic declarations must be made, that we cannot have our virtue (or the viciousness of our critics) taken for granted, is one of the many signs of the increasing pressure against freedom that I think now I did not take sufficiently into account in this article.

(*1954*)

Some Observations on Changes in Leisure Attitudes

. . . our sole delight was play; and for this we were punished by those who yet themselves were doing the like. But elder folks' idleness is called "business"; that of boys, being really the same, is punished by those elders; and none commiserates either boys or men. For will any of sound discretion approve of my being beaten as a boy, because, by playing at ball, I made less progress in studies which I was to learn, only that, as a man, I might play more unbeseemingly? and what else did he who beat me? who, if worsted in some trifling discussion with his fellow-tutor, was more embittered and jealous than I when beaten at ball by a playfellow?

—*The Confessions of St. Augustine*

Ten years ago, I sat as a member of an international committee engaged in drawing up a Bill of Rights to be presented to some presumptive postwar agency. Among the rights proposed was one stating that all men and women had a right to "reasonable leisure," and that it was the duty of governments to make this right effective. In the ensuing debate, this was dubbed (by a Harvard professor) "Riesman's freedom from work" amendment, and, though the amendment carried, many of the hard-working delegates regarded it as a concession to the modern cult of effortlessness. Others thought the issue irrelevant, on the ground that, until the right to work was secure, the right

"Some Observations on Changes in Leisure Attitudes" was first delivered as an address to a group of school superintendents at the Harvard Summer School of Education. It was first published in The Antioch Review, *Vol. 12, No. 4, 1952. It was later reprinted in* The Antioch Review Anthology, *ed. Paul Bixler, World Publishers, 1953, and in* Perspectives, *USA, No. 5, Fall 1953.*

to leisure could wait. This was my first introduction to the discovery that many people are uncomfortable when discussing leisure: as with sex, they want to make a joke of it. And there is no doubt that most of us feel vulnerable in a milieu that increasingly asks us whether we are good players as well as good workers—a problem St. Augustine's serious-minded, self-deceiving elders do not appear to have faced. For us, at any rate, there is nothing easy about effortlessness. I want here to trace some of the sources of vulnerability.

I. In his novel, *The Bostonians,* written about seventy-five years ago, Henry James describes a week that his hero, Basil Ransom, passed at Provincetown on the Cape. He smoked cigars; he wandered footloose to the wharves; perhaps he read an occasional book; it does not appear that he swam. He was, *pro tem,* a "gentleman of leisure." It may be that a few fossils of the species are preserved in the Athenaeum, but I rather doubt if they can be found in Provincetown. At least my impression is that people who go to such places for the summer appear to lead strenuously artsy and craftsy lives: even if they lie on the beach, they are getting a competitively handsome tan, but most of the time they appear to be playing energetic tennis, taking exhausting walks, entertaining children and guests by that mixture of grit, insects, and tomatoes known as a picnic; and in the evening attending lectures, the experimental theatre, and colloquia in private houses. While they may be less systematically engaged than many students in laying by credits, they are gainfully improving themselves in body and mind; and, perhaps unlike many students, they are subject to the additional strain of having to feel and to claim that they are having a good time, being victims of that new form of Puritanism which Martha Wolfenstein and Nathan Leites in their book *Movies* have termed "fun-morality."

All this in a country in which the average industrial work-week has declined from 64 hours in Henry James' day to around 40 in ours, not including the mid-morning coffee break and the other sociabilities which have crept into the hours which the census registers as working ones. We are in the ambivalent position described by Lynn White, Jr., President of Mills College, commenting on a roundtable on "leisure and human values in industrial civilization" of which he was chairman at the Corning Conference a year ago:

> We said, "Ha, ha, I have no leisure; why am I involved in this?" It was a sense of guilt and, at the same time, a sense of pride. In other words, we feel leisure is a cultural value. Theoretically we would rather like to participate in it, but we are sort of proud that we are such responsible members of society that we really have no time for leisure.[1]

Our responsibility extends, in fact, to a concern for how other people—our children, our pupils, our union members, the community at large—are spending their leisure. In fact, those of us who are in the education industry and its allies, such as the library industry, have developed quite substantial interests—vested interests—in other people's leisure. We see their loose time, as others see their loose change, as our problem and our responsibility. This is, I suggest, one reason why the "gentleman of leisure," whose portrait Thorstein Veblen drew so sardonically in the '90's, is obsolete today. Instead, we are all of us—that is, almost all—members of the leisure class, and face its problems. As Eric Larrabee pointed out at Corning, the expansion of the leisure "market" has brought "friction" in its wake.

It is, of course, characteristic of American life that our bonanzas, our windfalls, whether treasures of the soil or treasures of the self, have been interpreted by the most sensitive and responsible among us as problems. I'm not sure but that the hue and cry against Puritanism isn't beginning to be overdone, and that we won't come to realize that our moral seriousness—in fact, our fun-morality—is not wholly negative. At the Corning Conference, the Wellesley-educated Hindu author, Miss Santha Rama Rau, scolded us; she commented:

1. For this and later quotations, see *Creating an Industrial Civilization: A Report on the Corning Conference*, Eugene Staley, ed., 1952. I have drawn on the materials prepared for this conference by Reuel Denney and myself.

I am wondering why leisure is a problem at all. Surely, nowhere else in the world do people fuss about what to do with their spare time. I think it is rather sad that some kind of guilt has been built up in this particular society so that people feel that they should be productive in their spare time. . . . What is wrong with lying on the beach and relaxing?

I suppose one, perhaps unfair, answer to her is to be found in the six- and seven-year old Indian children standing guard over their families' fields all night long, lest a sacred bull trample the crops down and leave the family to starve. It is Puritanism that, in considerable part, has brought us to the point where leisure is or can become a problem for the vast majority. In fact, so great is the sheer quantity of our available leisure and leisure resources, that I do not think we can find very helpful models in other countries.

Recent reading and reflection, and discussion with Mark Benney of the London School of Economics (now visiting lecturer at the University of Chicago), has convinced me that this is true enough, at any rate, for England, from which we once derived our working model of the gentleman of leisure, and from which, too, I suspect the Hindu aristocrats such as Miss Rama Rau have learned more than many will admit. The English remain torn between the aristocratic leisure pattern, which is rural, sportsmanlike, casual, and on the edge of such quasi-criminal activities as cockfighting, and the middle-class leisure pattern, dating from the sobersides of the Puritan revolution, which is urban, uplifting, strenuous. (The urban working-class pattern, as represented in the London music hall and a vivid "street culture," is pretty much dying out.) A recent extensive survey by Seebohm Rowntree and G. R. Lavers, entitled *English Life and Leisure,* was evidence to me that the English today on the whole know even less than we how to spend leisure—that there is a sameness and lack of imagination about their pastimes and pursuits. The English aristocrats with their natural allies, the lower class, have won the day in the sense that the Victorian middle-class morality appears to be almost dead in England, and sexual intimacy seems the chief leisure resort after puberty. But while the young people are uninhibited, they are not joyful. They have to watch every penny they spend on liquor, but again seem to take no great pleasure in it. They gamble, but often with desperation. The truth is that they can no longer afford the aristocratic vices which are now, with the decline of religious sanctions, psychologically available to them. And the middle-class values of self-improvement are still strong enough so that many are dissatisfied with the aimlessness of their lives; I recall one young middle-class girl, for instance, who told the interviewer that she slept with young men who asked her to, but wished she could find something better to do.

What, then, do Rowntree and Lavers, who are distinguished students of English social life, recommend? They plug the old middle-class model, only more of it. After touring the Scandinavian countries to study leisure practices there, they urge more folk-dancing, more hobbies, more adult education, better books—and, I need hardly add, fewer Hollywood movies.

In fact, their attitude towards Hollywood may be regarded as symptomatic of the attitude of a great many students of leisure—"recreationists" perhaps we'd better call them—here and abroad. In their view, Hollywood is a source of disruptive leisure patterns, of vulgarity, spendthrift living, and false values generally. You know the indictment, I'm sure—an indictment which includes most of our popular culture, radio, TV, and bestsellers as well. Rowntree and Lavers put themselves up, as many school officials have, as angry competitors with this commercial popular culture, waging a losing fight. If they can offer nothing better, I am afraid that both the old aristocratic pattern, which is too expensive, and the old middle-class pattern, which is too didactic, will evaporate from England, leaving nothing of much quality to take their place.[2]

2. Mr. Benney believes that English leisure is not quite so dreary as this book indicates: the interviewers seem to concentrate on the activities that shock them and, indeed, to encounter a high proportion of rather sad and isolated

II. Now it is my opinion that Hollywood movies not only are often shoddy but are often profoundly liberating and creative products of the human imagination. And I am not referring to so-called "message" films, pleas for better race relations or labor relations. I refer rather to such films as *The Asphalt Jungle,* or *All About Eve,* or *An American in Paris,* or *The Marrying Kind,* or *The Great Gatsby,* and many others without any patent social message; some successful, some not; movies which take us out of ourselves or force us back in; movies which open a window on life, and movies which exhibit a nightmarish fantasy. If English leisure is sterile and mean-spirited, I doubt if such movies have made it so. Rather, I think English, and American life also, would be enriched if people learned to understand and appreciate the movies, and could enjoy them in the spirit, at once critical and friendly, with which people at different times and places have enjoyed literature. The thought occurred to me some years ago that our schools and colleges, and particularly our altogether too pious adult education ventures, might begin experimenting with courses on movie appreciation, and popular culture appreciation generally—a movement which would require us to develop something we have not yet got in this country: a corps of gifted movie and radio and TV critics. The beginnings are evident in the work of John Crosby, for instance; what is lacking is any program for developing such critics, operating in the different media and at different levels of irony and sensibility. I argued that such a program might help close the gap which now separates the literary culture of the schools—the culture which such men as Rowntree and Lavers narrowly regard as the only true and genuine culture—from the popular culture of RKO and CBS.

I argued too that such a program might help us get rid once and for all of the current distinction between active and passive recreations—"active" being such things as sports, hobbies, and square dancing, and "passive" such

people; moreover, nothing appears in the book about such gregarious leisure pursuits as political meetings and dart matches in the pubs.

things as movie-going, TV-watching, and other things parents and teachers wish their children wouldn't do. For I am convinced that this is not a real distinction: much leisure which appears to be active may be merely muscular: its lactic acid content is high, but there may be little other content, or contentment. And conversely, such supposedly passive pursuits as movie-going can obviously be the most intense experience, the most participative. Indeed, Hollywood movies could hardly corrupt England and Europe if they were as passive and as pacifying as is charged! And so I wanted to teach people to enjoy the movies as participants in a fine performance, and not merely as a place to pass the time out of the old folks' reach. In fact, I was particularly eager to develop courses just for the old folks in the understanding of popular culture, thinking in this way not only to open up to them a wide range of imaginative experience but also of helping to close the gap which separates the young, who have been raised with movies, comics, radio, and now TV, from the old who have come to them late if at all. . . .

But now I am not so sure that the problem I have in mind can be solved by courses, or possibly by any sort of conscious social program. I vividly recall my experience a few years ago when, asked to talk informally at a men's dormitory at the University of Chicago, I chose the movies as my topic, and started to say some things about the contemporary tendency among educated Americans to regard the movies as "just a show," to be "taken in" when one has nothing better at hand. I was talking to an audience most of whom devoutly believed that Hollywood movies other than Chaplin and the early Griffith are without exception junk, and that only England, France, and Italy make movies seriously worth seeing. I was trying to rebut this prejudice by saying something about the differing film conventions on the Continent and in this country: how, for example, we had had a convention of a happy ending which our more arty directors were now tending to exchange for an equally conventional, though Continental, unhappy ending, and that no necessary superiority lay in one convention rather than another, any more than in one sonnet form rather than another. Likewise, I sought to show how the undoubted inanities of the Production Code often resulted in a movie treatment—the so-called Lubitsch touch, for instance—which was a creative surmounting of the constricting forms. And then suddenly I stopped in the middle of my lecture, and for a while could not continue.

For I had realized, as I looked at the intent faces of the students, that I might well be engaged in closing off one of the few casual and free escape routes remaining to them; that I might be helping to inaugurate a new convention: namely, that one had not only to attend Hollywood movies but to understand and appreciate them. I might be imposing on a group of students already zealously engaged in self-improvement, in social and intellectual mobility, still another requirement—and this in the very act of seeking to liberate them from a common prejudice against American movies. I could continue my lecture only after I had made some of these misgivings explicit, and had indicated that I came to offer some of them an opportunity, not another extra-curricular curriculum.

I realized the problem here was not so much mine of becoming a possible taste-leader, as it was one for the students who were looking for such leadership, if not from me, then from somebody. Contrary to the situation in my own undergraduate days, when we were, at least for external consumption, stoutly individualistic, these students were more malleable, more ready to be told. One reason for this is that the general level of teaching has improved, despite all the attacks currently being made against our educational system. Not only has the teaching improved, but the teachers have changed their pace and style; we try to get close to our students, to be good group leaders rather than platform ham actors, and to concern ourselves with more aspects of student life than simply classroom performance. We are perhaps today less distant from the student than we once were, both in terms of social class position and in terms of intellectual attitude. . . . The students I was talking to, were ready to shift their leisure behavior at a moment's notice; I could envisage a group of them going to a Sam Goldwyn movie and, coming out, being very self-conscious as to how they ought to respond to it, whereas earlier they would have gone to it with the excuse that they needed to relax a bit before hitting the books again. Since so much of their leisure was already highly self-conscious, I hesitated to add to the burden. All planning for other people's leisure has to face this fundamental ambiguity, a form of the ever-present problem of the unintended consequence.

To be sure, leisure is a burden of the sort I am describing only among the educated, among the great many high school and college graduates who have some aspirations towards culture; men and women who, in the absence of any visible aristocratic model of leisure in American life, look to their fellows for clues, look to the magazines and the press, and the "how to" books. For the working class, there is leisure now too, and often money to spend, but it is not usually a burden, not perhaps a burden enough. Hunting and fishing and bowling; puttering about the house, garden, or car; watching television with and without discrimination; playing the numbers—these are recreations, not so very different from those turned up by Rowntree and Lavers in England, which my students have observed among steelworkers in Hammond and Gary. To be sure, there is considerable aspiration towards improved taste on the part of some of the younger wives, who read the women's service magazines. And the unions make sporadic efforts to give political education to the men; you will hardly be surprised to hear that some of the leaders blame the mass media for seducing the rank and file away from meetings—a charge which Mark Starr, educational director of the Ladies Garment Workers' Union, leveled at David Sarnoff of NBC at the Corning Roundtable. I think the charge is quite unjust, for I see no reason why people should spend their leisure in political activity unless that is their form of sport and they enjoy it, save in those cases where conditions are really so terrible that every good man has to come to the aid of the party—and, contrary to what is so widely urged, I believe such conditions are rare in this country.

One reason why the steel workers have so few problems with their leisure is that their work today is itself often quite leisurely and gregarious. It was not like that even thirty years ago when, as we know, there were ten- and twelve-hour shifts, and when the work was so hot and heavy that many men, on returning home, lay exhausted on the kitchen floor before they could get the energy to eat and tumble into bed. Now at the big sheet and tube mill in Gary the men often take naps on mattresses they have brought in, and cook meals on burners attached to the fiery furnaces; if a new foreman doesn't like the practice, production is slowed down until he does like it. Think here, too, of the extent to which the schools train young people in this kind of comradely slow-down against the teachers and against the system generally, so that I sometimes think of school teachers as foremen who conspire with their pupils, the workers, to conceal the true state of affairs from top management, the principals, and from the parents who are the absentee stockholders, who grouse now and again about their dividends. At any rate, since work has now become so relatively lacking in strain—though it is not nearly so routinized in feeling as it may seem to be to observers of factory life—the worker leaves the plant with a good deal of energy left, which carries him readily through his leisure hours.

By contrast, the professional and business person is apt to leave his work with a good many tensions created by his reactions to interpersonal situations, and as a result his leisure "needs" may have to be satisfied before he can rise above the level of needs—before he can rise from the level of re-creation to the level of creation. But it is just this very person on whom fall most of the demands for participative, active, constructive leisure which we have been examining earlier; and he may move from a job, where he is constantly faced with others and their expectations, to leisure pursuits, again in the company of others, where workmanlike performance is also expected of him. While he may nominally have a short work-week—though in many middle-class occupations such as medicine and teaching, hours are as long or longer than ever—he has not got much time which is not filled with stress. As my colleague, Nelson Foote, likes to put it, he has very little reverie as a balance to his sociability.

III. Let us look at a concrete example. A friend and former colleague, Professor John R. Seeley, is now engaged in directing a large research project on the relations between school and community in a wealthy, upper-middle-class suburb. It is a suburb which has one of the finest public school systems on this continent, one which is often held up as a model to others; in fact, the magnificent new modern high school dominates the community, even physically, as the cathedrals did in the Middle Ages. The very fact that this elaborate research is going on there—it is to take a period of at least five years before any final conclusions are reached—is indicative of the alertness of the school officials, the school board, and the other community leaders. Yet, from my own very limited observation and from what has been reported to me, it is plain that the community, despite all material advantages, is not happy. The parents have neuroses; the children have allergies; and the teachers—well, I don't know. What has gone wrong?

If we follow the life of the children after school, we can perhaps get some clues. They are being prepared now for their later careers and their later rather hypothetical leisure. Their parents want to know how they have fared at school: they are constantly comparing them, judging them in school aptitude, popularity, what part they have in the school play; are the boys sissies? the girls too fat? All the school anxieties are transferred to the home and vice versa, partly because the parents, college graduates mostly, are intelligent and concerned with education. After school there are music lessons, skating lessons, riding lessons, with mother as chauffeur and scheduler. In the evening, the children go to a dance at school for which the parents have groomed them, while the parents go to a PTA meeting for which the children, directly or indirectly, have groomed *them,* where they are addressed by a psychiatrist who advises them to be warm and relaxed in handling their children! They go home and eagerly and warmly ask their returning children to tell them everything that happened at the dance, making it clear by their manner that they are sophisticated and cannot easily be shocked. As Professor Seeley describes matters, the school in this community operates a "gigantic factory for the production of relationships."

Since, moreover, the same interpersonal concerns dominate life within this "plant" and outside it, there is no sharp change of pace between work and play, between school and home activities. The children and their mothers—the fathers who work in the city at least make a geographical shift and also something of an emotional one—are characterized by a pervading anxiety. This is connected, I think, with the fact that the older, clear goals of achievement have been called into question, and these family units must decide not only how to get what they want but also what it is they should want. To answer this question, the community makes much use of professionals—the school principals and teachers themselves, who have a very high standing; child guidance experts and mental hygienists; and the packaged professionalism which can be bought in books or over the radio. The result is a well-known paradox: here is a suburb devoted to the arts of consumption and leisure, where these arts are pursued with such dogged determination that leisureliness as a quality of life is very largely absent. While all the appurtenances of variety are present, life is monotonous in the sense that it is steadily gregarious, focussed on others, and on the self in relation to others. As I have observed among some students, at Harvard and elsewhere, even casualness can be an effortful artifact.

IV. Yet it is all too easy to deride these parents and children and assorted experts, to urge them—as some people are now doing in the anti-progressive education movement—to drop all this new-fangled nonsense and get back to hard work and traditional curricula and nineteenth century or classical "values" generally. It is perhaps not surprising that both aristocratic and working-class stances towards leisure combine in this derision. When, for example, this suburban community was recently discussed in my seminar on leisure, many people, both faculty and students, took the position that what these suburbanites needed was more direct and uninhibited aggression, more toughness and less talkiness. They compared the community unfavorably to a working-class community where, for reasons I indicated a moment ago, leisure is undoubtedly more casually dealt with. What they admired was aristocratic or artisan insouciance, as against upper-middle-class anxiety and preoccupation. Yet I do not know by what standard of value one prefers a broken nose to asthma, or lumbago or gout to ulcers. There is no doubt that the suburb in question, and others like it, is anxious and vulnerable, individually and collectively; otherwise, it would not be quite so receptive to a team of researchers. But I think that overadmiration for toughness is part of a romance which the middle class, in Europe as well as in America, has been carrying on with the lower class for a good many years. . . .

Thus, I think we can look at the people of this suburb rather differently from the way I have been doing so far, or from the way my seminar reacted to them. We can see them, for one thing, as explorers. Whereas the explorers of the last century moved to the frontiers of production and opened fisheries, mines, and mills, the explorers of this century seem to me increasingly to be moving to the frontiers of consumption. They are opening up new forms of interpersonal understanding, new ways of using the home as a "plant" for leisure, new ways of using the school as a kind of community center, as the chapel of a secular religion perhaps. But frontier towns are not usually very attractive. And frontier behavior is awkward: people have not yet learned to behave comfortably in the new surroundings. There is formlessness, which takes the shape of lawlessness on the frontier of production and of aimlessness on the frontier of consumption. In both instances, the solid citizens who stayed home are likely to feel superior, both to the formlessness and to whatever may be emerging from it, just as most Europeans of the educated strata have felt superior to most aspects of America throughout most of our history. The move to the suburb, as it occurs in contemporary America, is emotionally, if not geographically, something almost unprecedented historically; and those who move to any new frontier are likely to pay a price, in loneliness and discomfort. When the physical hardships are great, as they were for earlier generations of pioneers, the psychological hardships may be repressed or submerged—though we cannot be too sure even of that, for (as Oscar Handlin makes clear in his book on immigration to America, *The Uprooted*) the most devastating strains on the newcomers were in fact the emotional ones, rough though the physical conditions were.

To carry my analogy further, I do believe that discoveries are being made on the frontiers of consumption. Take the American diet, for instance. Once upon a time, and still in many quarters, this was in charge of the nutritionists, the exponents of a balanced meal, adequate caloric intake and colonic outlet, and plenty of vitamins. These good people bore the same relation to food that recreationists do to leisure: they want it to be uplifting, salubrious, wasteless. But now, among the better income strata at any rate, their work is done: it is incorporated into the formulae of bakers, into the inventories of chain-stores, the menus of restaurants and dining cars. We have, as I sometimes like to put it, moved from the wheat bowl to the salad bowl. In consequence, in the suburb I have been describing, and elsewhere throughout the country, there is an emphasis, which was once confined to small sophisticated or expatriate circles, on having the right responses to food, on being a gourmet. Save for a few cranks, the housewives are not concerned with having enough wheat-germ, but with having enough oregano, or the right wine—and more than that, with having the right enjoyment of the wine. In the middle of the shopping center in this suburb is a store which stocks a stupendous array of delicacies, spices, patisseries, delicatessens, and European gadgets for cooking; the casserole replacing the melting pot!

Now, as I have indicated, the residents of this suburb are anxious about food and their attitudes towards it. They want to be knowledgeable about it and also to enjoy it, but they are not yet easygoing in the matter. Among men particularly, the demand that one must enjoy food, and not simply stow it away, is relatively new, and again these pioneers are awkwardly self-conscious. (Let me make clear in passing that I am not talking about old-fashioned conspicuous consumption. I am not talking about the hostess' fear of making a gastronomic *faux pas,* or fear that her children's table manners will disgrace her; no doubt these fears may still exist, although greatly muted, in the group I am describing. No, these parents are afraid that they are missing some taste experience, which in turn reveals the lack of a basic personality attribute.) We are observing these families, it appears, in a time of transition, when they have left old food-conventions behind and are exploring, without settling on, new ones. They are, in effect, paying the society's cost of research and development.

And can there be any doubt but that the result will be—in fact, has already been—an addition to the stock of American leisure bounties and benefits? The self-service supermarket, with its abundance of foods capably displayed, where the shopper's caprice and imagination can roam without interference from officious clerks or sabotage from indifferent ones, seems to me as significant an invention on the side of consumption as the assembly-line on the side of production. But the invention would be meaningless without a group of experimentalist families prepared to develop new eating patterns, new combinations of color and taste. And here enters still another service industry: the cookbook and recipe industry, which has ransacked the world's cuisines and produced a host of books and newspaper columns, as well as those restaurants which serve as pilot plants. I think there can be no doubt that the children of the children now growing up in our demonstration suburb will be reasonably free of fears, guilts, and awkwardness about food: prepared as a matter of course for the pursuit of happiness in this area of existence. In fact, I see only one caveat: the return of the nutritionist ghost in the craze for reducing, which makes not only women but men choose between food and figure, with one eye on mortality tables and the other on the way one appears in the hall of mirrors which is society! Even so, the reduced diets on which these figure-chasers bravely live are, item for item, unquestionably superior to anything known before in the American provender—which a generation ago made our food, like our bootlegging, an international joke. Moreover, the cult of one's figure, as of one's dress and one's coiffure, is certainly not an illegitimate one for one's happiness and aesthetic sense.

In other fields of consumption such as music, painting, and literature; in the whole subtle field of sociability and conversation; in sports; in the changing style of vacations I think the pioneers are also paying a high price in emotional outlay, particularly in anxiety. I have already raised the question of whether our intellectual and literary culture is not too severe and derisive about the middle-class vice of anxiousness, compared with its benign tolerance for the aristocratic and lower-class vices of brutality and indifference. Such very general questions of value judgment are of great importance in determining contemporary attitudes towards leisure. I think, for example, that we make life and leisure harder for the already anxious person—whose anxiety is in fact thoroughly understandable in the light of our discussion so far—by making him also anxious about his anxiety, so that we heap on him a cumulative burden. . . .

Teachers also feel it compulsory not to be anxious, but to be always easygoing, warm, and relaxed—what a burden this puts on teachers in the better public and private schools!—whereas lack of discipline and firmness would have worried teachers in an earlier day. I am inclined to think we should form a union of the anxious ones, to defend our right to be anxious, our right to be tense, our right to aspirin and to our allergies. I was shocked when one of my colleagues remarked, after our seminar had had a description of life in the suburb I have here used as a case, that children were worse off there than they had been under the *ancien régime*. Historical amnesia had blinded him, as it blinds many now-fashionable critics of progressive education, to the brutalities and savageries in the treatment of children a hundred years or so ago. Then children were harnessed to the engine of society with often little concern for their own development. Many were too frightened or too cowed to be anxious.[3] . . .

V. I have stressed as much as I have the conflicts in our attitudes towards the proper use of leisure, and the kind of training children should get with their later lives of leisure in mind, because I feel that a recognition of ambiguity at the very heart of our problem is a first step towards perspective and a certain necessary detachment. I can't emphasize enough how rapidly our country is changing, and how hard it is even for the best informed among us to grasp what is going on.

Let me give just two illustrations: Recently a friend of mine who works for one of the pocket book companies visited an Ohio Valley city of about 75,000. There is no bookstore in the town, but a few books are kept, along with stationery and oddments, in the main department store. My friend asked at the department store why they didn't put in a real bookstore, and was told, "Well, this is a steel town. People here don't read; they just look at television or go to the taverns." Yet over three-quarters of a million pocket books were sold in this same town in 1951 at restaurants, at newsstands and in drugstores, many of them in the Mentor line of modern classics. This is well over a book a month for those old enough to read. I wish we had some knowledge and understanding of what these citizens made out of all they read: the Faulkner novels, the Conant *On Understanding Science*, the Ruth Benedict *Patterns of Culture*, along with the Mickey Spillane and other mixtures of sadism with sex. But studies of this kind in the field of leisure have not yet been made, as far as I know.

3. Stephen Spender's novel, *The Backward Son*, and George Orwell's account of his schooldays, "Such, Such Were the Joys" (in *A Collection of Essays*, Anchor Books, 1954), can remind us that even a generation ago the English public school could still treat the sensitive young with ferocious bullying. Likewise, the fictional hero of Salinger's *Catcher in the Rye* might have profited from some of the humaneness and sensitivity introduced by the now maligned progressive educators.

I draw my other illustration of the laggard state of our knowledge even of the basic data from an article by Gian-Carlo Menotti which appeared in a recent issue of the New York *Times Sunday Magazine*. As you know, Menotti is a gifted and widely hailed young composer who, after some twenty years' residence here, considers himself an American. He was complaining about the precarious position of the creative artist in American life, particularly in the field of music. Here, he points out, we bestow all our adulation on the performer: the glamorous conductor or singer, the Menuhin or Serkin or Reginald Kell, who interprets music but does not create it, while the modern composer, unless he writes for the movies or gets some help from a foundation or a rich wife, will starve (as Bela Bartok did)—and is certainly not in any case featured in the billing along with the star performers. And he goes on to say that many parents in America are ashamed if their sons choose an artistic career; not only do they fear they will not make a living—even if they (the parents) could afford to support them—but fear, too, that they will be sissies; fathers try to force their sons to become businessmen or doctors or something else equally reassuring. Now I am sure that Menotti has a very good case about the plight of the composer, who seems so much worse off than the painter or writer, having more impresarios standing between him and his public. However, it seems to me that Menotti does not take account of the rapid and widespread change which has been going on in just the attitudes he is attacking. Through amateur chamber music groups and through the fabulous growth of the long-playing record industry, many thousands of Americans are today discovering modern music with a rush, just as they are discovering wine and other pleasures that were once confined to a small cultivated indigenous group and a somewhat larger group of immigrants who brought this culture with them from the old country. Likewise, it seems to me unlikely that millions of middle-class parents would not in 1952 be pleased if their sons exhibited artistic gifts and interests, even if not commercially promising. . . . When I said as much, however, at the Corning Conference, Miss Rama Rau and others said I was mistaken: parents would only accept art if it was advertised in *Life* magazine. . . . I would be greatly interested in comments on this topic, for I feel that here again we simply do not know.[4]

VI. So far we have been looking at our culture from inside. We have asked ourselves some questions about what is going on, about what attitudes are prevalent towards it, what models of competent use of leisure exist, what differences there are among different social strata, and so on. But there is another way of going at our problem which is to ask, not what play and leisure are like, or were like, in our culture but what they are like in any culture. Is there, for instance, any natural or biological basis for leisure or is it entirely conventional? *Homo Ludens*, a book by the late Dutch scholar Huizinga, offers some interesting clues to this. Huizinga points out that every language he examined had a word for play which is different from the word for work, and that many cultures have a pattern of sport, of noneconomic serious and yet playful competition. Many if not all cultures, moreover, operate on a periodic or seasonal rhythm between heavy work and heavy play—and I might add that many societies also have feasts even if they do not suffer from famines. That there is a cross-cultural solidarity of play may be indicated by a well-known example. Our Army advised soldiers and aviators to always carry a piece of string with them and when downed in a Pacific jungle to start playing cat's cradle if a suspicious

4. In discussion [at the Harvard Summer School], it was argued that parents will now often accept art as a glamorous stairway to quick success, but that this makes it even harder than earlier for a youngster whose interest in art cannot be readily commercialized: his parents are impatient with him, not because he is an artist or composer—which would lead to a total break and a relatively good conscience on the artist's part—but because, being in a glamorous field, he has not made his way; since the youngster in part also wants success, he finds it harder to cut himself off from his parents' values and anxieties. For thoughtful discussion of this problem, and a critique of the art schools which cash in on this craving for success, see Lyman Bryson, *The Next America*.

native approached; the native would sometimes start to play, too.

All this must rest on something basic in the biological substratum of man and many animals. We know of course that children play even without instruction, provided certain basic minima of security are met. Thus, while children's play has aspects of artifice which the ever-renewed child's culture elaborates, much of it is simply given. In fact, work and play are not yet, for the child, independently organized; and what he makes of play as he develops depends to a very considerable extent on the society's interpretation of his play—is it regarded as "child's play," as useless, as preparation for life, or is it disregarded?

I think we can say, indeed, that the child's play serves as the principal model for all later efforts to free leisure time from its burdens and to cope with its puzzling ambiguities. We all of us know, if we think about it, that children's play is by no means always free and spontaneous; it is often filled with terror and morbidity; but at its best it is surely one of the unequivocally good things of this earth, and no wonder we try to recapture it as Paradise Lost. But if we look closely at children's play we can observe something else which may even give us a clue as to how that recapture can, in part, be achieved, namely that the child's greatest satisfaction appears to arise from experiences of mastery and control. As Erik H. Erikson has noted in imaginative detail, the developing body provides a graded set of experiences; anyone can observe this who watches children play with their new-found mastery of walking or running or talking or diving. Play seems to reside in a margin, often a narrow one, between tasks which are too demanding, and those which are not demanding enough to require the excited concentration of good play. A child or adult who is simply going through the motions is not engaged in play or leisure as we have been talking about it here, however the society may define it. But without some social forms for leisure and play, forms which have to be broken through, yet have to be there to be broken through, I do not think we will have much play either. For the demand that play be constantly spontaneous, unchanneled by social forms, is too overwhelming; spontaneity, as we have already seen, is lost if we strive too hard for it. Thus, play would seem to consist in part of giving ourselves tasks, useless in any immediate sense, which challenge us but do not overwhelm us—tasks which allow us to practice our skills on the universe when not too much is at stake. Some of us, who lose this ability in our waking lives, retain it (as Erich Fromm points out in *The Forgotten Language*) in our dreams, which can be astonishingly witty, brilliant, and artistic—an indication, perhaps, of the child still buried within us, not so much in Freud's sense of the vicious child but rather of the child natively gifted with the capacity for imaginative play.

I have spoken of mastery of tasks, but I do not want to be understood as implying that this necessarily means physical activity—that is only one example. The child in the front of a subway train who intently watches the motorman, the signals, and the tracks may be quiet, but is undoubtedly playing, and may be playing very well—a point Reuel Denney eloquently voiced at the Corning Conference. When we speak of "role-playing," we should have something of this sort of vicariousness in mind. And this leads me to the complicating point that many of our workaday tasks as adults can be handled with a certain quality of leisure if we are able to regard work as a series of challenging tasks to be mastered, where the net of expectations surrounding us is at the same time not too frightening. On the other hand, we can be playful at work as a way of *evading* demands, sometimes by being one of the boys, pretending to ourselves and others that, if we really worked, we would get to the top. Students often play such games with themselves. But this is not really carrying out in adult life the effort at competence which is our lesson learned from the play of the child. That requires that we work at the top of our bent, while at the same time enjoying the very processes of accomplishment—enjoying our awareness, for example, of all that is going on in a classroom; enjoying our understanding of a technical problem; enjoying ourselves, in other words, as functioning and effective human beings.

We get here, it is apparent, into very deep waters indeed, where the boundaries between work and play become shadowy—as I think, for other reasons, they are tending to become in our society anyway—waters where we are looking for a quality we can only vaguely describe: it is various and rhythmical; it breaks through social forms and as constantly recreates them; it manifests itself in tension, yet not too much of it; it is at once meaningful, in the sense of giving us intrinsic satisfaction, and meaningless, in the sense of having no pressing utilitarian purpose. It is some such model as this, I suggest, which haunts us when we consider leisure and judge its quality in ourselves and others. It is a model which has been elaborated in our culture, and yet which transcends most, and perhaps all, given cultures.

New Standards for Old: From Conspicuous Consumption to Conspicuous Production

I. In a recent column, John Crosby affectionately quoted a remark of Sylvester L. Weaver, vice-chairman of the board of NBC: "The kids," said Weaver, "are already getting the full picture. 'The kids running around in space suits are smarter than the adults who are laughing at them.'" The parents' imagination, Weaver implied, is localized, whereas that of their children floats free even of planetary boundaries. A recent story in the science-fiction magazine *Galaxy* preaches a similar moral. It is a tale of two children, aged ten, who take off on a Moebius ring for other times and places. These children, at home in an Einsteinian universe, patronize their parents, are sorry for them, and obey them, not out of fear or favor, but lest they cause them pain. The parents are bound to a specific time and place, a specific job, whereas the children, free of chores for the most part both at home and school, are not hindered, as they would have been in an earlier day, from rapidly overtaking and surpassing their parents' know-how on the frontiers of consumption. It would be my guess, for instance, that more children than parents today favor "modern design" not only in space suits but in cars, bars, houses, and furniture.

Margaret Mead and others have pointed out that immigrant parents in America have always been on the defensive, because their children were more "American" than they. But the tendencies I am discussing seem to extend

"New Standards for Old: From Conspicuous Consumption to Conspicuous Production" was given as a lecture in the Barnard College series on "The Search for New Standards in Modern America," March 10, 1953, and is here reprinted with the permission of Barnard College.

beyond this country, for they are the consequences of industrialization and urbanization and the growing leisure that, in later stages, accompany these developments. Indeed, when countries without a long Christian and Puritan heritage adopt the techniques of modern industry, they may appear more "American" than America in their readiness to slough off older ideologies of thrift and workmanship; they may hanker for leisure and consumption before they have solved the problems of production. The Coca Cola bottlers, the Hollywood film distributors, and other consumption missionaries preach a gospel that may be premature in Thailand or Egypt. But whatever the gospel, it is doubtless the young—lacking the trained incapacities of their elders—who catch on to it most quickly, but at times, as I myself think may be true with space suits, most shallowly.

II. I am going to illustrate some of these matters by referring to a play many of you have doubtless seen: *Death of a Salesman.* Whereas in 19th-century literature, children often fear that their parents will catch them out in some frivolity, it is Willy Loman, the father in *Death of a Salesman,* who is caught out by his son in a hotel room. And the other son, Happy Loman, openly ridicules his father as a fool for working hard; Happy—how meaningful his nickname!—has latched on to American consumption know-how at its most garish: his eyes are on the pleasure frontier while his father's are still on the production-achievement frontier. Not that Biff or Happy escape defensiveness towards their father—today as in an earlier day sons are still trapped by the irrelevance of their parents' hopes and fears for them—but the initiative is certainly changed.

The changes that have taken place can scarcely be fitted into a simple chronology of parent-child relations. Too many other factors are involved. The east coast is different from the middle west—and the differences, despite our stereotypes, are not well understood. There are very great differences in social class. It has been said that the upper class is oriented to the past, the lower class to the present, the middle class to the future. The upper class therefore tends to be strongly family-centered—think of the social memories of the Apleys, cemented by estates, portraits, memoirs, family names, and other impedimenta, as these are portrayed in Marquand's novel. Willy Loman, by contrast, seems to live always in the future, even though he spends much time listening to voices out of the past which point him to a future he didn't take or that didn't take him. Willy, in fact, appears to have no past, which is part of his pathos. . . . And Willy faces the problem that he is not really identified with salesmen but—as happens among some particularly outstanding salesmen—with the customers. It is often taken for granted that the good salesman should identify with the customers on whom he is dependent. Actually, the motives of men in business are more complex, and ambivalence towards the customer is common. Recently, a friend of mine, a market researcher, told me how a shaving lotion manufacturer stubbornly refused to alter his product, even to meet complaints of customers: it was the best on the market, and that was that. Similarly, another client, a pie-mix maker, while steadily losing business, would not agree to change his advertising to suit what market research had uncovered as to its effects: if potential customers who read his copy were "biased," that was their hard luck. Here, strikingly enough, resentment of the customer survives in firms highly dependent on sensitivity to consumers, companies which go so far as to employ market researchers but not far enough to cater to what they regard as customer prejudice. . . .

Willy Loman, however, failed to establish such emotional distance from his clients, and lacking support from his own occupational group, he became something of an anomaly among salesmen, exceptionally vulnerable, without the occupation's long-built-up defenses against the demands of work. In his ignorance of the ropes, Willy again strikes me as unusually deracinated—something Arthur Miller mislocates, I suggest, in the intangible nature of the occupation.

III. So much may be regarded as an overture to a somewhat more systematic account of why some of these developments have come about, why our work and leisure have changed so considerably. Naturally, such an account must be speculative and abbreviated; I will have to confine myself to institutional changes and to such intellectual currents as *Babbitt* or *Death of a Salesman* represent.

Let me emphasize, first of all, that such changes are never wholesale. Thus, the attitude towards the middleman in *Death of a Salesman* is nothing new. The idea that the middleman doesn't produce anything can be found in medieval thought and in the Reformation; the idea was very strong in 19th-century American populism. Populism, though it appears to have vanished, has left its mark. For example, nostalgia for a rural past is still very strong in America. Even so urban a writer as Arthur Miller is obsessed in *Death of a Salesman* with the fencing in of a once-rural Brooklyn and with the virtuousness of working with one's hands close to the soil. What is interpreted as "close to the soil" is, to be sure, partly a matter of cultural definition; thus, in Kansas City the leading annual social event, at which debutantes are presented, is the American Royal, a stock show at which grain traders and cattle buyers parade around under huge Stetsons—perhaps believing for a moment that they can identify with ranch life although they make their living as down-town brokers, and although ranchers themselves would seldom wear such head-gear. These identifications, as they become ritualized, have much more influence on our conceptions of our work than anything "intrinsic" to that work (such as the soil itself) or to man's biological potentiality for work and for avoiding work.

An illustration of the slow way in which cultural definitions change lies in the fact that, as Americans have sloughed off to a considerable extent the Puritan's exalted valuations of work, we have nevertheless not on the whole sought jobs that would provide a maximum of income with a minimum of work. Rather, what has happened is that our aims have become more complex: we now seek "the right kind" of work, including the right blend of leisure with work and inside work. For instance, a recent series of articles in *Fortune* indicates that we are witnessing the death of our salesmen in general: companies are finding it more and more difficult to recruit salesmen, even or especially when they work on a commission basis. The old-fashioned salesman set his own pace; he had a great deal of leisure, and, if he was good and business was good, he could make money. But today such opportunities seem often to go begging, and corporations engage in all kinds of semantic niceties, such as redefining sales jobs as sales engineering to get around the problem; they try to replace direct selling by advertising, and by using the retail store as the point-of-sale as in the Supermarket. College graduates today want jobs in personnel work or other "service" occupations, rather than in the exposed and isolated position of the salesman. For one thing, their wives make more demands of them than Willy's wife did: they want them home, and free of ulcers—and these new-style wives are more help to their men than the neutral misery of Mrs. Loman was any comfort to Willy. In the old days, Biff might have become a salesman without afterthought, but his ambitions are confused by some of the newer currents.

One reason for this is that young people seem to be increasingly choosing the role of an employee in a large organization, with pensions and perquisites, rather than the chance to make a quick killing by commission selling or other risky and entrepreneurial job. One company reported to *Fortune* that they now look for salesmen among Greeks—an ethnic group not yet acculturated to the newer American values; another, that they do their recruiting for sales in Texas and Oklahoma—states where also old-fashioned crazy millionaires can still be found. Sometimes people refer to high income taxes as a determining factor, but I think taxes, though certainly an element, are frequently used as rationalizations by men who don't want to take risks. Taxes are simply part of the managerial climate in which enterprise is now carried on, in which innovation is entrusted to a research and development staff trained at the Columbia School of Industrial Management and the Harvard Business School—men who take courses which deal with human relations in order that they will be able to get along with their colleagues in the office, or at least to discuss problems of human relations at American Management Association meetings.

And this leads me to a further reflection on *Death of a Salesman.* You will remember the terrible scene in which Howard Wagner fires Willy, while listening to an idiotic recording. Some of my colleagues at Chicago have recently been studying retirement practices and find that one reason many companies have a firm rule compelling retirement at, let us say, 65 is that people today are too soft-hearted to fire other people. At one large steel company, a number of older men have jobs which are make-work because no one can bring himself to discharge them. A retirement rule locates the responsibility elsewhere, makes it impersonal. This is true of the retirement regulations in universities also. Indeed, wherever I have observed such matters—in business, in government, in academic life—I have noticed the lengths to which people will go before firing somebody. Howard Wagners are hard to come by. (You will notice that I am criticizing the play on the basis of a sociological estimate, but I must say that the play invites such criticism by its own effort at documentary realism.)

IV. So far, I have spoken as if fear of risk was the chief factor in the actual dearth of entrepreneurs and of salesmen in the American economy at present. But there is also a growing desire to be serviceable to others—this is one reason for the current high prestige of the medical profession. The attraction of personnel work for many college graduates rests on their urge to work *with* people (the fact is, they more often work with files—but that is in a way beside the point) rather than, as they interpret selling, *against* people. People want to be part of a team, part of a group. Work is done in groups, research is done in groups. It is this security which is often more important than pension plans. (I am discussing at such length the problem of work and the salesman today, because in order to see clearly the changes in the standards for judging consumption, we have to see how work itself has changed. For work and play seem to be fundamental dualities in culture, like day and night, male and female, parent and child, self and not-self.)

It may be that the changes I have been discussing are partly kept from clearer view by the American belief that men must be tough, not soft and sentimental; thus, we tend to conceal from ourselves as well as from others our conciliatory attitudes, our moods of fearing success and display, our sensitivity to envy. And so we continue to talk about free enterprise, about getting ahead—about all the older values which the Loman family, in its several ways, has taken so literally. But often this talk is big talk, or whistling to keep up our courage.

Such interpretation of contemporary talk, in fact, requires us to go back historically and raise the question whether in the 19th century, underneath all the Horatio Alger talk and the Samuel Smiles talk, similar ambivalences towards an all-out individualism were not present. The Christian values which are so strong in Mr. Gosse's group of Plymouth Brethren not only helped to spur the rise of a competitive, individualistic capitalism, but also moderated that capitalism by feelings of social responsibility, of concern for the other—after all, they were called "Brethren." And Christianity always contains the latent dynamic of a potential return to the values of the early Christian era, before the Church became a great going concern; in other words, there is always the available material for a reformation—within Catholicism as well as within Protestantism. Christianity may have become something of a shell in the 19th century, for many pious frauds, but it was always more than that and was not for long successfully allied with the more ferocious forms of competitiveness. Bruce Barton's notion of a generation ago that Jesus was really a big advertising man would hardly go over today among people of Babbitt's station, let alone among the advertising men who relish Mead's satiric *How to Get Ahead in Business without Really Trying*.

By the same evidence, we may conclude that there *have* been changes, very profound ones, although their origins can be traced back to an earlier day. Values once confined to a small elite group, or to an elite place within the hearts of many people—a kind of Sunday rather than weekday place—have now become much more widespread. For example, we can see this in attitudes towards conspicuous consumption. Veblen noticed in his book on the leisure class, published in 1899, that some small groups among the very rich were learning to be offended by conspicuous display, they were going in for "natural-looking" estates, "natural-looking" contrivances, and presumably "natural-looking" dress, too. He realized that when a leisure class gets large enough, and sufficiently in touch with itself, it can depart from grossly vulgar display—it can whisper rather than shout. And he saw how renewed attitudes of "workmanship," as against the earlier "wastemanship" at the top of the social pyramid, could spread downwards, as more people gained leisure, and as more came in contact with leisure class values.

Yet even he, perhaps because of his farm origin and midwest experience, did not see fully the extent to which nonconspicuous nonconsumption (or, as one of my friends more appropriately terms it, "conspicuous under-consumption") was already a powerful American pattern. He seems to have escaped contact with Boston Unitarians or Philadelphia Quakers whose display was much more veiled. Although in Henry Adams' novel, *Democracy*, we are treated to an inauguration ball more gaudy than the un-top-hatted one of a few weeks ago [January, 1953], when we read Henry James's *The Bostonians*, which appeared in 1876, we are confronted with wealthy young women who were plain of dress and disdainful of display. For them, good intangible causes took the place of good commodities.

I should add, in fairness to Veblen, that he saw some of this. But he largely overlooked the possibility that these attitudes were being shaped by intellectual as well as by merely technological currents. Thus it would not have occurred to him that his own books would influence people's attitudes towards consumption, that he would be the godfather of the consumers' movement—that, indeed, a whole series of books, including his own and coming right down to Marquand's novels or *Death of a Salesman*, have helped inter certain American values with irony and sarcasm. For him, as for Marx, men always conform eventually to economic necessity, not to cultural or ideological necessity.

Nevertheless, Veblen's *Theory of the Leisure Class* fitted not too badly the American scene from the gay 90s to the not quite so gay 20s. The hero in the novel *Jefferson Selleck* who suffers agonies on his wedding night because he is of lower social origin than his bride; the drama of *The Great Gatsby,* and the miseries of Charlie Gray in *Point of No Return* and of Mary Monahan and her intimidated Beacon Street lover in the *Late George Apley,* are so many testimonies to the Veblenian cruelties of the American status system, with its unmerry emulative chase. And yet the last novels I mentioned are testimony also to a newer note in American life and literature, that of the failure of success, rather than, as in *Death of a Salesman,* the failure of failure.

V. It has, I believe, been the bounteousness of modern industry, especially in America, which has done more than almost anything else to make conspicuous consumption obsolete here. It would go much too far to say that consumption bores us, but it no longer has the old self-evident quality; it no longer furnishes our lives with a kind of simple structure or chronology of motives, as it did for William Randolph Hearst, for instance. To collect objects in Hearst's manner required a certain confidence, even arrogance, a certain imperviousness to ridicule and criticism. Hearst's "whim of iron" appears to be a thing of the past.

It is not only or primarily, however, that our interest in goods has been drowned by the boundless cornucopia of goods, by analogy with Engel's law that food consumption declines proportionately as income rises. The same expansion of the economy has created new fortunes much faster than their possessors could possibly be tutored by the old rich in the proper consumption values of the latter. No mere "400" located in a single city can any longer dictate appropriate leisure-class behavior in terms of what estates, houses, furniture, and so on to collect. The absence of titles in America, and of many old-family names equivalent to titles (judging by names, many Negroes and onetime

Kabotskys belong to some of the best families), also makes such hegemony very difficult—indeed, from the point of view of an Italian count (unfamiliar with American distinctions even in the days of Daisy Miller), a Dallas oil heiress in seven figures and Neiman-Marcus clothes may be preferable to a Saltonstall in six figures and Jordan Marsh clothes. In this situation, the more established wealth and its auxiliary leaders of high taste have sought to fight back, not by a futile outspending, but by a conspicuous underspending. A Hearst has been ridiculed, not only for poor taste in *what* he bought, but *that* he bought in such quantity.

No doubt, universal education—itself part of our bonanza of good fortune—has exposed many people, who later have come into means, to tasteful critiques of working-class extravagance. The mass media, too, carry along with the prodigality of their advertising the relative emaciation of their judgments on expenditure: the *Vogue* style of restrained elegance is made an accessible model for millions. However, the movement of style has not only been from the top down—and how could it be when people can't tell, for reasons already indicated, where the top is? A relaxation of standards has spread upwards: the new rich gentleman needs no longer to struggle into a dress suit to hear Mary Garden at the Opera House, nor need he learn to ride to hounds or to send his sons to Groton or St. Marks. All he has to learn to do—and this, as Robert L. Steiner and Joseph Weiss point out in "Veblen Revised in the Light of Counter-Snobbery," is not easy for him—is to mute the wish for wild and gaudy spending that he learned as a lower-class lad, the very wish that may have helped propel him into the millionaire ranks. Frictions on this score are indicated by the concern of the Cadillac people with the consequences for their older clients of the fact that the Cadillac (rather than, as some years ago, the Buick) has become "the" car for well-off Negroes.

Today, men of wealth, fearful of making a wrong move, harried not only by taxes but by public relations and their own misgivings, are apt to give over the now-dreaded responsibilities for spending to a foundation, which then on their behalf can collect research projects or artistic works

—protected by bureaucratic organization and corporate responsibility from imputations of extravagance. (As I write this, however, the big foundations such as Ford and Rockefeller are under Congressional Committee scrutiny—there seems to be no escape from money save anonymity!)

Another form of putting spending at arm's length is to delegate it to one's children. Whether for toys or for schools, for space in the home or advice on child management, more money is being spent on children and by them than ever before. The trouble with children, of course, is that they grow up—unlimited amounts cannot be spent on them. Before too long, in the same strata that Veblen and Arthur Miller have influenced, the children now grown up are denouncing advertising and disdainful of waste and extravagance. The parents, of course, can have more children, and as you may know, this is what has happened to the country in the last decade, much to the bewilderment of the demographers, who thought that the American urban middle classes would continue to have fewer and fewer children and more and more commodities. Demographers do not know, and I do not know, why the shift has occurred; doubtless the causes are complex and ramified—the same thing has happened in France and elsewhere. But I do suspect that the changes in value-patterns we have been discussing have been among the factors. I started several years ago reading college class books for the light they might shed on subtle shifts in attitude. I was struck by the emphasis on the family that began to appear in my own and other college classes of a few years back. People in writing about themselves no longer started off by saying they were Vice-President of Ozark Air Lines and a director of the Tulsa National Bank, and so forth; they began by telling about the wife and five kids and how they had a home in the suburbs where they all enjoyed barbecues in the back yard. The occupational achievement was played down; the family scene, with its pastoral virtues, played up. Since then I have found similar tendencies in other groups. This would seem to hang together with the devaluation of individual success we have been discussing: children are a kind of unequivocal good in a world of changing values, and we can lavish on children the care and emotions we would now feel it egotistical to lavish on ourselves. The younger age at which people are marrying today is a further factor; having started to go steady at fourteen, they want to settle down at twenty. Whereas a generation ago a career man and a career girl would have considered marriage an obstacle to their work aims, today marriage and children are in a way part of the consumption and leisure sphere, the side of life currently emphasized.

VI. Thus, children absorb some of the surplus and foundations some more of it. Especially the biggest foundation of all—the federal government. Conspicuous consumption has been socialized, and appears of necessity largely in the form of weapons, with something left over for national parks. When we speak of government spending for armaments, it is clear that the line between consumption and production is hard to draw, and the much more general point I want to make is that with the decline in conspicuous consumption—a relative rather than an absolute decline perhaps—has come a great rise in what we might call conspicuous production.

As I have implied earlier, the company for which Willy Loman worked did not engage in conspicuous production —else they would have kept him on, finding a place for him in overhead. The companies that do engage in it begin by locating and designing their plants and offices for show as well as for "efficiency" in the older sense of nearness to suppliers, distributors, and other facilities. It would be interesting to know to what extent the immense tax-facilitated rebuilding of American industry since World War II has been influenced by management's desire to have a plant that looked like the *Fortune* ads of the Austin Company and other designers of low-slung, "streamlined" factories. To be sure, if such factories are good for morale, they are by definition efficient, but the Hawthorne experiments are some evidence that workers respond more to interest taken in them than to lighting, cooling, or other circumambient factors—very likely, such factories are good for executives' and directors' morale. (These experiments were made nearly a generation ago and it may be that the subtle relations between the effects of physical and social environment have altered since then.)

Conspicuous production takes a great variety of forms. If a company leads the procession in granting paid vacations or in providing some new service for employees—that may be partly conspicuous production. Many additions to overhead both constitute such production and spend time advertising it—even some incumbents of the president's chair may have that as their principal role. Officials, who would no longer be as eager as their predecessors were to buy their way into an exclusive country club, suburb, or resort, are most eager to have their companies' ads appear in the pages of *Business Week, Fortune,* or on television, whether or not their market research can wholly justify each instance of space- or time-buying. I understand that some large companies have issued manuals to their officials on how to live up to their expense accounts, and we may properly regard such manuals as successors to all the educative literature by which previous ruling groups have been taught to spend—something which, strange as it may seem to some of you, needs always to be learned.

Professor Richard Hofstadter has suggested that these practices should be called conspicuous corporate consumption rather than conspicuous production. Certainly, it is as difficult to distinguish one from the other as to distinguish work from play among many of the managerial work-force. It would take a very close scrutiny of factory lay-out, for instance, to be sure what changes were the result of desires for corporate prestige rationalized as cost-cutting methods, and to know whether to allocate the costs of prestige itself to the production or the consumption side of the ledger. The aesthetics of the machines of production, factories and plants express a slightly different kind of conspicuous production. It is only when we adopt an "economizing" point of view that we can distinguish, in the activities centered around the economy, between the end of maximizing the product and the other ends, ceremonial, religious, prestige-laden, that are contextually being pursued. The conspicuousness of these other ends is the result, as Professor Martin Meyerson has pointed out to me, of our taking for granted as the sole end of work that of maximizing product—from that distorted, if traditional, perspective other ends embedded in the context of social life appear out of order, even garish. Men who in the nineteenth century or today have seemed to be pursuing wealth or efficiency as a single uncomplicated goal certainly have been self-deceived as to their total gamut of motives. Nevertheless we can say, I think, that corporate consumption, in which each company goes into business as a junior welfare state, does currently rearrange our motives in a new configuration.

One factor, as I have already indicated, is the increasing professionalization of management, a development which has had consequences rather different from those Brandeis or Taylor hoped for. The eighteenth- and nineteenth-century industrialist came out of a rural background or ideology: he regarded his firm as a farm, and his work-force as hired hands, often transient and easily replaced, or as a small-town business, paternalistically run. He did not think of himself as having to be an expert on human relations—that could be left to the clergy, the main professionals in his purview. Feeling, moreover, some doubt as to where he stood socially, vis-à-vis the clergy and vis-à-vis Eastern aristocrats, he built a big feudal castle of a house for himself to show everybody that he had arrived, as if to declaim that he was personally worthy by visible evidences of his net worth: if he could not outshout the clergyman and the statesman, he could at least outshine them. And his wife, lacking the cultural tutelage of aristocratic wives and excluded by patriarchal convention from any contact with the workaday world, had nothing more to occupy her than to act as his deputy in conspicuous spending, his ambassadress to the dominions of culture he was too busy and too bored to bother with.

Such an industrialist, when he met his competitors, frankly regarded them as such, and whatever conviviality he might show, he kept his secrets of production to himself. He met with others, that is, in terms of money, not in terms of a specialized profession which freely exchanges its own secrets while keeping them from the lay public. Today, the communication of industrialists and businessmen with one another is frequently quite different. Meeting as professionals, the former individuality which distinguished the American businessman is rubbed off. He seeks status in his ability to run a smooth, attractive, and pleasant social and technological organization. Unions obviously have done something to encourage this, and so has government, in its tax and labor policy, but the desire of businessmen themselves to become professionals in human relations seems to be a major element.

And their wives, too, have changed. If they are college trained, it isn't enough for them to spend their husband's income. Often they have had jobs themselves; they may be professionals in their own right, or potential professionals. They want to become pals and companions of their business spouses—sleeping partners, so to speak—aware of what goes on at work, and vicarious consumers of corporate conspicuousness, flaunting not so much their own now-standardized fur coats but their husbands' firms—a more indirect display. Both husband and wife are urban, not small-town and rural, in their orientation; and they tend to view the factory work-force as a human collectivity in which there are roles to be played and maneuvers to be made. The earlier nineteenth-century horrors of rapid urbanization, in which human relations tended to become depersonalized and older social groupings disintegrated, now appear to be giving way to new institutional forms adapted to the conditions of contemporary city life. The presence of women on this scene, in fact or in feeling, helps alter the atmosphere, introducing a consumption mood into work relations, with its refreshing congeniality of association as contrasted with a male society of tycoons.

The divorce of corporate ownership from control and the consequent disenfranchisement of the stockholders (plus federal tax policies) have put responsibility for spending the corporate surplus on the executive in his capacity as an official, for corporate savings are only to a limited extent distributed to stockholders but are increasingly retained in depreciation funds or other concealment or reserve accounts. Business management schools play a part in deciding what it is that the corporation should now spend money for—whether it is for training directors, or market research, or philanthropic activity (which now supports much "pure" research)—all the multifarious forms of conspicuous corporate consumption.

In general, I think it can be said that many of the motives which were in earlier decades built into the character structure of individuals are now built into the institutional structure of corporate life. On the whole, I would rather see our surplus used to allow individuals a still greater amount of leisure, so that each of us would work, let us say, a four-hour day, than keep us at work eight hours so that our large organizations can generously spend the difference. And yet, in making such a judgment, I know I must continuously keep in mind the complex and stratified nature of the changes going on in our American life. If I had to choose between having Lever Brothers spend the American surplus on its beautiful Park Avenue offices and having the Happy Lomans and Glenn McCarthys spend it, I could easily come down on the side of Lever Brothers. Corporate consumption may be, as it has often been in architecture, a pleasure in its own right and sometimes a model for individual consumption.

Some Clinical and Cultural Aspects of the Aging Process

If we observe the aging of individuals, in the period after middle life, it seems to me that we can distinguish three ideal-typical outcomes. Some individuals bear within themselves some psychological sources of self-renewal; aging brings for them accretions of wisdom, with no loss of spontaneity and ability to enjoy life, and they are relatively independent of the culture's strictures and penalties imposed on the aged. Other individuals, possibly the majority, bear within them no such resources but are the beneficiaries of a cultural preservative (derived from work, power, position, etc.) which sustains them although only so long as the cultural conditions remain stable and protective. A third group, protected neither from within nor from without, simply decay. In terms more fully delineated elsewhere,[1] we may have autonomous, adjusted, and anomic reactions to aging.

THE AUTONOMOUS

In the case of someone like Bertrand Russell or Toscanini, one feels an essential aliveness of spirit that reflexively keeps the body alive, too, in the face of the inevitable

"Some Clinical and Cultural Aspects of the Aging Process" is based on a memorandum submitted in January 1953 to the Kansas City Study of Middle Age and Aging being conducted under a Carnegie Foundation grant by the Committee on Human Development of the University of Chicago. It was first published in the American Journal of Sociology, *Vol. 59, No. 4, 1954.*

1. See chapter 14 of *The Lonely Crowd,* Yale University Press, 1950; or chapter 12 of the Anchor edition of *The Lonely Crowd,* 1954.

physiological catabolisms. Such men create something new every day through their own reactions; in their work as in their general style of life they exhibit what Erich Fromm calls the "productive orientation."[2] It is most important to realize that such men are not necessarily "balanced" or "well-adjusted" people: they may have terrible tempers, neurotic moods; they may be shut out from whole areas of existence; they may get along well with very few people, or as historians or musicians prefer the "company" of dead people; they may relate themselves to the cosmos more through an emphasis on objects and ideas than on social relations. One can see in such cases that a passionate interest or preoccupation which has remained alive since childhood—though perhaps newly justified or rediscovered in middle life—may matter much more than the roundedness of interests we are today inclined to encourage among our two vulnerable groups of "clients": children and older people. It might be valuable to study, for instance, professional chess players of distinction; my guess would be that they suffer very little deterioration as a social-psychological process, however constricted their lives may appear to the therapist whose norm is a superficial integration of a bundle of diverse activities.

Such individuals, I repeat, are fairly immune to cultural changes, or to cultural definitions of their own physical changes: they carry their preservative, their "spirits," within. Freud could continue to live with vigor in the face of cancer of the mouth which made eating embarrassing and difficult; as his life went on, it seems to me that he grew steadily more alive and imperturbable—*Civilization and Its Discontents,* written when he was over 70, belies its pessimistic theme by the very vitality of its presentation. Likewise Franz Boas, though he suffered from disfigurement and though he was in many ways a cramped person, does not appear to have experienced any decline of powers. The misfortunes brought by Nazism could no more shake either man than the misfortunes brought by their own bodies. Men of this sort exhibit in a dramatic way the

2. *Man For Himself* (1947).

specifically human power to grow and develop on a superphysiological level (with, of course, physiological consequences); as long as the body does not actively prevent, these men are immortal because of their ability to renew themselves.

In lesser degree, anyone who can experience anything for himself—whether he is a "man of distinction" or not—staves off by so much psychological death. Paradoxically, the premonition of death may for many be a stimulus to such novelty of experience: the imminence of death serves to sweep away the inessential preoccupations for those who do not flee from the thought of death into triviality. It is apparent that we enter here a cultural dimension and raise the questions how death is regarded or disregarded in America, compared to how it is viewed, for example, in existentialist philosophy.

I can think of several reasons why we have not paid very much attention to these autonomous reactions to aging. Such reactions are rare, and a spurious democracy has influenced both our research methods (I am sometimes tempted to define "validity" as part of the context of an experiment demanding so little in the way of esoteric gift that any number can play at it, provided they have taken a certain number of courses) and our research subjects (it would be deemed snobbish to investigate only the best people). Moreover, the period of life I am describing and its attendant qualities do not last long: men react productively to waning physical and often social power, only to die shortly thereafter. And we tend to view individuals as we do entire cultures: while we can admire the Hellenistic period although it was weak and vulnerable and soon perished, we do not on the whole admire declining empires nearer to us in time. We read their future fate—death—into our present judgment of them.

THE ADJUSTED

I should, I suppose, always put quotation marks around my use of the term "adjusted," for I define this, not in terms of my own value judgments but in terms of given cultural definitions. For instance, we all know the type of American executive or professional man who does not allow himself to age, but by what appears almost sheer will keeps himself "well-preserved," as if in creosote. For the most part, he lacks inner aliveness of the sort just discussed; the will which burns in him, while often admirable, cannot be said to be truly "his": it is compulsive; he has no control over it, but it controls him. He appears to exist in a psychological deep-freeze; new experience cannot get at him, but rather he fulfills himself by carrying out ever-renewed tasks which are given by his environment: he is borne along on the tide of cultural agendas. So long as these agendas remain, he is safe; he does not acquire wisdom, as the old of some other cultures are said to do, but he does not lose skill —or if he does, is protected by his power from the consequences, perhaps the awareness, of loss of skill. In such a man, responsibility may substitute for maturity.

Indeed, it could be argued that the protection furnished such people in the United States is particularly strong since their "youthfulness" remains a social and economic prestige-point, and wisdom might actually, if it brought awareness of death and what the culture regarded as pessimism, be a count against them. In a way, nothing happens to these people, which leads them (save possibly in rare moments of self-doubt and self-questioning) to regard themselves as well-off. They prefigure in complex and often imperceptible ways the cultural cosmetic that makes Americans appear youthful to other peoples. And, since they are well-fed, well-groomed, and vitamin-dosed, there may be an actual delay-in-transit of the usual physiological declines to partly compensate for lack of psychological growth. Their outward appearance of aliveness may mask inner sterility.

Like the women of an earlier day who were held up by stays, such "adjusted" people of the middle and later years are held up by endoskeletal (mesomorphic?) tensions. As I have said, they are literally held up: nothing advances, save their careers, their responsibilities. This sort of energy must surely be ranked among the world-conquering assets of Western man: it is impressive to Indians to find Englishmen, as well as mad dogs, out in the noonday sun—they are gods of a sort, who tell the sun to stand still. Only at night, perhaps, coming home from a party, does the mask drop or crack, to be ritualistically reorganized the following day. We who are the beneficiaries of such accumulated energies in the past cannot lightly scoff at their possessors.

Nevertheless, I am inclined to think that many of the geriatric suggestions currently made for improving the adjustment of the elderly are aimed simply at finding ersatz preservatives, not at any inner transformations that would allow self-renewal to occur. Thus, we may seek to persuade a retired doctor or executive to take up golf or fishing with the same undiscerning ferocity he once threw into his work and its social context; we may shift someone from the faculty club or the Kiwanis into the Golden Age Club; and so on. It would be unjust to criticize too severely these ameliorative measures in the absence of understood and institutionalized ways of assisting more basic transformation—ways it is often, one fears, too late to start with by the time of retirement. (We know, in principle, it is never too late; but, as with other therapeutic questions, it is a matter of available help, of the allocation of scarce resources.) Yet we may occasionally discover dilemmas in which too quick an effort to assure a smooth adjustment results in this merely substitutive activity, whereas allowing a person to be confronted for a time with nothingness might save him—or destroy him—depending on what inner resources he could muster in reaction to the challenge.[3]

And in this connection let me bring up reservations about our usual social-psychological discussions of roles and role theory—discussions which too easily assume that people *are* the roles they play, the willing or unwilling puppeteers of the social drama. In my own view, the ability to play roles not only involves, in a great many instances, some rewriting

3. I have just come upon the excellent article of Dr. Martin Gumpert, "Old Age and Productive Loss," *Bulletin of the Menninger Clinic*, 17:103–109 (May 1953). Dr. Gumpert stresses that the very bodily defeats and impairments of the aging person may be and often are more than compensated for by inner growth.

of the socially-provided script, but some saving grace of potentiality not bound up in the role; the role itself is what allows people to give to it less than their full selves; it clarifies one's economy of affects. Hence there are reservoirs of inner life in a great many individuals whose roles, almost by definition, do not wholly absorb them. (The same is true, as Toynbee observes in terms of world history, of many cultures and what had been thought to be their "roles.") We see in wartime or other socially-structured emergency the great efflorescence of unsuspected potentialities in people—unsuspected often enough by the very individuals concerned. Where do these potentialities come from? It is hard to say, though we are tempted to refer them, as we refer so many mysteries, to childhood, and to say that the cultural preservative is a deep-freeze in the sense, too, that childhood potentialities, though long neglected, are seldom wholly crushed. (Very few projective test experts, in my limited observation, focus sufficiently on the discovery of such potentialities; the "deeper levels" they look for are ordinarily those that foreshadow trouble rather than liberation: they are understandably more worried that they will miss a hidden flaw than a buried asset.)

Professor Martin Loeb, the field director of our Kansas City research, in discussing these notions with me, has been inclined to question the making of such explicit value judgments, the positing of an ideal of aging as the basis for setting up a typology. He suggested that I might be in danger of projecting into a typology my own dream that the autonomous person does not "really" age, at least in any deleterious way. And he asked what was wrong with a grandmother's way of aging who had had a hard life and now preferred to sit passively on the porch and watch her grandchildren and the passing traffic? Who was to tell her she should be spontaneous?

I doubt if this was meant as a warning against value judgments as such, for we cannot avoid them, but rather against shallow and ethnocentric ones. Still, I sometimes feel that middle-class social scientists are today almost too ready to throw over their own values, as class-biased, while accepting values from groups whose life-conditions have permitted them fewer alternatives. Our circle of sympathy should not be too narrow—should even perhaps include the lower-middle-class grandmother who wears too much grease paint in a pathetic effort to look like a cover girl. And certainly a grandmother who decides out of her life-experience to observe her progeny and the passing show and who is capable of observing people as individuals and not entirely as stereotypes would strike me as making a productive reaction to aging—spontaneity and aliveness are of course not to be equated with activity and hep-ness. In general, I feel that we can sharpen our scientific awareness of what aging does to people, and vice versa, by bringing into play our preference for more creative as against more stultified ways of meeting the challenge of aging in individuals and in cultural groups.

As the Eisenhower Administration takes office, I think we shall have an unusual opportunity to observe the working out of some of these ways. Some of the military and business leaders newly drafted into government will be unable to grow and develop when robbed of the protective surroundings their social systems gave them; they may even appear to age rapidly, to decay. (Others, sufficiently high up, can try to recreate analogous protective systems, down to the secretary, the staffs, the shape of the desks and perhaps of the subordinates too—so as to avoid the need to leave "home.") Still others, however, will prove to have, or to gain, the quality of inner aliveness that enables one to adapt to radically new surroundings; fear does not prevent their seeing that these are new, or force them simply to curse the newness as "bureaucracy," "politics," or whatnot; rather, they will be stimulated.

One would want to watch, also, for the consequences of different occupational experiences before entering the government. Are the department store executives whom William E. Henry has described as having a tropism towards decision-making better off than bankers who are in the main accustomed to constrict decision-making? Is it a question of the nature of different preservatives in different occupational groups, as these mix or refuse to mix with the occupational experience of government officials? Can we develop tests that will help answer such questions, not for young people early in their careers, but for middle-aged people suddenly given a new lease on a new office, if not on a new life?

An illustration of how difficult it is to predict which of these several "careers of aging" an individual will pursue is presented by the notorious misjudgments teachers are apt to make about the prospects of their students. Some who appear to have spark and originality lose it very shortly. Then, retroactively, one can see that while young they were kept alive partly by physiological changes and that aging started for them at 25 if not before; nothing new has happened after that. In such cases, it depends hardly at all on the individual whether the culture keeps him going until death or does not prevent his obvious and grievous deterioration. In contrast, other individuals who in their 20s appeared to be quite set in their ways, without much ability to have new experiences, turn out to have been harboring reserves which slowly come to reshape their whole orientation. Whereas for some and perhaps most men the possession of power protects them from having to develop (others are compelled to adapt to *them*), there remain a number of men for whom power serves as a stimulant to late flowering.

Thus, it is plain that for the "adjusted" group it matters decisively what institutions they hitch or are hitched onto, and whether such institutions encapsulate them or awaken them or destroy them. Their one-and-only life-cycle gets fatally mixed up with the larger institutional cycles. And, to recur to our image of the aging business or professional person, it sometimes seems as if his tenacious efforts to keep himself from sagging into a flabby or relaxed age provide much of the motive power for our entrepreneurial expansion combined with institutional conservatism.

THE ANOMIC

Real decay sets in when the physiological vitality is lost, and when the culture does not carry the individual onward but drops him. Here we get the sudden decompositions, as they appear, of some men who are forced to retire, where it becomes evident that the job and its emotional ambience kept the job-holder together: he held a job less than the job held him. Or we get the spouse who—though he or she did not greatly love the other spouse—cannot survive him or her, but dies shortly thereafter in a metaphorical Suttee. (We find the same pattern among the "quasi-families" of people who are not married, but are tied to each other in a similar symbiotic way.) Such people live like cards, propped up by other cards.

At first blush, they may look very much like the people who have a better cultural preservative, but the paths soon diverge, and their decay sets in earlier. They are not the lawyers and engineers and businessmen of springy step, but the prematurely weary and resigned. As against the person who, in a way, never grows up, never faces death, they sometimes appear never to have been young. But in both cases—the adjusted and the anomic outcomes—there is a truncation of the "seven ages of man," the variety and contretemps of the life cycle; there is an insufficient dialectic between physiological decline and psychological increment.

Moreover, both the autonomous and the anomic reactions to aging are alike in that the individuals concerned make little use of the standard cultural preservatives—the former because they transcend and reshape them, the latter because they cannot attain them or maintain them. If responsibility accompanies maturity for the autonomous, and takes the place of maturity for the adjusted, the anomic find their way to neither. Like a person who is afraid to overshoot the green when he drives from the tee (or, more probably, gives up acting as if he wanted to make the green at all), they start out in life with aims that will not carry them through a career. And they do not succeed in getting onto an institutional escalator that will define for them what it is to have a career.

Our research in Kansas City, having moved out of the clinic and into the community, will probably have to develop typologies less "universal" than this one I have proposed here. For the three types I have sketched have nothing to do with Kansas City as such—with its conflict of rural and urban ideologies, its history as an entrepot, its prospective future as an industrial base. Differences of sex (I have said almost nothing about women in this paper) and of social station have decisive consequences for the forms of aging felt to be appropriate—but these differences, too, while illustrated in Kansas City as elsewhere, are not peculiar to it. Nevertheless, as we examine different occupational groups in the metropolitan area, we may find this typology useful as a critique of each group's way of aging. Thus the well-to-do and ceaselessly energetic medical men of Kansas City may buy a cultural preservative at the expense of being run ragged from the days when they did autopsies to the day when they are the subject of one—perhaps a bit raggeder because busier, more successful, and slightly more traditional, than medical men elsewhere. As against this, we may find the pattern Warren Peterson suspects to exist among Kansas City high school teachers, that they are "old maids" at 30 and for 40 years thereafter (they must retire at 70) do not appreciably age, being kept alive by their young charges, their community obligations, their summer school courses, and the rest of the diurnal round to which this helplessly exposed target of community hopes, fears, and envies is committed.

Even here, I doubt if we shall find patterns exclusively Kansas City's, or exclusively metropolitan. But it is in any case fortunate that our research objectives, and our setting in Kansas City, both force and encourage us to move back and forth between clinical and cultural considerations, in search of a typology, or a set of typologies, that encompasses both.

The Themes of Work and Play in the Structure of Freud's Thought

The process of incorporating Freud's thought into our living heritage of social and humanistic studies has moved bewilderingly fast, especially in America. But incorporation, as always with great thinkers, has been partial. There has been a tendency, among Freud's medical followers, to "empiricize" him, to forget about his philosophical interests and outlook in order to get on with the clinical job. Among nonspecialists, however, it is this philosophical side of Freud's thought that has often been most influential. In generally accepting it at face without an effort to refer it back to its base in Freud's own experience, people have neglected the very kind of reference he taught us to make. In my opinion, it is not possible to separate his technique from his cultural outlook and setting. It is sometimes said that he was a therapist and medical man in his earlier writings and a gloomy and speculative philosopher in his later writings. But we must be wary of such dichotomies by which, for many, the "good" Freud is separated from the "bad" Freud as, by similar measures, the "good" early Comte is separated from the "bad" later Comte, or the "good" Marx of *The German Ideology* from the "bad" Marx

"The Themes of Work and Play in the Structure of Freud's Thought" was first published in Psychiatry, *Vol. 13, No. 1, 1950.*

For many of the ideas in this article and the three following, I am indebted to Philip Rieff and Murray Wax, and particularly to Erich Fromm. Since they were written, a number of important works have been published on Freud, but I wrote the articles knowing Freud, for all practical purposes, only from his own published writings. Were I rewriting them today, I would change emphases here and there.

of the *Manifesto* or *Capital.* Though of course there are important differences in emphases, these men are of a piece —this, too, Freud would teach us—and their earlier writings contain the germs of the later views.

I have sought to establish this wholeness of the man in the light of certain important themes in Freud's philosophic and social outlook, by examining some of the implications of his early writings, making particular use of his own reported dreams. The later explicit statements in such writings as *Civilization and Its Discontents* or *The Future of an Illusion*[1] often merely confirm and elaborate a position that can be inferred from the "Dora" history, for instance, or from the book on dreams. I have, so far as possible, avoided coming into contact with biographical material or gossip about Freud, in order to see what the works themselves, so bravely revealing, have to say.

For my purposes here, it is not of very great importance to decide at what point Freud's writings reveal him as a unique person—reveal, that is, his own deep affective involvement in an idea—and at what point he simply speaks, without much affect or individuation, in terms stereotypical of the general attitude of the era.[2] Certainly, his utilitarian and Philistine attitudes toward work and play were both central to his own view of life and a dominant note in his cultural environment. But what really matters for us is that

1. *Civilization and Its Discontents,* first published in 1930, develops, *inter alia,* certain themes set forth in "'Civilized' Sexual Morality and Modern Nervousness," *Collected Papers* 2:76, published in 1908, and the Clark University lectures of the following year.

2. To decide this question, in each specific case, could be often highly speculative and difficult. Problems of the same sort arise when one seeks to interpret contemporary interview material, at least of a nonpsychoanalytic sort. There one must always ask: Does what the respondent reports say much about him as an individual, or is it mainly testimony—and, of course, that he gives this testimony says something about him—to the norm of his group, his social class, or the group or class to which he aspires? In Freud's case, we have the advantage of his reported dreams and associations, and many stray remarks, which it is sometimes possible to reinterpret by use of the method he discovered.

by virtue of his greatness—by virtue, too, of the fact that he was on the whole a liberator of men—Freud has succeeded in imposing on a later generation a mortgage of reactionary and constricting ideas that were by no means universally held even in his own epoch. Like so many original thinkers, he was ambivalent; he provides the texts for the partialities of incorporation, and for contradictory life-paths and social policies.[3]

In this essay, I deal with Freud's basic attitudes to work and to play. They were formed in a society that was primarily job-minded; they circulate today in an American society that has much more chance to be leisure-minded and play-minded. While my preoccupation is with the social and cultural implications, it will I think be clear that the more technical contributions of Freud—for instance, his theory of dream interpretation, or his concept of the analytic transference—were to a very considerable degree shaped by his class and cultural outlook. This, of course, does not mean that the contributions are wrong; rather it helps us understand them, and puts us on the lookout for unsuspected pitfalls of ideological bias that may be hidden beneath questions of technique.

WORK: FREEDOM OR NECESSITY

Freud viewed work as an inescapable and tragic necessity. Although he was no student of population problems, he implicitly agreed with Malthus' gloomy conclusion that men would be forever caught between the drives of hunger and sex—lucky to be one jump ahead of starvation. And sex, too, was for Freud a realm of necessity. He saw it, not as presenting men with a problem to be solved, nor with a game to be played, nor, coupled with love, as a road to human closeness and intimacy, but rather as a "teleological" prime mover, charged with the task of socializing and civilizing men and thus preserving the species. Sex could

3. See Erich Fromm, "Individual and Social Origins of Neurosis," *Amer. Sociological Rev.* (1944) 9:380; reprinted in Clyde Kluckhohn and Henry A. Murray, eds., *Personality in Nature, Society, and Culture*, 1948.

fulfill this task because of its ability to bribe with an elemental pleasure and to appease with an elemental release. Work was, then, the means by which the species maintains itself while performing its endless procreative mission.

This outlook, heavily influenced by Puritanism, took shape in the early nineteenth century, in part as a reaction against the views of utopian visionaries—men such as Condorcet, Godwin, and Owen—who envisaged the possibility that, beyond this realm of necessity, might lie a realm of freedom where work had social meaning and where the economy would be our servant, not our master.

Needless to say, men are producing animals and must work in order to live. Moreover, it is altogether likely, men being the creatures they are and work being what it is, that some drudgery will continue to be associated with it. The question of the meaning of work, of how it is experienced, is primarily a cultural problem; and cultures differ enormously in the way work is interpreted in their value-scheme. In some, work is not sharply differentiated from other aspects of life. It may be viewed as fulfilling religious duties; it may have the pleasurable variety, creativeness, and interpersonal texture which is associated with some kinds of farming, or artisanship, art, or science. It may be viewed in other ways. Only, probably, in our Western industrial culture, has work in fact the features Freud attaches to it; is it sharply set off against love, against pleasure, against consumption, against almost every sort of freedom. Only here is it a curse for most people, mitigated as such, often enough, not by its own nature, but by the fear of boredom, which can be even greater than the irksomeness of toil.

In the nineteenth century, dominated by scarcity economics and Malthusian fears, work could nevertheless be given the rational meaning of the avoidance of hunger. And hunger and gain (ambition) could be viewed as the self-evident motives of a market economy, the former operating on the poor, the latter on the well-to-do.[4] In the

4. Cf. Karl Polanyi, *The Great Transformation* (1944).

mid-twentieth century, in the countries of the Industrial Revolution and especially in America, it is likely that with very little human toil a full abundance can be assured to all inhabitants as the result of the machine technology. But although the result has already been a great lowering in the hours of work and vast improvement in physical conditions, work itself is still subjectively felt as a duty, without meaning in its own terms. This is most striking evidence of the fact that the pattern of a culture can disguise, even distort, the inescapable problem of work. Neither the basic physiological drive of hunger, nor the basic equipment of production—man's brain and eyes and hands—instruct him in what meaning, what pattern, he shall give to work, any more than the basic drive of sex, and its genital equipment, tell him what meaning, what pattern, he shall give to love.

It is, as I shall try to show, the more pessimistic, middle-class, nineteenth-century attitudes that are reflected and elaborated in Freud's thought. I shall consider, first, his view of the "real," the workaday world, including his view of his own role in it, and, second, his attitude towards the subordinated world of play.

THE WORKADAY WORLD

Freud, like so many scientists of a system-building cast of mind, was always in search of simplifying dichotomies, of polar opposites. As the "self" was the opposite of the "other," as the pleasure-principle and the reality-principle —or Eros and Thanatos—divided life between them, so the workaday world with its productive machinery, its markets, its other economic processes, was sharply marked off from the play-world, the world of fantasy and gratification. The former world, Freud took for granted as he found it; he reserved his insight and his unconventionality largely for the latter.

Freud regarded the world of business and professional life—of all areas where hunger and gain were alleged to hold sway—as unquestionably real. The views of critics, such as Veblen or Thurman Arnold, who see the mythical or fantastic elements of business enterprise,[5] are foreign to his mode of thought. It did not seem to occur to him that much work was obsessive busy-work, that businessmen often fled into work to avoid women, or that the seeming pursuit of business self-interest might be the sheerest rationalization for activities that were quite differently motivated. To be sure, the European businessman is more of an "economic man" than his American counterpart; his compartmentalization of work, separate from home and from play, is more complete; he *does* seek gain as his principal end, rather than friends, prestige, or an agenda. Nevertheless, Freud's attitude towards the work that men do in their occupations was almost that of a behaviorist who does not probe into motives.

Indeed, Freud concluded his book on dreams on the qualifiedly behaviorist note that "actions, above all, deserve to be placed in the front rank" in judging human character, since the dark and daemonic psychic forces he had been describing had usually only the most limited consequences in the real, that is, the workaday, world.[6] In the same volume, Freud described the dream-experiments of his colleague, Dr. Schrötter, and concluded: "Unfortunately, the value of this important investigation was diminished by the fact that Dr. Schrötter shortly afterwards committed suicide."[7] There was no note of sympathy or grief for this human tragedy: what mattered to Freud was the work and not the man. Such behavioristic views seem to be a reflection of the psychology of a market-economy: it does not matter what men think or how they feel, but only that, overtly, they react "appropriately" to the stimuli of hunger and gain.

5. See, for example, Thorstein Veblen. *The Theory of Business Enterprise* (1904); Thurman Arnold, *The Folklore of Capitalism* (1937).

6. Freud, *The Interpretation of Dreams*, in *The Basic Writings of Sigmund Freud*, Modern Library, 1938, p. 548. This citation will hereafter be referred to as *Interpretation*. All books cited are by Freud, unless otherwise noted.

7. Ibid., p. 386.

Middle-Class Conventions Concerning Work

Freud's friends and patients, mainly upper-middle-class folk, were not supposed to be motivated by the spur of hunger, but by the hope of gain. Freud knew penury as a youth—financial needs drove him out of the laboratory and into practice—but it was still the penury of the rising student, not of the destitute proletarian. He assumed that the individualistic motives of getting on in the world, the desires of fame and success, were perfectly "natural"; it did not occur to him that they might be culturally stimulated or produced, let alone that they might be, in themselves, neurotic drives. While he was apt to minimize the extent of his own ambition, it did not trouble him to avow his wish to be a full professor, to be famous, to be "an authority." With the exception of the cases where he had personal experience of bigotry or incompetence, he rather easily assumed that his teachers such as Brücke or Meynert were "great masters," entitled to "veneration";[8] there was nothing unreal about their attainments and position. And, just as he assumed without question the conventions about greatness, he also assumed the other conventions of the workaday world—for instance, about the great importance of priority in scientific work. In one of his dreams he is anxious to "give Professor N. due credit for his diagnosis."[9]

The Playboy Classes

Three social groups seemed to Freud to be immune to the demands of the workaday world. These were the aristocrats, who needed only to be born in order to be fed;[10] the professional artists and writers, who were privileged not only to live in the play-world of illusion but to draw from

8. Ibid., pp. 407, 409, 417. For a disavowal of ambition, see p. 219, and cf. pp. 257, 446.
9. Ibid., p. 333.
10. See Freud's dream of Count Thun; ibid., p. 415.

it the realities of fame and fortune;[11] and the monks and priests.[12]

The artist, as Freud viewed him, had the gift of being able to sell his day-dreams, his fantasy productions, even his megalomania, on the market; he could appeal to the hidden dreams and desires of his audience who responded by bestowing on him the admiration he could not have won in direct economic or sexual competition. The artist, moreover, was free from the arduous conventions of the scientist; by his gift, he could obtain a release from what others have to do and gain as direct an access to truth as to the hearts of mankind. While for the scientist, too—such as Freud—dreams and fancies might be real data, he must work and not play with them in order to make a profit.[13] But he must on no account "waste" his talents; Freud found Leonardo da Vinci infantile when, instead of turning his powers to account, he employed them in ephemeral toys and antic jests.[14] In a different vein, he also found Leonardo's passion for investigation neurotic: where one investigates the universe (instead of acting on it, or moving one's fellowmen by great art), one obviously misses real values for which a normal person would strive.[15] Naturally Freud applied to his own work a similarly conventional

11. "A kindly nature has bestowed upon the artist the capacity to express in artistic productions his most secret psychic feelings hidden even from himself, which powerfully grips outsiders, strangers to the artist, without their knowing whence this emotivity comes." *Leonardo da Vinci*, 1947, p. 84. Hereafter referred to as *Leonardo*.

12. See, for example, "A Neurosis of Demoniacal Possession in the Seventeenth Century," in *Collected Papers* 4:436; see especially pp. 470–471.

13. However, even a scientist may sometimes be lucky; thus Freud writes: "From the reports of certain writers who have been highly productive, such as Goethe and Helmholtz, we learn, rather, that the most essential and original part of their creations came to them in the form of inspirations, and offered itself to their awareness in an almost completed state." *Interpretation*, p. 543.

14. *Leonardo*, p. 108.

15. Ibid., pp. 42, 43.

judgment: what helped him to cure patients was "real"; all else was "speculation."[16]

While, however, the artist had a privileged position in the native ease with which he won success, he remained, in Freud's eyes, a mere decoration upon the economic and political processes which mattered in the workaday world. Freud, the middle-class patron of the theatre and collector of figurines, wrote of art as a monarch might speak of his court jester: "Art is almost always harmless and beneficent, it does not seek to be anything else but an illusion. Save in the case of a few people who are, one might say, obsessed by Art, it never dares to make any attacks on the realm of reality."[17] Freud's attitude towards Count Thun, the aristocratic "do-nothing" Prime Minister of Austria, was not very different: he, too, was a privileged idler.[18]

Work as the Man's World

Only in one respect did Freud deal with success as anything but an obvious, self-evident goal which justifies the expenditure of immense efforts: he observed that in daydreams men seek to throw their laurels at the feet of beautiful women. Does it follow from this that the real world, too, was in Freud's eyes subordinate to sex? The question raises all sorts of ambiguities. On one level, Freud saw men's libidinal drives, coupled in various harnesses with their aggressive ones, as the source of all their productions: work was a channelling and sublimation of these drives. But on another level, the nighttime sphere of sex was clearly subsidiary to the daytime sphere of work, of accomplishment in the real world. For one thing, in Freud's eyes the man of potency and means, unintimidated by cultural taboos, would have no difficulty in finding appropriate sexual outlets. Achievement—making a dent in the world—this was the problem. Indeed, women were only trophies, to be

16. *New Introductory Lectures on Psycho-analysis,* 1933, pp. 207, 218. Hereafter referred to as *Psycho-analysis.*
17. Ibid., p. 219.
18. *Interpretation,* p. 415.

tied, metaphorically, at the conqueror's wheel: they were a by-product, pleasant enough, of his achievement, but only incidentally an aim.

The workaday world then was clearly a man's world. Speaking again of Leonardo, Freud referred to his "manly creative power" prior to his homosexual, reflective and investigative stage;[19] Freud's attitude towards Hamlet's indecision expressed a quite similar judgment. This "man's" world was threatened, not only by homosexual tendencies, but by an excessive, uncautious interest in women. In connection with one of his dreams, Freud tells us his fear that his sons' talents will be "ruined by women," just as the great Lassalle was killed in a duel over a lady.[20]

The place of women in this man's world was rather like that assigned to them in Veblen's ironic *The Theory of the Leisure Class.* Their very narcissism makes them desirable objects of display; their role is to be fed, tended, exhibited. But they must remain tractable in their gilded cage, and neither lure men to failure by giving them syphilis or otherwise draining their work-potential, nor, above all, enter the world of men as competitors.[21] Indeed, any effort of a woman to take part in the real world, in any capacity other than consumer of goods and libido, was interpreted as a desire to make up for her lack of a penis, the organ of power and creativeness. So strong were Freud's psychoanalytic rationalizations of the conventional Victorian—or, as Veblen would hold, predatory—attitude towards women, that they still impress many psychoanalysts, even women

19. *Leonardo*, p. 115.

20. *Interpretation*, pp. 333–334. Freud does not see that Lassalle was lured to his death, not by feminine wiles, but by his highly ambivalent ambition for social status and fear of social humiliation. The plebeian Jewish Lassalle, despite his leftist views, was moved by the unconscious wish to prove his patent of nobility; therefore, his real "folly" lay precisely in acceptance of the motives and outlook which Freud took as the highest, most realistic wisdom. Cf. Georg Brandes, *Ferdinand Lassalle*, 1911, pp. 202–215.

21. "We say also of women that their social interests are weaker than those of men, and that their capacity for the sublimation of their instincts is less." *Psycho-analysis*, p. 183.

psychoanalysts.[22] Freud seems to have coped with the inconsistency, from his viewpoint, of his own daughter's entry upon analytic work by assigning to women analysts the field of child-analysis—very much as women in industrial management today are assigned the job of handling the morale problems, not of men and women, but of women only.

MAN'S NATURAL LAZINESS AND THE FUTILITY OF SOCIALISM

The grimness of today's workaday world, as Freud saw and accepted it, is so great that it is understandable that men should exhibit signs of laziness, as if to justify the charge that they would not turn a hand, without the spur of hunger and gain. It is not surprising therefore to find Freud falling in with the hoary argument which seeks to derive the futility of socialism from the observed laziness of the working class.[23]

The Passive Paradise

This attitude Freud expressed in his interpretation of the myth of the Garden of Eden, which he saw as meaning that man longed for the idyllic idleness of the womb, or of childhood—the next-best in dependent passivity. But man was driven by his "original sin"—apparent in the sexual-aggressive Oedipus complex—to violate the conditions under which he might be taken care of in carefree bliss. Forced out of Paradise, he had ever after to work in the world, as sign and as penance; only in illusion could he momentarily return. Freud, who was accustomed to over-

22. Cf., for example, Helene Deutsch, *The Psychology of Women*, 1944, vol. I, chapters 7 and 8.

23. *Psycho-analysis*, p. 246. Freud found socialism impossible on other grounds as well, namely man's natural aggressiveness, which departs somewhat from the conservative Malthusian pattern; but aggressiveness, too, comes down, though only in part, to the scarcity of possessions and men's desire to seize them from each other, rather than to work for them.

turn many myths and see through them, accepted this myth as an historical truth, or rather as a primitive anticipation of the Victorian conviction that "life is real, life is earnest." A similar view is implicit in Freud's theory that man, as child and primitive, passed through a stage of belief in the omnipotence of thought. This magical thinking, in which wishes are automatically gratified, as they almost are for the infant, seemed to Freud to constitute one part of the charm of Paradise; men give it up for reality-thinking only under the pressure of frustration and pain. "If wishes were horses, beggars would ride"—or, more accurately, would fly. By a word, men would annihilate bothersome rivals, as Freud actually did in one of his most striking dreams.[24] The intensity of wishes and their violent ability to propel a dream thus arise from the fact that wish-fulfillment was once effortless, and that men never become reconciled to a workaday world in which this is no longer so. Freud assumed that men do not grow psychically, that nothing new happens to them in the course of development which might lead them to desire activity for its own sake.

Thus Freud had no doubt whatever that man needs to be driven into reality, by an angry God or his earthly deputies. Children, he felt, naturally did not want to grow up; they must be forcibly socialized, forcibly adapted to reality.[25] Parents who fail early to acquaint the child with pain, with what he must expect from the world, will create neurotics, recusants to their workaday tasks. Freud had no faith in his own children's talents as self-realizing, and he enjoined upon his wife the "training" by which these would be husbanded.[26]

In all this, I feel that Freud patronizes infancy and childhood. Even small infants seem to want to explore the universe—and not only in search of food and sex. Children—though, of course, like all of us, they have moments of

24. *Interpretation,* p. 406. Freud says in the introduction to the second edition of the book on dreams that many of the dreams reported were connected with the poignant and emotionally significant period of his father's death.
25. *Psycho-analysis,* p. 201.
26. *Interpretation,* p. 333.

regression—often are stifled in their wish to grow up, to accept responsibility and arduous tasks, by adult authorities who underestimate them. Conversely, adults, and children, too, forced to work at a pace that is not their own, react by rejecting work, in fantasy if not in featherbedded fact.

FREUD'S ATTITUDE TOWARDS HIS OWN WORK

Freud's very definition of pleasure as release of physiological tension contains, in capsulated form, the essence of his attitude towards work. Even though he might, under certain conditions, regard work as a sublimatory release of tensions which are sexual in origin—which permits him on occasion to speak of "intellectual pleasures"—still he viewed these as only a poor second-best, purchased through a stunting of the primary, libidinal releases.[27] But if pleasure is release of tension, then toil—ordinarily the opposite of release—is by definition arduous. Nevertheless, despite the elaborateness of Freud's physiological and metapsychological explanations, despite all his talk about pleasure-principle and reality-principle, we must not forget the cultural setting: How could he as a self-respecting Victorian admit that his work was anything else but a chore? To speak of his job, as Americans today often do—usually with like conventionality—as "good fun," would hardly befit a practitioner of the Harley Streets of the world; we need merely remind ourselves of the unspeakable boredom from which even the most exciting case could hardly rescue the languorous Sherlock Holmes.

The Slave of Science

Freud's work, as I read his own account of it, seems to me of the very greatest intellectual interest; beside such detective work, even that of Sherlock Holmes is pallid and limited. But Freud seems to have found—or at least admitted to—almost no pleasure in it; on the contrary, his writings are full of references to his weariness, to the ar-

27. *Leonardo*, p. 46.

duousness, rather than the ardor, of his unique intellectual adventure. "It is a habit of mine to run up two or three steps at a time"[28]—how blithely he speaks of "habit" rather than symptom when it is himself he is describing. His hurried days were almost incredible: ten or twelve hours of analysis—made especially anxious by the novelty of the task and the dangerously isolated position of the therapist—followed by writing up his notes on his cases;[29] then working far into the night on his writing, lectures, and correspondence; at night, writing and interpreting his frequent dreams, sometimes pages in length—only *once* did he not make "careful notes" on a dream;[30] finally, rousing himself in the morning with the greatest effort to begin another weary round.[31] Even when he suffered from the most painful boils, he refused to rest from "my peculiarly strenuous work,"[32] until ordered to by the doctor. And of course in later life, his agonizing cancer of the throat gave him no excuse to slow the pace of his labor. Like other middle-class, self-made, self-driven men, he could only relax at the conventional times: on his vacation, or at the parties to which he infrequently went. He said of himself, characteristically, after a summer evening's lecture: "I was tired; I took not the least pleasure in my difficult work, and longed to get away from this rummaging in human filth. . . ."[33] But, even on vacation, Freud could not abandon his vocation. Just as he "amused" himself by examining starfish on his first visit to the Irish Sea at the age of 19[34]—how different his preoccupations from those of James Joyce by the Irish Sea—so he drove himself even in his beloved Italy, like any harried tourist.[35] Though he reproaches himself,

28. *Interpretation*, p. 290.
29. Ibid., p. 197.
30. Ibid., p. 349.
31. Ibid., p. 210.
32. See Freud's dream of not working; *Interpretation*, pp. 284–285.
33. Ibid., p. 441.
34. Ibid., p. 475.
35. Ibid., p. 414. Freud speaks of wearing out his brother "by rushing him too quickly from place to place, and making him see too many beautiful things in a single day."

or permits himself to be reproached, for his hobbies,[36] as for his other "vices" such as smoking which did not directly contribute to his work, he did in fact manage to turn most of his "play" to economic account, like a cook who saves her leftovers for a stew. He enjoyed jokes—and collected them for a book on wit; he loved Michaelangelo—and wrote a long analysis of his "Moses" statue; his wide reading of novels and poetry was automatically and unaffectedly ransacked for analytic clues. So in fact, nothing was "wasted" —nothing, that is, but Freud, who took for himself Claude Bernard's motto, "*Travailler comme une bête.*"

In return for his Spartan zeal, Freud allowed himself to take pride in his conscientiousness, especially in cases involving no admixture of interest, like the twice-a-day injections he gave a cranky old lady;[37] while he scolded those "spoilt" gentlemen, the devout, who "had an easier time of it with their revelation."[38] And, indeed, the Sisyphus task of science, endlessly pursuing truth, becomes for Freud the very core of his personal philosophy of life.[39] Nevertheless, while Freud would agree with Spinoza that "the joy by which the drunkard is enslaved is altogether different from the joy which is the portion of the philosopher,"[40] still he would have insisted that there is little joy, but much enslavement, in the philosopher's quest.

"*Per Ardua ad Astra.*"

In one very important respect, Freud's Puritan attitude towards work in general, and to his own work in particular, had a profound influence on the whole psychoanalytic method. For he assumed, as a matter of course, that any answer to which one came without arduous toil must be wrong. It was this feeling, that truth must cost something if

36. See the dream of the botanical monograph; ibid., p. 243.
37. Ibid., pp. 204, 206 *et seq.*
38. *Psycho-analysis*, p. 237.
39. Ibid., pp. 236–238.
40. *The Philosophy of Spinoza*, edited by Joseph Ratner, Modern Library, 1927, p. 245.

it is to be worth anything, which, among other factors, led Freud to feel that the more far-fetched and "difficult" the solution, the more probable its correctness. Thus, despite his reference, which we have earlier quoted, to the successful "intuitions" of his admired Goethe and Helmholtz, he distrusted intuition in psychoanalysis. Repeatedly, he attacked the "intuitive" method of dealing with dream-symbolism.[41] Moreover, not only in dream-interpretation, but in all his work, Freud played down the role of intuition, just as he distinguished between mere "speculation" and real scientific work. Again and again, he referred to himself as a sober-sided, meticulous investigator, who never jumps to conclusions, but constantly acknowledges his dependence in observation and theory, on "the real external world."[42] Understanding is the reward, not of the gifts of genius, but of the "expenditure of effort."[43] Undoubtedly, Freud expended tremendous effort, but of course it is not only this which led him to his genuine innovations. While he accused intuition of arbitrariness, the very logical, and often pedestrian, rigor of his own treatment of symbols led repeatedly to highly arbitrary, indeed quite fanatical, constructions. But, of course, these were "work"; they did not spring from an alerted, but at the same time unstrenuous, "listening" for what the symbol was attempting to convey, but rather from a forceful, categorical insistence that the symbol surrender its meaning to Freud's intransigence. Perhaps his relative disregard for his own imaginative gifts was not only a defense against the critical pettifogging researchers of his day, but also a rationalization of his envy for those whom he considered still greater geniuses such as Goethe, who appeared to him to have had an easier, sunnier path.

Every so often, however, Freud did refer to his pleasure in mastering difficulties.[44] But, like most political conservatives, he did not assume that men generally could share

41. For examples, *Interpretation,* pp. 369, 371, 374, 401.
42. *Psycho-analysis,* p. 239.
43. *Psycho-analysis,* p. 238.
44. For example, *Interpretation,* p. 275n.

his own loftier motivations.[45] Among Puritans, such a hierarchy of toilsomeness is not uncommon. Compare the statement of Mrs. Gromyko: "Oh, Andrei does work hard, yet not as hard as Mr. Vishinsky, and even that is not so hard as Mr. Molotov works."[46]

Freud's Own Dream-work

A single, magnificent example illustrates Freud's method, and at the same time these limitations. In his famous "Dream of the Botanical Monograph," Freud says:

> I have written a monograph on a certain plant. The book lies before me; I am just turning over a folded coloured plate. A dried specimen of the plant, as though from a herbarium, is bound up with every copy.[47]

His associations to the dream were manifold and revealing. Among other things, Freud noted an association to his own monograph on the coca plant. He has told us elsewhere of his frustration because he did not become known as the discoverer of the anaesthetic properties of cocaine, the reason being that he let a friend continue the research so that he (Freud) might take time out to become engaged to his future wife.[48] He also made reference to the fact that his wife often remembered to bring his "favourite flower"—the artichoke—from the market where she diligently shopped, while he was less "thoughtful" of her, seldom bringing her flowers.[49] The artichoke reminds him of a childhood scene where he tore up a book containing "coloured plates" and of his later fondness for collecting books; he reproaches himself, both for this expensive hobby, and for the "onesidedness" of his *Gymnasium* studies, which had led him close to failing his botany examination.[50] In sum, after pages and pages of examining separately each

45. *Civilization and Its Discontents*, 1952, pp. 24–25.
46. *Time*, August 18, 1947; p. 25.
47. *Interpretation*, p. 241.
48. *An Autobiographical Study*, 1935, pp. 23–25.
49. *Interpretation*, p. 242.
50. Ibid., pp. 243, 323.

dream-detail, he permits himself in his analysis a slight awareness of his "thoughtlessness" towards his wife, of envy and grandiose ambition, and a memory of destructiveness, safely remote in childhood and in any case blamed upon his father. The worst thing he can say about himself is that he has expensive and distracting hobbies! In fact, he calls the childhood memory itself a "'screen or concealing memory' for my subsequent bibliophilia."[51] A curious "screen" in which he concealed the amiable and redeeming veniality of a hobby for collecting books behind the less amiable vice of destroying them—perhaps the vice of destructiveness itself! But play—that is, preoccupations and hobbies, especially if expensive, not directly advancing one in one's profession—did appear to Freud as sinful.[52]

In his associations to the dream, Freud pushed aside his unconscious recognition of what the dream was about and disregarded the significance of flowers as a symbol. Instead, he tore the dream word-from-word like the leaves of an artichoke; he viewed the dream, not as a *Gestalt,* but in a series of concentric verbal associations. I would like to suggest another possible interpretation of the dream, on a fairly obvious symbolic level. Freud seems to have been aware in the dream that flowers—a symbol which he else-

51. Ibid., p. 243.

52. In speaking of the absence of affect in this dream, Freud writes that the dream "corresponds to a passionate plea for my freedom to act as I am acting, to arrange my life as seems right to me, and to me alone." *Interpretation,* p. 439. But the "freedom" he refers to is that of his collecting mania, against the reproaches of his own conscience and those of his even more puritanical friends like the eye specialist, Dr. Koenigstein, who had told him the evening before that he was "too absorbed" in his hobbies. *Interpretation,* p. 243. He reproaches himself: for not inventing cocaine, for "neglect" of botany; but he answers "I am entitled to freedom for, after all, I am conscientious and have made some good monographic studies." Thus, he assumes that he must justify not driving himself 100 per cent —"allowing himself," as he says, some small vices. By his standard, even his meagre vacations from the workaday world were sinful, especially where he "missed something," such as the cocaine discovery, as a result. *Interpretation,* p. 268.

where recognizes as plainly sexual[53]—do not speak to him; his love has become "a dried specimen of the plant, as though from a herbarium. . . ." Is it not also correct to assume that he is unconsciously aware that he has sacrificed his wife's love to his ambition—that *this* is screened by the mild, and yet symbolic charge he elsewhere makes against her that, but for his devotion to her, he would be famed as the discoverer of cocaine? Indeed, he scarcely permits himself to realize that he is readier to buy himself a monograph—he speaks of his "fondness for . . . possessing books"[54]—than to buy flowers for his wife; this, although the dream commentary refers to his seeing at a bookseller's on the previous day a monograph on the cyclamen, his wife's favorite flower.[55] (His wife has, in fact, become "puffy," like a stuffed animal, while Mrs. "Gardener," whom he met the night before, is still "blooming," presumably from Mr. "Gardener's" care.)[56] Flowers are, by their very nature, a symbol of emotional feeling, even waste; in the act of "possessing" them, they dry up; the artichoke, on the other hand, is not a real extravagance—it is edible. Yet there is more than "possessing" involved; Freud has imprisoned love within the covers of an illustrated monograph; he has crushed it; in penetrating to the heart of the artichoke, he has a lifeless specimen in his hand. I strongly suspect that the mild scene of childhood destructiveness, which Freud treats as screening his bibliophilia and, on a deeper level, his sexual curiosity, actually conceals the way in which his own life and that of those around him is torn by his almost total incapacity for love and spontaneity—this is his true "onesidedness." It is like the Irish Sea, which means little more to him than the examination of a starfish and the recollection of its Latin name.

Dream-work and Entropy

The concept of "dream-work" attributes to the process of dream-formation the same economics of affect which Freud

53. *Interpretation*, pp. 382–383.
54. Ibid., p. 243.
55. Ibid., p. 241.
56. Ibid., p. 245.

employed in the process of dream interpretation. He writes, "we take pains to dream only in connection with such matters as have given us food for thought during the day";[57] that is, the dream-work is the processing plant which prepares the material with an eye to the driving wishes behind it, the inspection of the censor, and the economical and convenient packaging of the imagery. Behind this concept, there lies again the assumption of man's laziness. If we had our way, Freud is saying, we would not even dream; we would lie in the blissful fetal state. But our wishes, and external stimuli also, prevent this; these create tensions in our otherwise flaccid state of rest; the *purpose* of the dream-work is to release this tension and thus, by permitting us to go on sleeping, to restore us to the workless state. As Freud divided his year between his workaday months and his vacation period, so he divided the day between the waking tensions and the night's release. But this is not the only way to live! A vacation may be restful, though strenuous, if it lends variety and enjoyment to life; likewise, sleep is not merely the opposite of waking tension. In fact, recent studies have shown that restful slumber is accompanied by frequent changes of position; motionless sleep is not nearly so refreshing. Dreaming, too, is assumed to be an almost continuous process, of which the dreamer is only occasionally aware.

This feeling of Freud's, that he needed to explain the fact of having a dream, and to find the energy-source for the amount of "work" involved, misled him in at least two ways. It was one factor in his insistence that every dream represents a—probably libidinal—wish-fulfillment, the wish being the primal source of energy; this insistence led him to over-elaborate explanations of those dreams, such as anxiety dreams, judgment dreams, and so on, which did not appear to fit his formula. Secondly, it made him suspicious of dreams which, by their baroque imagery, their eloquent speeches, or other luxuriance, seemed to have required much "work"; since work is unnatural to man, this effort must hide something, must cover up a most forbidden

57. Ibid., p. 245.

thought. Thus, when Freud recalls in a dream the formula for trymethylamin, he takes this as "evidence of a great effort on the part of my memory,"[58] and goes off accordingly on a long, interpretative search.

This attitude towards effort pushed Freud towards over-interpretation in his analytic thinking generally. Being a strenuously effortful man, his thoughts and dreams, even without further elaboration on his part, would naturally tend to be complicated and far-flung. Moreover, Freud's work-drive compelled him to go beyond even his initial reaction, towards sometimes over-intricate structures of thought—the *Moses* book is a final and brilliant testament of this obsession which was at the same time part of the drive which made him great and courageous. And yet, concealed beneath all this work, is it possible that Freud is occasionally "playing" with us, and with himself? Is it not likely that, outwardly denying himself any playfulness or frivolity as doctor and scientist, he may have unwittingly sublimated his play-impulses, so that they can be glimpsed only in an "unnecessary" metaphor, a fine-spun interpretation of a dream, a tenuous reconstruction of history?

However that may be, it would seem an important task to track down, in Freud's more technical writings, some of the over-interpretations that may have resulted from his attitude towards effort. Here all I can do is to indicate some of the implications of this attitude. It seems clear that Freud, when he looked at love or work, understood man's physical and psychic behavior in the light of the physics of entropy and the economics of scarcity. For him, life was not self-renewing, or self-producing; he viewed the process of life as drawing on the given natal store, as on a bank account. Hence, for him, effort, expenditure, was problematical: it needed to be explained; something must lie behind it.

One views dreams quite differently if one holds a different view of the nature of life itself. If one thinks that growth is characteristic of life, that life can unfold unsuspected potentialities and resources, one feels that it is

58. Ibid., p. 203.

not *effort* that needs to be explained—that is life itself—but the *absence* of effort. Then it is the absence which appears pathological. So, if one comes upon a dream which is rich in invention and the use of symbolic expression, or which exhibits indignation, or judgment, or wit, or other human faculties which one appreciates in waking life, one will not feel that this is strange and that the dream must *necessarily* be about something altogether different. Any dream ordinarily requires interpretation, but its prima-facie opacity need not be due to a censorship over malign or outrageous wishes; the necessity for interpretation may result from the fact that symbolic expression is simply a different language, often a more abundant one than the dreamer allows himself in waking life.[59] Or it may be due to the fact that the memories called up in the dream have not been pigeonholed into the dreamer's organized, waking categories and thus appear with a freshness and intensity of experience which he may have had as a child.[60]

THE WORLD OF PLAY

Already, in order to talk about the world of work, as Freud saw it, I have had to picture in contrast the opposing world of play. For, indeed, Freud saw these two worlds as sharply separated as was the Aussee where he spent vacations, from the urban Vienna where he did his analytic work. Freud's world of play, as we shall see, is a world of children, of artists, and, only surreptitiously, of adults—that is, those adults who are real men and not idlers or escapists.

The Nursery Years

Freud regarded childhood as an auto-erotic haven where all one's pleasures are within reach. Nor is there any con-

59. I have leaned heavily on Erich Fromm's lectures on dream interpretation. See his article, "The Nature of Dreams," *Scientific Amer.* (1949) 180:44.

60. See Ernest Schachtel, "On Memory and Childhood Amnesia," *Psychiatry* (1947) 10:1; also Evelyn T. Riesman, "Childhood Memory in the Painting of Joan Miró," *Etc.* (1949) 6:160.

flict between the drives of hunger and sex: "Love and hunger meet at the mother's breast." Soon, moreover, the child discovers the pleasures of onanism; these, too, require no work, not even the labor of object-choice. But this cannot go on; Freud writes:

> This age of childhood, in which the sense of shame is unknown, seems a paradise when we look back upon it later, and paradise itself is nothing but the mass-phantasy of the childhood of the individual. This is why in paradise men are naked and unashamed, until the moment arrives when shame and fear awaken; expulsion follows, and sexual life and cultural development begin. Into this paradise dreams can take us back every night. . . .[61]

But this view of childhood as not subject to the laws of the adult world of reality was only one side of Freud's position. He noticed that children liked to play at being grown up, and indeed wished to grow up;[62] and he had a clear vision, unusual for his epoch, of the terrors, phobias, and conflicts which beset even the most protected child. Unlike most adults, he did not condescend to the battles and nightmares of the nursery; these he accepted as real. And with his usual pessimistic sense, he observed that "the excited play of children often enough culminates in quarrelling and tears."[63] Thus he saw the child as more adult, and the adult as more child, than was the conventional opinion.

This contradiction in Freud's thought can be reconciled if one observes that he saw through the current myths regarding "the innocents of the nursery" only insofar as sex and aggression or matters related to them were concerned —and, obviously, this was no small achievement but one of his most decisive contributions. He saw, clearly enough, the sexual elements in children's play, the onanist practices, the animistic fantasies.[64] But he was at one with his adult generation in looking down on play in general as childish; he did not entirely grasp its reality-testing and reality-ex-

61. *Interpretation*, p. 294.
62. *Leonardo*, p. 107.
63. *Interpretation*, p. 315.
64. See, however, his discussion of children's food wishes and disappointments; ibid., p. 214.

panding functions, its nature as a part of or an aspect of preparation for human adult existence, any more than he respected the creative functions of the playful moods which he criticized in Leonardo's life.

Indeed, even to talk about "functions" when discussing play runs the risk of catching us in an anthropological or psychoanalytic functionalism from which we may escape only through the paradox that human freedom is limited to being "unfunctional." . . .

Play and Foreplay

This divorce between work and play which sharply separates the world of the adult from the world of the child is not reconciled by maturity. Rather, once the genital stage is reached, play becomes attached primarily to the sexual function and continues in an underground, often unconscious existence. In his utilitarian attitude towards sex, Freud was much interested in what he called "foreplay," the preliminary stages of lovemaking. Foreplay seemed to him a kind of come-on which tempted couples onto the path of biological fulfillment; by its tension-heightening nature, it seemed to violate the pleasure-principle and to demand ejaculative release. By this ambiguity, it impelled otherwise reluctant people to comply with the "laws of propagation."[65] (The term "foreplay," itself, seems to carry its own linguistic self-contradiction: if it is play for a purpose, it is robbed of most of its spontaneous, amiable, frivolous, or tender playfulness.) In other words, just as Freud "allowed himself" his book-collecting and other hobbies for their recreative functions, so he "allowed" mankind this apparent frivolity of foreplay for its procreative functions: in both cases, pleasure is not really free, it merely baits the trap. After intercourse, so Freud felt, there is sadness; after play, one pays by sorrow and work.

65. The phrase is from *Leonardo*, p. 70.

Dreams and Day-dreams as Play

Fantasy and art are among the secondary and derivative efforts of mankind to obtain sexual pleasure; they constitute a kind of bargain basement, in which a meed of pleasure is sublimated—no other pleasure could equal direct sexual pleasure in Freud's view—in return for a modification in the ensuing pain. The discovery of this *ersatz,* inexpensive pleasure is made by the child, Freud argued, in the form of a hallucinatory wish-fulfillment, a kind of mirage in which the hungry infant, for instance, can persuade himself that he is being fed.[66] In later life, the adult can restore this state in dreams and day-dreams.

Freud perhaps tended to exaggerate the extent to which one can actually escape reality, unless one is crazy, by means of these fantasies. For although he is correct in believing that in the passive state one can afford wishes which would endanger one in real life, by the same token one diminishes one's satisfaction: somehow one realizes that "it's only a dream"[67] or a day-dream—and that it will never come to pass. Moreover, our individual and cultural imagination sets limits to wishes; they are often as poverty-stricken as that of the woman in the famous tale, which Freud quotes, who used the first of her three fairy wishes to procure some sausages which she had smelled next door.[68] The "damned wantlessness of the poor," against which Lassalle protested, is not dissipated when they sleep.[69]

My conclusion here is that Freud was romantic about dreams, as he was about more overt sexual life. By his in-

66. *Interpretation,* pp. 509–510.
67. Ibid., p. 513.
68. Ibid., p. 520n.
69. In a recent *Fortune* poll, a cross-section of the American people was asked what income they would like to have, if there were no limits to their demands. The average person gave a figure less than 25 per cent above what he was at the moment making; the mean figure was less than $4,000. See "Portrait of the American People," *Fortune* (1947) 35:10.

sistence that, underneath the manifest dream, there must lie a wish, and that this wish, in an adult, would have a dark, luxuriant, and forbidden quality, he avoided seeing how flat and conventional, how sorrowful and anxious, many dreams actually are. There is, for example, little that is wish-fulfilling in his own "Dream of the Botanical Monograph." Actually the censorship, to which he himself called attention, is not so easily evaded as he supposed; the most daring, and therefore frightening, wishes do not even exist in our unconscious, let alone rebel in the night against the dictation of the censorship.

But though there is a romantic element in Freud's view of the dream, this did not prevent him from subjecting it, like every other psychic performance, to the laws of scarcity economics. One dreams, he says, in order to continue sleeping, for otherwise the ungratified wish or outside stimulus, would wake one—one continues sleeping, of course, to prepare for the labor of the following day.[70] Thus the dream represents an elaborate compromise, a deal between the psychic forces: with the censorship relaxed by sleep, the repressed wishes are able to go in search of pleasure, using the thought-residues of the day, but at the same time the dream-work "binds the unconscious excitation and renders it harmless as a disturber . . . of sleep," while satisfying through displacement and other devices of evasion the censorship's one open eye. This involves, Freud writes, a lesser "outlay of . . . work, than to hold the unconscious in check throughout the whole period of sleep."[71]

70. *Interpretation*, pp. 518–519.

71. Anxiety dreams do not seem to fit in this economy, and their explanation caused Freud no end of trouble. He finally concluded that anxiety is the response of that part of the dreamer's psyche which is displeased by the forbidden wish; this part, at least, is pleased by the suffering the anxiety occasions, which is felt as punishment. *Interpretation*, p. 520; *A General Introduction to Psychoanalysis*, 1943, p. 192.

Art as Play and Display

So far, I have been discussing the play-world in its private aspects, to which one has access principally in sexual "play" and in dreams. There is also a public play-world; it has virtually the same economy as that of the dream. It is built on fairy-tales[72] and other folk-myths, on wit, and on art.

The artist's job is that of giving public expression to his private fantasies, fantasies which others may share; his work is others' play. Moreover, art, as Freud viewed it, is not bound by the rules of the workaday world—it is free. Like religion, the other great operator in the play-world of illusion, it can dissolve the dichotomies of human existence; it can deny the fact of death, or, as in the Greek and Egyptian sculptures which fascinated Freud, it can unite man and woman.[73] The pleasure in art is, as one would expect, partly Oedipal and rebellious sexuality, partly narcissism, in which both artist and audience identify with the hero. Licit gratification of illicit wishes is secured by these projections.

The relative thinness of the role assigned by Freud to art is surprising, in view of the amount of attention which he gave the subject both in his own writings and in his "hob-

72. Freud had the genius to see that fairy-tales were "*nichts für Kinder,*" that they had an adult meaning though one which the adults did not permit themselves to see. He applied to them the same interpretative process he had used on dreams; he analyzed their symbolism; he tried to see what really happens in them beneath their decorative screen. He found it typical that the heroine, for example, Cinderella, marries the prince; he took the status-striving, as well as the sexual, even incest, elements, as "real"; naturally, every girl would want to marry a prince and lead the do-nothing life of an aristocrat. *Interpretation,* p. 371. Moreover he held that in fairy-tales we commit the Oedipal offenses; we are the "great criminals"; we indulge in the totem feast, with its sacrilege. All this gives us pleasure whose true nature, like that of dreams, is concealed from us by its apparently harmless, innocent garb.

73. *Leonardo,* p. 96.

bies." Of art as critic of society, as transcending the given cultural divisions and definitions of work and play, as conscious creator of new values, Freud does not speak. His own tastes in art seem to have been conventional for his time, place, and class. Like so many nineteenth-century bourgeois, he admired the Renaissance, perhaps finding in it an age less cramped than his own. His great hero was Goethe, regarded as a late-Renaissance figure. He seems to have had little taste for music. Though he admired Ibsen, who was also a defier of sexual convention in his writings, he was not in general interested in "modern art." But it is modern art which has most strongly rebelled against being a plaything for rich patrons; sometimes it has done so by its very "ugliness" according to accepted patterns. Moreover, Freud paid little attention to the formal problems of art, being primarily concerned with its psychological causes and effects; when he thought about form at all, he said that the problem was insoluble.[74] Thus, his attitude towards art, as well as his taste, was conventional: by assigning it to the world of play, of regression, of sex, he patronized it, as a sober, cultivated bourgeois should. Perhaps one could say that he viewed it, as a modern city-planner views a zoo or park, as a territory zoned off from the workaday world, which is there to delight but not to be taken with full seriousness.[75]

The Play of Words

Somewhat the same attitude governs Freud's view of wit. He saw the role of language as a reality-instrument in a way that could hardly have been done before the development of his theory of dreams. For by means of words, one delays gratifications, and tests reality experimentally before, so to speak, setting foot in it. Though the infant, like the primitive, uses them as magic handles, in his phase of thought-omnipotence, they nevertheless become tools,

74. Ibid., p. 120.
75. See Freud's remarks on the uselessness of beauty, including parks, in *Civilization and Its Discontents*, 1932, pp. 54–55.

not pleasures. By their nature, moreover, they are logical, un-autistic: they relate us to the world and to the other people in it; only children and lovers are permitted a private language. But even here, in this instrument of communication, there is a domain reserved for pleasure: this is word-play or wit. At one point in his dream-theory, he speaks of comical effects as a "surplus" which is discharged by laughter;[76] wit is, indeed, the theatre and poetry of the poor. But the pleasure which Freud found in wit is not only that of release of the tensions of obedience to the laws of language;[77] it is also that of direct rebellion. He enjoyed the satiric and sardonic elements in the Jewish jokes and stories he collected for his studies. And even the sexual elements which Freud emphasized in his analysis of wit are not only pleasurable in their own right, but in their rejection of convention. Freud, so meticulously clean as a physician, was quite "rebelliously" fond of "dirty" stories, just as he enjoyed spitting on the stairs of an old lady patient whom he detested.[78]

CONCLUSION

I have indicated that Freud's ascetic rationalistic dichotomy between work and play, and the very limited role he assigned the latter, belong to the work-morality of nineteenth-century Europe—to the years when the advancing industrial revolution had still not shown its potentialities for drastically shortening labor and expanding leisure horizons. The chances are, moreover, that Freud went much further in the direction of asceticism, of eliminating "waste," than did most of the members of his class and culture: he actually did what it was only their ideal to do. But when one looks at contemporary American attitudes towards work and play, one cannot be too critical of Freud—one can, indeed, see much in his view that is refreshing. Thus he never adopted the notion that work and play must alike

76. *Interpretation,* p. 538.
77. Ibid., p. 332n.
78. *Interpretation,* pp. 269, 272, 291.

be "fun"—and, more particularly, fun with people. This notion forces men in the American upper-middle class to merge the spheres of work and play, often without advantage to either. An anxious gregariousness and concern for the expression of appropriate consumer tastes can permeate a business or professional conference as easily as a cocktail party. To a degree, Americans have substituted fun-morality for work-morality. But this, among other things, makes it difficult to admit that one is tired: one has not done enough to "deserve" it. Conversely, one tends to exploit his vacations not, as Freud did—when he was not traveling or climbing mountains—by doing productive work, but by seeking to train oneself for advances in status or in the solution of vexing interpersonal problems.

I can put my point another way by saying that there are certain advantages to making fun and play surreptitious—even sinful. For then, play is less apt to be socially guided, less apt to be compulsively gregarious. Freud's view of play as a kind of underground in adult life protects it—gives it some of the same chaotic freedom that the carnival provides in Catholic countries. As against this, the contemporary social focus on recreation sometimes tends to leave no room either for whorehouses or for underground passages of any sort; everything must be out in the open. And while in a utopian society this would not be so bad, today it often means that play is exploited in fact—as it was for Freud in principle—for physical and psychic hygiene.

Indeed, Freud's own account, in a somewhat distorted version, is one of the factors which has shaped this modern view. Many women, for instance, indulge in sexual play not because they seek pleasure but because they have been told, and tell themselves, that repression is bad. Men justify their vacations on the ground that they "owe it to themselves." Emancipated parents are anxious if their children do not masturbate, lest they become neurotic. Men who have stomach trouble feel that they must "relax," must have more fun, to avoid further psychosomatic disorder—the give-away clue of psychic imperfection. And those men who cannot play are robbed, both by cultural developments and by the loss of psychological innocence Freud helped bring about, of the older defenses provided for them in a work-oriented society. So it turns out that, under the guise of fun and play, we remain today almost as truly ascetic as Freud, often enough without the very real satisfactions which—in spite of himself and in spite of his views as to the supremacy of sexual pleasure—he derived from his intellectually demanding and adventurous work. The threat of work today is not that it is arduous, but—in the some ways far worse fact—that it is boring and without meaning.

As against this, Freud, despite his skepticisms and reservations, had no doubt that work was worthwhile and that scientific work, whatever its uncanny "primal" sources in sexual or aggressive drives, had its own logic, its own convention, and its own tradition. Moreover, while he was a utilitarian in his attitude towards play, and, in a way, towards life in general, he was actually much less of a utilitarian about science than many of his successors. The pursuit of truth was for him self-justifying: man had every right to penetrate the secrets of nature without giving an account of himself to academic, priestly, democratic, or other moralizing authority. Although he thought the truth would set men free, he was, nevertheless, far from the mood of many "policy-oriented" researchers today, who hedge their curiosity about by all sorts of expediential considerations and concern for various good causes. One of the things that makes Freud such perennially exhilarating reading is the sense of the "play of the mind" that he communicates.

It may be a long time before middle-class people, in America, will feel themselves free to play when they are not free to really work—if their work has degenerated into sociability or featherbedding. Those who are excluded from meaningful work are, by and large, excluded from meaningful play—women and children, to a degree, excepted. The kind of passionate fondness and excitement about his work that Freud had, although he would seldom admit this to himself, is also a good base from which to learn to play. And people have to learn to play—or stop unlearning; in this enterprise they are faced with the whole long tradition of the driving and driven men who created Western industrial society, Western political organization, and Western scientific thought, including psychoanalysis.

Perhaps it is time now for the analysts, and for other social scientists, to pay more attention to play, to study blockages in play in the way that they have studied blockages in work and sexuality. Yet, in studying play, one must be aware of the ambiguities that haunt play, be aware of the elusiveness and privacy that are its main defenses. We have far to go before we move to a new integration of work and play unreservedly superior to the Freudian dichotomies—an integration allowing us more work in work and more play in play.

Authority and Liberty in the Structure of Freud's Thought

Sufficient time has elapsed since Freud built his system—not perhaps in years but in the movement of thought—to permit and require critical re-examination of the sort undertaken here. Such re-examination depends for its very method on Freud's own work, and its aim is less to point to weaknesses in that work, which have already been sufficiently discussed, than to contribute to the sociology of knowledge and to the ongoing effort, both in psychiatry and in the other social sciences, to separate what is essential in Freud's thought from the garb, determined very largely by the time and the culture, in which that thought made its debut. The texts of Freud which I will primarily use are not those in which he himself spelled out his *Weltanschauung*, but rather those more technical writings in which his outlook on such problems as those of authority and liberty appears only inferentially, and often without his own full awareness.

THE MEANING OF HUMAN HISTORY

Kenneth Burke observes, in a remarkable essay on "Ideology and Myth," that when historical thinking succeeded philosophical thinking in the West, writers who wanted to establish some thing or some authority as essential declared that it was temporally prior:

> Thus, whenever they wanted to say that man is "essentially competitive" or "essentially good," they said that the "first men" were constantly at war or that men were "orig-

"Authority and Liberty in the Structure of Freud's Thought" was first published in Psychiatry, *Vol. 13, No. 2, 1950.*

inally" good but were later corrupted by society. They postulated such "firsts" in some hypothetical past time, their thinking in this regard often being much more mythical than they suspected, and no more based on actual scientific knowledge about the past than was the "mythical" doctrine of "original" sin (which, translated philosophically, would mean "essential" sin, that is, some ineradicable difference between individual and group which the individual, eager to socialize himself, might experience as a sense of guilt).

Freud was similarly concerned with establishing status-rankings between different orders of the given, either on the basis of temporal priority or on the basis of what essentially *belongs* and what is merely additive or artificial. For him the "essentially" human was the ur-human—one reason, perhaps, why the myth of the primal horde held such attraction for him. Likewise his view of original sin—namely, the primal crime of Oedipus which is both deposited in our racial memory and repeated by each of us in the modified form of childhood fantasy and feeling—fits Kenneth Burke's description.

A concept of original sin is typical of a view of life which makes the past an authority over the present, in which the individual is mortgaged to society, and both the individual and society are mortgaged to the preceding generations. All through recent history, one finds secular variations of this outlook, and secular castes who, replacing the priests, have the duty of collecting the interest on the mortgage. The most striking, because extreme, example of this is in the work of Auguste Comte who was so impressed with the legacy of past ages that he invented quantities of new holidays to celebrate a calendar of secular saints; immortality was, for him, the continuation of the hold of the past over the present. Though he did not believe in original sin, he did believe that the individual owed to his parents, and to all the past, so enormous a debt that it could never be repayed even by a lifetime of altruism. In Ruth Benedict's *The Chrysanthemum and the Sword,* there is a recent analysis of this principle in operation in Japanese society.

In Japan too the individual feels that he must spend his life in repaying his debt to his parents, and to society—symbolized by the Emperor. Payment of the debt in all such cases is never a mere matter of contract; it is always a matter of morality, enforced by feelings of shame and self-abnegation.

Freud's metaphorical doctrine of original sin is, at first glance, emancipated from such rigors. He does not believe in altruism, nor, of course, does he give a literal meaning to original sin. Nevertheless, in his manifest thinking, he seems to stand on the side of the past's authority. The most striking illustration appears in *Moses and Monotheism.* He suggests there that anti-Semitism may be due at least in part to the "stubborn" refusal of the Jews to acknowledge their share in the primal crime, which in their case took the historical form of the killing of Moses, their "father." And he points out that the ascetic renunciation which he attributes both to Jewish ethics and theology—the bare bones of monotheism—are the consequence of unconscious guilt feelings for this consciously forgotten offense. But the reader may well ask: Does Freud not accept here the authority of those of the dominant majority who are hostile to Jews and rationalize their hostility by swinging the club of the past over the present? Freud took his own Jewishness very seriously, as shown in his well-known letter to the B'nai B'rith.[1] To some extent he seems to be renouncing the present claim of the Jews to equal and decent treatment, and justifying this renunciation on the basis of the past as forcibly reconstructed by him.

In fact, Freud traced all authority back to this source of the original father; as he writes in his book on dreams:

> The sovereign is called the father of his country (*Landesvater*), and the father is the first and oldest, and for the child the only authority, from whose absolutism the other social authorities have evolved in the course of the

1. "On Being of the B'nai B'rith," reprinted in *Commentary* (1946) 1:23.

history of human civilization (in so far as "mother-right" does not necessitate a qualification of this doctrine).[2]

It is significant to see what short shrift he gives, here and elsewhere, to matriarchy. The possibility of the ur-existence of matriarchy is obviously inconvenient, if one wants to justify contemporary authority by throwing over it the mantle of the primal father. Freud takes this latter step explicitly in his *Group Psychology and the Analysis of the Ego.*

Freud had, however, to face the fact that some children do not know their fathers, or know them only as lenient ones; and the fact that it was not easy to find convincing evidence for the existence of repressed Oedipal desires in every adult whom he analyzed. One way in which he dealt with this problem was by the concept of racial memory: from this, no one can escape. This memory included a realization of the primal crime, which, however, needed usually to be revived by some symbolic repetition; it also included a kind of ur-language and universal symbolism.

The concept of ur-language and ur-symbolism is of particular importance in Freud's thought. For its implication is that language and imagery are prisons, set up in the long-distant past, from whose categories and modes of thinking man cannot free himself; it is a kind of phylogenetic rather than epistemological Kantianism. Since mankind originally thought dichotomously, with ur-words meaning two polar opposites, the implication is that all real or basic thinking continues to be of this sort; neither cultural diversity nor individual style can do much but add trimmings to the racially inherited pattern.[3] Even in our word-play when,

2. *The Interpretation of Dreams,* in *The Basic Writings of Sigmund Freud,* Modern Library, 1938, p. 275n. Referred to hereafter as *Interpretation.*

3. "'The Antithetical Sense of Primal Words,'" *Collected Papers* 4:184, London, Hogarth Press, 1925. In his essay on "Ten Levels of Language," Albert Guérard has shown the differentiated richness of the lingual inheritance, which both groups and individuals are free to alter in many ways; no one level is superior. *Amer. Scholar* (1947) 16:148.

according to Freud, we put aside adult reality for a moment, we fall back upon puns and images which are part of the racial stock; so, too, with symbols, whether found in dreams or works of art. A small number of these have a given, usually sexual, meaning: a tool or stick is always a penis; a lake or river signifies birth or the womb; a room or wood means a woman; a dream of flying symbolizes sexual intercourse. No deviations are permitted; the racial memory controls the individual or cultural experience.

Yet in Freud's position there is a concealed element which is not at all authoritarian; this is the notion that, since all have the same memory, there are no fundamental differences between classes of men or between nations. The upper classes are subject to the same crude unconscious memories as any peasant: "None is so big," he writes, "as to be ashamed of being subject to the laws which control the normal and morbid actions with the same strictness."[4] Underneath, he is arguing, men are, after all, the same. Thus the dialectic of history is turned around so as to deny privilege as well as to defend it.[5]

The same mortgage which binds society to its past, and to the reincarnation of its primal father, also of course extends to every single individual. Freud's ultilitarian teleology led him to see the individual as a piece of somatic tissue indebted to its own sperm or ovum until released by death —"the common fate . . . which subdues us all."[6] Everyone is bound to procreate;[7] that is his purpose on earth, and all else is preparation. This task he inherits, just as he inherits his unconscious memories and passions; the neurotic tries to subdue these—to escape their domination—and falls ill as a result.[8] From this point of view, Freud's attack on narcissism is quite understandable: narcissism is, so to

4. *Leonardo da Vinci*, New York, 1947, p. 28. Hereafter referred to as *Leonardo*.

5. Cf., *Wit and Its Relation to the Unconscious*, in *The Basic Writings of Sigmund Freud;* p. 778. This citation will hereafter be referred to as *Wit*.

6. *Interpretation*, p. 411.

7. *Leonardo*, p. 70.

8. *Interpretation*, p. 520.

speak, the last refuge of the individual from his creditors, social and personal. And yet—here again we see the ambivalence of his view—he was the inventor of a therapy designed to lift from the individual his oppressive mortgage, or at least to provide for a stay of foreclosure and a remission of payments long since due.

It is now necessary to see somewhat more particularly the ways in which mankind is bound to its destiny, at once phylogenetic and teleological. Just as all are guilty of the primal crime, even if they did not participate in or even consciously remember it; so all are saddled with the prospect of a future which is not capable of much voluntary change. Immutable laws limit man's control over his physical environment and over his own desires for aggression and nirvana. The most that could be hoped for is the slight amelioration of the inherited framework; no radical transformation of society has any chance. This is a curious position for a thinker who discovered whole areas of untapped human resources, richer than the wealth of the Americas, and who in his clinical practice actually assisted men and women to make abundant use of their own latent energies which had been crippled by conflict and repression.

Since this *is* an ambivalent position, it is not surprising that Freud's whole attitude towards history combines elements from both the progressive and the cyclical theories which were current in his time. The progressive theorists, both before and after Darwin, saw mankind's development as linear—up from the ape, up from slavery, up from animism, as the case might be. Thinking of this sort goes back to the Enlightenment, to men like Turgot and Condorcet; it was refined by nineteenth-century writers who, like Hegel and Marx, introduced dialectical elements—or, like Comte or Maine, conservative ones—without changing the fundamental pattern. That pattern viewed history not as a series of alternatives which were rather accidentally chosen, but as entirely "necessary": what happened had to happen in accordance with the laws of progress. In such a late thinker as Bergson, even the laws evolve; nothing is static; everything moves forward according to a vital principle or spiritual gyroscope.

Cyclical theories of history, though old, did not find favor until late in the century. Antibourgeois writers such as Brooks Adams and Pareto reacted against the optimistic assumptions of the linear theorists. Whether they spoke of the circulation of elites or of the rise and fall of civilizations, their cynical platitude remained: *plus ça change, plus c'est la même chose.* Moreover, increasing historical and anthropological knowledge made the simple progressive theories difficult to maintain. Despite the efforts of the nineteenth-century ethnologists, for instance, no single sequence of tribal social development could be discerned. Those who were attracted to cyclical theories were not only rejecting modern capitalistic society as the best of worlds to date or even the prelude thereto. They were also rejecting the parochialism which viewed the fate of the planet from the perspective of Western Christianity or even, as in Comte's case, from the perspective of a single country thereof; that is, these thinkers chose their illustrations from a wider range of cultures—seeing less to respect in their own, and more to respect in the others. Thus, with the assistance of such men as Sumner, they laid the foundations of cultural and historical relativism.

Freud picked and chose among these contrasting attitudes. His notion of the gradual development of a phylogenetic inheritance, of the linear change from primitive to modern times, as recorded both in language and in social organization and as deposited in the unconscious—this borrows from the progressive theorists. On the other hand, his conception, most explicitly set forth in *Civilization and Its Discontents,* that epochs of repression and refinement are always succeeded by epochs of explosion and barbarity, and his further, more implicit belief that, from here out, nothing new can happen in history—these are reminiscent of the cyclical theorists. This ambivalence follows not only from Freud's ambivalence towards authority but also from his feelings towards his own civilization. Sometimes he was inclined to view this, ethnocentrically, as the height of human attainment, and to accept without question the values of science and cultivation and the middle-class world generally. But, except for the value of science—which he never questioned so far as I can find—he could also be quite sharp in his hostility towards the culture in which he lived, and admire, without condescension, earlier ages and earlier civilizations, such as the Egyptian. About the shape of the future, however, no such conflict was necessary: this was virtually governed by the past. Under these circumstances, Freud advised mankind to "submit to the inevitable."[9]

To a degree, this attitude towards the future may be closely related to Freud's acceptance of scarcity economics. Where scarcity prevails, there will authority also be found —the authority of the generalized past and the more direct authority of the ruling class which must control the distribution of the limited resources. Freud was quite skeptical that there could be alternative outcomes or abundant ways of organizing man's relations to nature and to his fellows. For where history appears as a series of determined events —and historical writing almost always makes it so appear— the future can hardly be regarded as open: at most it will present a dichotomy, an either-or.

Today, we are all short-run pessimists. But Freud's long-run pessimism has also become fashionable, perhaps prevalent, though it is often linked to a religious base which Freud explicitly rejected. How radical it was when he first expressed it may be gathered from an essay by Bertrand Russell on "Current Tendencies,"[10] written in 1920. This essay attacks the "cosmic impiety" of such thinkers as Bergson—their delusions of omnipotence, of automatic progress, which he felt ignored or trivialized man's existential problems. In such a climate of late Victorian evolutionary optimism, Freud's pessimism was challenging. Today, we stand

9. *New Introductory Lectures on Psycho-analysis,* 1933, p. 221. (Hereafter referred to as *Psycho-analysis.*) Compare, however, his high hopes for the spread of psychoanalytic modes of thought in "The Future Prospects of Psychoanalytic Therapy," in *Collected Papers* 2:285.

10. Bertrand Russell, *Selected Papers,* New York, 1927, pp. 312–46.

in need of more impiety, cosmic and otherwise. It is pessimism which has become complacent.

Freud's pessimism, furthermore, was strictly limited. In his day-to-day clinical task, he acted without question on two progressive beliefs: the unfolding nature of science, and the linkage of knowledge to therapy. At least once, moreover, in his published writings, he permitted himself to face the possibility of economic abundance and its social consequences, saying that "a fundamental alteration of the social order will have little hope of success until new discoveries are made that will increase our control over the forces of nature, and so make easier the satisfaction of our needs."[11] History, then, is not hopeless after all. From this it follows that man, far from bowing to the inevitable, must imitate Prometheus; he must not only understand, but act: "He has the right to make an effort to change that destined course of the world. . . ."[12]

To sum up, it may be said that Freud's view of history is a compromise among ambiguous and contradictory elements. On the one hand, there is evolution and advance; there are great men who "make an effort to change that destined course," men such as Moses. On the other hand, there are definite limits, now in all probability reached, beyond which neither man as a biological product nor society as a bio-historical product can move; the future holds neither miracle nor messiah.

INDIVIDUAL DESTINY

Only late in life did Freud begin to write on these general social and historical problems, although as early as 1900, in his book on dreams, his attitudes were already fairly explicit. For most of his life he was concerned not with social but with individual destiny. Some of his case records constitute what today would be called a "life history," and what medical men in any case term a "history"; from analyzing these, one can see what Freud thought of as open in human history and what as closed.

11. *Psycho-analysis*, p. 248.
12. *Leonardo*, p. 43.

The theory of the birth-trauma can be a starting point. If all of a person's life is viewed as determined by the one crucial event which commences his independent history, all later events have been reduced to mere repetitions or reminders, over which the person has no control. That is why the theory is so forcibly reminiscent of the strictest Calvinist predestinarianism; it has the same universal, uncontrollable quality.[13] In this strict form, Freud rejected the theory as it was developed by his disciple, Otto Rank; but he continued to believe that this trauma was the prototype, though not the source, of all later anxiety, while the womb became the prototype of the Garden of Eden. To the constitutional inheritance, the phylogenetic memory, and the birth experience, Freud added a fourth source of the later life-pattern—namely, the early years of childhood. Though "the development of the individual is only an abridged repetition" of the phylogenetic experience, it can nevertheless be influenced "by the fortuitous circumstances of life," particularly of the first five years.[14] It is in these "circumstances" that liberty lies, as against the authority of the past.

The childhood experiences, however, are not fortuitous in any extensive sense. The child has no more control over who his parents are—except in dreams where, Freud delighted in pointing out, children always create different parents for themselves, or in the myths of birth such as that of Moses—than over the manner of his obstetrical delivery or his sex. And in his early years, the child is unavoidably helpless, dependent for life itself on the surrounding adult world. Freud's great contribution was to relate these "obvious" facts to a dynamic theory of character. Character is determined, once and for all, in the childhood situation. Writing of Leonardo's illegitimate birth, Freud states: "The love of the mother became his destiny; it determined his fate. . . ."[15]

13. The theory of the birth-trauma pretends to be scientific, but it was never actually tested, though as Freud pointed out it offers itself easily to empirical scrutiny. *The Problem of Anxiety*, 1936, pp. 94–96.

14. *Interpretation*, p. 497.

15. *Leonardo*, pp. 94–95.

In Freud's theory of character, the final (genital) stage is reached with the physical and psychic changes of puberty. This is the terminal; beyond puberty there are no further stages; before it, lie the various way-stations—oral, anal, phallic—at which the destined neurotic or pervert lingers too long or to which he returns. Just as the sex role, given at birth, is unalterable—short of castration—so these childhood phases determine the interpretation of the events of adult life: choice of mate, of livelihood, of *Weltanschauung*. Even the most dramatic and unexpected experiences, such as those of war, serve chiefly to revitalize and repeat a childhood pattern; that is, the traumas of war and death are perceived within the characterological limits which are already set. After puberty at the latest, and probably much earlier, nothing new can be added; the life pattern is already fixed—short of psychoanalytic therapy. . . .

If all men are prisoners of their childhood character-structures, over whose formation they have had no control, it easily follows that all their later motives, tastes, and judgments are not, in any real sense, theirs at all. Men are viewed less as individuals than as the representatives of their sex-and-character roles. In what is perhaps his most famous case history, that of "Dora," Freud dates the onset of the patient's hysterical neurosis from her rejection of a sexual advance from an older, married man, a long-time friend of the family. Freud assumes that not to be excited by a reasonably presentable and potent male is itself neurotic, and some of his analysis is based upon this assumption. He scarcely grants Dora, or any other woman, the privilege of taste and idiosyncrasy even—indeed especially—in the most intimate relations of life: a penis is a penis, and that is enough for a "normal" woman who has physically attained, as 14-year-old Dora had, the genital stage. That Freud believes this, may be inferred from a footnote to his report on Dora's case, in which he remarks, as if in answer to possible critics, that he has seen the man who attempted Dora's seduction, and that he is attractive![16]

16. "Fragment of an Analysis of a Case of Hysteria," in *Collected Papers* 3:38. The case of Dora is, of course, exceedingly complex, and Freud could argue that Dora was

Hence Dora's refusal must be neurotic. Of course, it *may* have been neurotic, though the man as Freud describes him seems rather a dubious character. Our quarrel is only with Freud's implication—to be sure, qualified by other arguments—that Dora had no freedom of choice, so to speak, in the matter: she *must* be neurotic since she refuses to "bow to the inevitable," the fact of being a woman.

But men are subject, in Freud's analysis, to an authority identical to that which women face in their sex roles. So when he finds a patient who, instead of visiting a girl about whom he has heard, takes a train in the opposite direction, this, too, *must* be neurotic—of course, it *may* have been. Freud insists that the biological equipment of men and women, rather than the cultural definition of that equipment, is determinative of normalcy.

Given the crucial importance of sex and sex-roles in the Freudian theory, little new can happen; whatever does happen will be explained as essentially a repetition or recombination of the past. The figures created in dreams Freud compares to dragons or centaurs.[17] These composite creatures, like the unicorn, seem to me to symbolize man's difficulty in imaginatively transcending nature. Just as deterministic theories of history, whatever their differences *inter se,* put the historian in the position of an authority who, in the name of History, sets limits to mankind's future development, so the Freudian analyst makes himself into an authority in the name of Character or Sex. In his view, motives are without opacity, and actions, though often ambivalent, are without ambiguity. If a person cares about justice, that must be because he is essentially envious; if he shows pity, that must be because he is reacting against a basic sadism; he gives himself away to the observing authority in the very act of concealment. One can see that the same deterministic principle is at work here as in the concept of universal symbolism or as in some of the histori-

in fact in love with Herr K. Note also Freud's reference (in "Further Recommendations in the Technique of Psycho-analysis," in *Collected Papers* 2:377, 385) to "all the individual details of [a patient's] way of being in love."

17. *Interpretation,* p. 350.

cal constructions—for instance, Freud's insistence that Moses *must* have been killed by rebellious Jews.

Now it may be argued that Freud in these instances is simply expressing the scientific postulate that everything is, in principle, capable of being explained, and that science has no room for the concept of freedom of the will or for accident. One might question so flat a statement of the postulate, by reference, for instance, to recent theories of probability; but that is not my purpose: it is not the fact of explanation but the nature of the explanation that I question. Just as in his psychic economics Freud applies the second law of thermodynamics and assumes that libido is indestructible, so he assumes in his analysis of the individual that one's childhood-formed character and role are indestructible; these form the real self, all else is trimming. His men and women are allowed little future, other than a repetition of the past; whatever happens to them is *"déjà vu."* Freud takes on himself the role which so fascinated him intellectually, the role of the Parcae; before him, as the representative of destiny, all men are humbled. Freud held that even in dreams man does not escape. He closes his book on dreams on this characteristic note: "By representing a wish as fulfilled the dream certainly leads us into the future; but this future, which the dreamer accepts as his present, has been shaped in the likeness of the past by the indestructible wish."[18] But even the predestining wish is not the person's own; it goes back to the childhood situation which was anything but unique and which in turn is merely a repetition of the primordial pattern. Would it be going too far to say that—for Freud—life itself, ever renewed in the individual, is subjected to the repetition-compulsion of the race?

THE STRUCTURE OF AUTHORITY WITHIN THE INDIVIDUAL

I have postponed consideration of the mechanics by which the person is, so to speak, held to his destiny, while being permitted a limited illusion of freedom. This is the function

18. Ibid., p. 549.

of the ego and the superego—the internal delegates of external authority.

The Walking Delegate from Economics: the Ego

The ego has the task of curing the child's addiction to the pleasure-principle and of encouraging his operation according to the reality-principle. This means somatic self-preservation—fundamentally coping with hunger; when that is taken care of, the ego can turn to its teleological duty of finding appropriate hetero-sexual objects, outside of the incest taboos, and thereby giving pleasure to the id. What is the nature of the "reality" to which the ego relates itself? It appears to be the given state of economic development in Freud's milieu, as interpreted by capitalist scarcity economics. The ego is concerned with survival, and with whatever happiness is attainable within this context. Thus from the viewpoint of the individual his ego is that part of himself which is charged with mastering reality; from the viewpoint of society his ego is merely the administrative organ which sees to the carrying out of the workaday tasks. In other words, the ego not only *develops* out of man's helplessness "in the presence of the great forces of life,"[19] but it exercises over the id the authority of those forces and administers their demands. It is an "official" agency, though of course on the lowest rung. But according to Freud it never achieves full control of its assigned internal territory.

The Walking Delegate from Ideology: the Superego

The ego, as the agent of economic or technical "reality," divides authority with the superego, which is the agent of parental and public opinion. This opinion is, in a sense, just as real a force as the other, for it depends on the given state of social ideals and patterns for identification. Nevertheless, Freud views the superego—as a Marxist might—as a sort of ideal superstructure. He does not credit it with

19. *Leonardo*, p. 103.

the full power he attributes to the material base. Hence enforcement here does not spring from the ego's role of adaptation to life itself but rather from emotional, indeed irrational, pressures in the child's upbringing. While at one point Freud remarks, "When our student days are over it is no longer our parents or teachers who see to our punishment; the inexorable chain of cause and effect of later life has taken over our further education,"[20] it does not follow that the superego loses its function with adulthood. As an unceasing source of guilt feelings, it cooperates with external authority in subduing the rebelliousness of the id. By holding the individual up to his internalized ideals—ideals he can never attain—the superego sees to it that he does not violate the cultural taboos appropriate to his social station.

If one assumes with Erich Fromm that the function of parents and teachers in any historical culture is to see to it that the individual will *want* to do what, under the given social and economic conditions, he *has* to do,[21] further light is shed on the relation between ego and superego in Freud's thought. Freud seems to realize, half consciously, that "reality" itself, namely what *has* to be done, is actually not a sufficient spur to human performance. By the reality-principle alone, mankind could not be governed. What is required is an actual reversal within the personality of its native attitudes towards work and play, as Freud regarded them: it must learn to enjoy what is inherently painful—its workaday tasks; and to fear what is inherently pleasureful—satisfaction of the desires of the id. This transformation of the affects of pleasure and pain is carried out under the aegis of the superego; it is never left to matter-of-fact "cause and effect."[22]

How does this come about? Freud's account is exceedingly involved; I will oversimplify for purposes of this paper. The motive power for this change of affect is the child's dependence on the parents, not only for physical survival

20. *Interpretation*, pp. 316–317.
21. Erich Fromm, "Individual and Social Origins of Neurosis," *Amer. Sociological Rev.* (1944) 9:380–384.
22. *Interpretation*, pp. 521, 533–534.

but for love. By using love as a reward for renunciation of pleasure, the child is trained in the way he should go; he becomes tractable, the word Freud uses in reference to his own sons.[23]

At first, this is an ego-adaptation; the parents represent "reality," and the child does what is necessary to manipulate them. But under the pressure of the parental demands for renunciation of instinctual gratification, this mode of adaptation proves economically inadequate. Some release for the suppressed impulses must be found. In this situation where the child is economically so hard pressed, torn between his need for further gratification and the necessity of not jeopardizing the margin of gratification that he does secure from his parents, he has recourse to the mechanism of identification. He internalizes the parental figures, particularly the one of the same sex, as part of his ego, and endows this new entity with his surplus of instinctual energy. So an outlet for the thwarted aggressive impulses is found—but at what a cost! For the superego now directs against the child the same aggression for which he could previously find no target. Continually the idealized parental figure is held before him as a norm, and every deviation in conduct or thought from this norm is followed by inescapable punishment. And since the energy for this punishment comes from the frustrated id, no actual conduct, no pure thought is satisfactory: the nobler the behavior, the less the id gratification, the more energy at the disposal of the superego, and the more the flagellation of the self.

To the historically-oriented Freud, the internalized parents were more than the child's idealization of his own particular parents. As well and beyond, they were historical figures, carried in the germ-plasm and evoked by the particular socialization process. The superego is not merely the precipitate of the particular Oedipus complex, but of the original Oedipal slayings. Thus, just as the child carries his ancestral germ-cell as both legacy and mortgage, so he continues in his superego a morality which springs not from his own direct experience, or even from that of his parents,

23. Ibid., pp. 333, 335.

but which springs from the phylogenetic past. This inheritance, Freud wrote, is only slowly altered in response to economic factors,[24] thus perceiving that the superego drives a person, in actual fact, not to the tasks required in his generation but to those required in the past. If there is rapid change in the economic environment, therefore, the superego and the ego would point in different directions; this, of course, is what actually happens when society moves from a technological economy of scarcity to a technological economy of abundance.

Ordinarily, and apart from neurotic outcomes, the ego and the superego divide between themselves the bureaucratic job of id-supervision, the role of authority shifting from one to the other depending on the balance of internal and external forces. Under conditions of civilization, this dual monarchy appears to grow very strong, while the original wishes of the id become more and more repressed or, with the transformation of affect, turned into their opposite. Moreover, with the transition to adulthood, the ideals of the superego undergo a change, attaching themselves no longer to the parents, but to outside powers—to God, to Public Opinion, and so on. Political leadership makes use of this mechanism; social groups are formed among people who have within themselves the same superego image. In this way, the internal bureaucracy and the external bureaucracy remain in touch with each other, with the former able to supervise the execution of not only the parents' commands but also those of the parent-surrogates of later life.

Mechanisms of the Internal Revolution

I rather doubt if any one would be as sensitive to the way in which authority actually operates within the individual as the foregoing shows Freud to have been, if he himself were not at least ambivalent towards authority. If Freud had been wholeheartedly on authority's side, he

24. *Psycho-analysis*, p. 244.

would have tended to overlook the extent of its power and the subtle infiltration of its operations, especially in modern society, into the very citadel of the personality. But beyond that, he would scarcely have been so aware of the seething rebelliousness which underlies outward conformity —of the civil war continually in progress within. For while many frightened bourgeois at the turn of the century were overanxiously afraid of socialism, few recognized, as Freud did, that the "revolt of the masses" was an affair not confined to the proletariat, and that hatred of civilization burned like an underground fire in even the strongholds of the bourgeoisie.

The fire burns in the id which, despite all efforts at repression, remains the stronger force—"the *daemonic* power," Freud calls it.[25] Indeed, the repressory forces must draw their energies from the great energy reservoir of the id, just as in modern society the masses supply the police force by which they are kept in check; the battle of revolution and counter-revolution—"cathexis" and "counter-cathexis," in Freud's terminology—goes on unceasingly. The proud ego and superego might be able to persuade both the outside world and the individual himself that everything is under control, only to be disestablished by the despised and rejected id.[26]

Thus in Freud's view the id is the great liberator, constantly struggling to overcome authority. The struggle is carried on according to the patterns familiar to us in a lenient, bureaucratic autocracy such as the Austrian Monarchy was in the nineteenth century: by sly evasion, by constant pressure, by satire, but rarely by open revolt. Freedom, then, is found in these interstices where the hierarchy is deceived or held at bay. Finally, the future lies with the

25. *Interpretation*, p. 543.
26. Cf. Freud, "The Origin and Development of Psychoanalysis" (Chase, tr.), *Amer. J. Psychol.* (1910) 21:181–218. Freud writes, in "My Contact with Josef Popper-Lynkeus," in *Collected Papers* 5:295, 297: "Our mind . . . is rather to be compared with a modern State in which a mob, eager for enjoyment and destruction, has to be held down forcibly by a prudent superior class."

oppressed id which will not take "no" for an answer.[27] This is one meaning of the well-known doctrine of "the return of the repressed." Let us see somewhat more precisely the forms taken by the internal fight for freedom.

Because the ego and superego draw their energies from the id, they are forced to relax their hold in sleep. They feel, moreover, that they can afford to relax since they have, as Freud puts it, closed the gates to motility;[28] nothing very serious can happen to the workaday authorities. Thus, every night is *Walpurgisnacht* for the id; in dreams these revels are recorded. But since the dreams are on the record, since they are recalled during the working day, they cannot express openly the desires and the revolts of the underground; in Freud's metaphor, they evade the censorship by the characteristic devices of obscurity and concealment known to all underground movements. These devices lull the censorship—viewed by Freud as just as stupid as the Austrian bureaucracy—by flattery, *double entendre,* and the invisible ink of symbolic language. Under these conditions, anything can be expressed, provided only that it is properly veiled.

In Freud's own dreams, for example, as interpreted by him, no authority is safe from attack. Count Thun, the Austrian Prime Minister; Meynert, the great psychiatrist to whom Freud in his waking life deferred; Brücke, Freud's inspiring teacher; the Emperor; Freud's own father—all are accused in his dreams of the vilest habits, the greatest absurdities; but all accusations are safely disguised by distortion, caricature, and obsequiousness.[29] Thus dreams, as Freud explained, play the role of the court jester, or of the Hamlet who is "mad north-northwest."[30] The authorities can rationalize their leniency with the remark, "After all, it's only a dream."[31] But it is the id which has the last

27. It is interesting to compare John Dewey's view of the liberating role of impulse. See his *Human Nature and Conduct.*

28. *Interpretation,* p. 510.

29. Ibid., pp. 269 (Count Thun), 417 (Meynert).

30. Ibid., p. 423.

31. Ibid., pp. 455, 513, 548.

word, for it maintains an unrelenting pressure; and since it forgets nothing and never misses an opportunity,[32] it will someday catch the censorship unawares and present the authorities with really frightening demands. The censorship will ring the alarm, and the sleeper will wake, frightened and anxious, finally aware that underneath the seemingly placid surface of his life there flow deep and dangerous currents—the "daemonic power." The play-world, to which Freud assigned dreams in one part of his theory, turns out to be not so innocent after all; in fact, Freud believed that there simply were, for adults at any rate, no guileless dreams.[33]

While dreams evade the bureaucratic censorship through their elaborate concealments of style, jokes and artistic productions escape by their wit and charm; it was indeed through these qualities that the Viennese often coped with their rulers and with the problems presented by the Empire's ethnic mixture. The id expresses its criticism by what Freud called tendency-wit, but then turns to its masters with a smile, saying, "After all, I don't mean it; it's only a joke." The censor is as humorless as he is stupid; he either misses the point of the joke or is tempted by it to let the villain through. To prove his point, Freud made an elaborate analysis of Jewish humor which, like so much of the underground humor which circulates in totalitarian states, is often a bitter attack upon authority. In the many jokes, for instance, which on their surface poke fun at the lies and sales talk of the *schadchen*, the Jewish marriage brokers, Freud saw that the underlying theme was an attack on the whole system of arranged marriage which put the fate of the young in the hands of the ghetto elders.[34] Similarly, in jokes of which poor Jews were the apparent butts, he saw that the real attack was on the dominant majority. Jokes, then, like dreams, are never guileless; they are skirmishes in the unending civil war within the individual and within the group.

32. Ibid., p. 268.
33. Ibid., pp. 250–251.
34. Cf. *Wit*, pp. 700–701.

Another evasion, in Freud's view, lies in the belief of adults that children's play is innocent and therefore need not be severely and closely supervised by the bureaucratic hierarchy. The "authorities" however are mistaken, just as mistaken as when they leave the dreamer, the jokester, the artist to their own devices. For children, Freud insisted, are naturally rebellious against authority; they hate their parents; they hate the sibling who displaces them; they have an eye, for which they are not given credit, for what goes on in their world.[35] When the individual child grows up, when his ego and superego take over their respective duties, a convenient amnesia covers over these early perversities and revolts. As Freud pictures the process, it is rather like the way in which American Negroes so quickly forgot their stirring history of slave revolts after emancipation. But the forgetting is only in the conscious mind. The id, which never forgets and never denies itself, is therefore constantly able to refresh its powers by harking back to these childhood perceptions and experiences. But as an adult, one is not aware on the conscious level of what one's own children are up to. Thus the internal authorities, despite their power, are not really able to suppress all claims for liberty, simply because they cannot get access to the claims; they are in the position of a jailer who has lost the records of his prisoners. No matter how he strives, the "liberation cannot be inhibited."[36]

Still another evasion rests on the fact that sexual activities, by their very nature, are carried on in private; the bureaucracy would have to have a far-flung network indeed to catch all evaders. Of course, as Freud saw, sexual intercourse is not quite free of bureaucratic regulation. He realized that a patriarchal society necessarily is an authoritarian one, since fatherhood, unlike motherhood, is not a palpable fact but must be inferred from circumstances. The inference is stronger or weaker depending on the amount of supervision—which in the Middle Ages took the form of chastity belts and in the Victorian Age of an overwhelm-

35. *Interpretation*, pp. 298–299, 499–500.
36. Ibid., p. 537.

ingly strong female superego. Even so, the civil war goes on. While virtually totalitarian pressures may limit illicit intercourse to a minimum, since interpersonal relations can be fairly well controlled, no pressures whatsoever can control the intrapersonal relations to the point of suppressing all sexual protests from the id. Masturbation, though carried out in private, and almost universally present in childhood, is too obvious to the waking self to escape censorship. But it was Freud's genius to see that in hysterical neurotic symptoms the sexual wish was, in spite of everything, expressed. To all appearances, and even in her own mind, a woman might seem most refined, but her gestures, her compulsions, her eating habits might betray an unmistakably sexual note.

Reference to the "refined woman" leads to still another area where the bureaucracy is easily evaded—namely, the lower classes generally, the peasants, the simpletons. While in the Marxian view these are the oppressed classes, in Freud's eyes they were freer from internal and external censorship than their "betters." Because they are not supposed to know any better, because their superegos are relatively weak, they can get by with assaults on the prison of language or the prison of sex; their transgressions will simply amuse the "authorities." In his book on wit, Freud explains that misuses of the language—obscenities, for example—which would make us indignant if committed on purpose, make us laugh if committed by a naive person; he is not dangerous, and we can afford to laugh. Such people are like children, except that they happen to be adult.[37]

But people of the upper and middle classes do not get off so easily.[38] A very few—the elite, the leaders—are strong enough knowingly to defy the hierarchy within and the hierarchy without; Freud admired them. The rest, however, adapt themselves as best they can to the world and its opinions as they find them, content to evade only in dreams and daydreams, and in jokes and art. Another residue are unable to adapt at all; they are too weak, the

37. *Wit*, pp. 766–767.
38. *The Problem of Anxiety*, p. 90.

pressures are too strong; moreover, they do not know how to achieve even the permitted evasions. These are the neurotics; Freud pitied them. Yet even they are not entirely devoid of liberty. They have, so to speak, a choice among neuroses. Perhaps they will become hysterical, expressing a sexual rebellion in a physical symptom such as vomiting. Or perhaps they will choose a phobia, refusing, for instance, to go out on the street lest they encounter temptation there. Or they may become obsessive as in the remarkable case of Dr. Schreber whose homosexuality took the form of constant preoccupation with thoughts of God's getting into him.[39] These "choices" hardly strike one as the essence of freedom. But one must remember that Freud did not believe there was much freedom to be had, even for the "normal" man. The point is rather that Freud did believe that the id was, in the last analysis, ungovernable; that the bureaucratic structure of civilization rested on a precarious foundation, since its agents were at the mercy of the oppressed; and therefore that the last word lay with the revolution.

AUTHORITY AND LIBERTY IN SOCIAL RELATIONS

As one might expect from his acceptance, in part, of cyclical theories of history, Freud was a believer in the theory of elites: that society was inevitably divided between a small class of leaders and a large class of led. Unlike the Marxists, he did not attribute this to any particular form of property relations; even under communism of goods, he felt that there would still be an elite, and the course of the Bolshevik revolution seemed to him to confirm his claims. His views rested not only on his belief in man's natural laziness, his need to be pushed into reality-work, but also on the theory of the death instinct, that man's aggressiveness would dissolve society into atoms if leadership ties did not hold it together. Thus authority has two independent psychological sources in the modern world: In the first place, it must ration those goods for which men will work;

39. *Collected Papers*, vol. 3, p. 390.

it does not matter so much whether these goods are directly economic commodities, as under capitalism, or are such things as fame and love, under communism. In this respect, the leader merely takes over the function of the parent who, as we have seen, brings children up by withholding love; conditional "love" is always the method of authority. Indeed, Freud attacked progressive education, which he felt would spoil children by giving them unrationed love. In the second place, the authority must keep order; without it, men's passions, envies, greeds, and superstitions would atomize society. With it, these same passions can form the basis of relatively enduring institutions.

These views are remarkably similar to those of the great theorist of autocracy, Thomas Hobbes; for he, too, tried to build a social order on a psychology—and one emphasizing men's fears and passions. Just as Freud imagined that society began from a compact of the brothers who had slain their tyrant father and realized that only in union and renunciation could they avoid the war of all against all, so Hobbes saw men in the state of nature as engaged in ceaseless combat, with peace attainable only by renunciation of virtually all individual rights. But there are significant differences, as well as striking comparisons, between Hobbes and Freud. The former, writing in a period of chaotic civil war, believed that men could be persuaded to make this surrender by an appeal to their reason—in Freud's terms, to their ego; that is, to their quite rational fear of being killed since no one man could be—like Freud's mythical primal father—strong enough to stand off all the rest. Hobbes said to men: Look here, is not death the worst thing? Is it not sensible to surrender everything else—freedom of speech, of religion, and so on—to assure plain physical survival? Moreover, if it should turn out that the leader on whose behalf you have surrendered these things does *not* bring peace, then you owe him no obligation; go find a better one.

In other words, Hobbes saw men endangered by their rational self-interest, which led them to aggressive striving to attain and secure the good things of this world. But he also thought men could unite through appeals to this same self-interest—self-preservation being, after all, a rational business for any living thing. And he thought all men equal, not only in the state of nature, but in the possession of this fundament of reason which could lead them to unification in a national state. He distrusted illusion—which he called superstition—because it clouded men's reason and led them to do fanatical things which were not in the interest of self-preservation.

While, like Hobbes, Freud saw aggression as native to man, he saw it as fundamentally an irrational striving rooted in the death instinct. He felt, moreover, that men could not be persuaded to renounce any desire by reason alone; the id is altogether too strong. Most men, that is; for only the elite could learn to live on a plane of sublimation. But the masses, in Freud's view, could be led to renounce aggression only through authority and what today would be called ideology—the cement of emotional ties. Thus the elite, producers of efficacious illusions, could live without these illusions, but not the masses.

While Freud did not publish his *Group Psychology and the Analysis of the Ego*[40] until after the first World War, his belief that the masses needed to be subjected to the authority of forceful leaders can be traced in his earliest psychological writings. Like Hobbes, he was afraid of anarchy; but he did not live in a period of anarchy, but rather, up until 1914, in one of the most stable and peaceful epochs in Western history. One of his dreams is especially interesting in this respect. It shows his admiration for Szell, the Hungarian parliamentary leader, who knew the arts of "leading men and organizing the masses" and was able to cope with the "anarchy" of the Hungarian delegates.[41] While Freud admired the rebel Garibaldi, who unified Italy, he seems from this dream to have had a typical Austro-German's contempt for the rebellious national minorities within the Hapsburg Monarchy. To one of these minorities, the Jews, Freud himself belonged; but he re-

40. Both this book and *Beyond the Pleasure Principle* reflect the impact of the war on Freud.

41. *Wit*, pp. 271, 411.

peatedly insisted on the need for scapegoats in order to maintain the national solidarity—outgroups and ingroups, in present-day terms. Indeed, notions of racial solidarity run through his work.[42] While Hobbes took the value of the nation for granted, he did not see it as the focus of sentimental ties.

For Hobbes, moreover, the leader had no special emotional qualities—no aura of charisma; he was simply the man who happened to take up the vacuum of power, and he was the leader only so long as he was powerful. Freud, following LeBon, saw the leader as having a quasi-magical influence on the mass. He was attracted to orators—such as Szell and Garibaldi—men who could cast a spell. In his article on the Moses of Michelangelo, Freud seems fascinated by charisma, by the physical and psychic strength which emanates from the great man—both the portrayer and the portrayed. So it is with his other historical heroes, such as Hannibal and Napoleon. These are the men who are above illusion, but who create it; above fear, but who inspire it; above loyalty, but who demand it.

All this sounds familiar enough today. But at the turn of the century, it was a far less conventional view. Nietzsche, for whom Freud had profound admiration, stood almost alone. Other elements in Nietzsche's theory are also found in Freud: the attack on reformers, the ridicule of humanitarians,[43] and the contempt for the bewitched masses,[44] who look always for the "happy ending" in their fantasies.[45] Nor, obviously, did Freud much care by what ideology the leader secured the necessary mass submission; late in life, he expresses considerable respect even for the Bolsheviks who, he feels, have known how to organize the masses.[46]

This, as will be apparent, is only one side of Freud's

42. *Psycho-analysis*, p. 242. Cf. *Interpretation*, p. 272. ("In the dream I am surprised at my German nationalistic feelings").

43. Note, however, that Freud states that he was a member of the Humanitarian Society. *Interpretation*, p. 240.

44. *Psycho-analysis*, pp. 194–195.

45. Ibid., pp. 220–221.

46. Ibid., p. 247.

view; perhaps it is the more conscious and explicit side. But before turning to the more libertarian themes, it is necessary to see how Freud, in his day-to-day writing and work, treated the powerless groups in his society. This will, I think, afford more insight into his personal authoritarian tendencies than will his writings on leadership. For the latter might, or so one could claim, spring from a realistic judgment of social needs; the former, while less explicit, had a more deep-lying effect on psychoanalysis itself.

THE HIERARCHY OF DIFFERENCES

I mentioned at the outset that Freud tended to view differences as implying relations of super- and sub-ordination; this, in fact, was my definition of authoritarian thinking. In comparison with man, for example, Freud saw the other animals as a powerless group, a downtrodden class. It is interesting that they never appear in Freud's writings, so to speak, in their own right; they are always the objects of phobias or the stuff of symbols. Where a little 5-year-old boy is afraid of draft horses falling down in the street, Freud cannot believe this could be pity, or any form of human sympathy; it is simply a sexual symbolism.[47] Of course, it might have been that alone, or that plus a special feeling for struggling horses in harness—a frightening sight to a sensitive onlooker. The point is that it seems hardly to have occurred to Freud that one might identify with oppressed and struggling animals, and that what might have been so frightening to Hans was seeing in these huge horses the same struggle that he felt himself engaged in.

Freud's attitude towards the lower classes of human society was actually not very different. Wherever servants, nurses, porters, and so forth, appear in his writings, they are viewed as dubious rather undifferentiated beings, scarcely credited with personality. Freud repeatedly warns parents against the damage that nurses can do to children; they

47. "Analysis of a Phobia in a Five-Year-Old-Boy"; *Collected Papers,* 4:149; but cf. p. 254, and also *Totem and Taboo,* in *The Basic Writings of Sigmund Freud,* pp. 906–907.

are viewed as seductresses, rather than as persons who might give a middle-class child the love and stimulation withheld by his parents.[48] As one gets glimpses of his own behavior towards the few lower-class people he came in contact with, such as maids and cabdrivers, one finds a tendency in him to be exploitative, even mean. He spits on the stairs to annoy a particularly neat housekeeper. He drives cabbies too hard. He seeks bargains from shopkeepers. He upbraids the conductor of an express.[49] In all this, he is the nineteenth-century bourgeois gentleman, for whom the lower classes are not really people, scarcely seen as individuals, and not respected.

Another social difference is that between adults and children; and here, too, Freud is partly on the side of the powers-that-be, the grown-ups. He frequently refers to children's questions as a "nuisance";[50] it seldom occurs to him that adults' questions of children—"And how old are you, my little boy?" and, "What are you going to be when you grow up?"—may also be a nuisance. More seriously, he makes the famous charge that children are "polymorphous-perverse"—that is, that their sexual life is not confined to the genital zone. Despite all his qualifications, this seems to me to be the application of adult standards to child behavior. He does not see that our language patterns, to which he was so sensitive in other connections, are adult-oriented; the child is forced into them both as object and subject. Likewise Freud speaks of children as immoderate,[51] lacking the ego and superego controls by which the adult has learned to govern his behavior. In this way, he justifies the authoritative controls which are applied to them. But it is at least an open question whether children are as wanting in moderation as Freud supposed. Just as recent experi-

48. For young men, actresses constitute a similar danger. *Interpretation*, p. 325.
49. Ibid., p. 269.
50. See, for example, *Wit*, p. 796.
51. Ibid., p. 796. But of course he also regards the adult demands made of children as immoderate. See, for example, "The Sexual Enlightenment of Children," in *Collected Papers* 2:36.

ments have shown that children, left to themselves, will choose the foods that their particular metabolisms need, there is evidence that they are far from immoderate in satisfying their other desires where they have not already been cramped by adult interference.

"The child's ambition," Freud writes, "is not so much to distinguish himself among his equals as to imitate the big fellows. The relation of the child to the grown-up determines also the comic of degradation, which corresponds to the lowering of the grown-up in the life of the child. Few things can afford the child greater pleasure than when the grown-up lowers himself to its level, disregards his superiority, and plays with the child as its equal. The alleviation which furnishes the child pure pleasure is a debasement. . . ."[52] Does this not sound a bit patronizing? So a white man would talk about Negroes, or a colonial about the "natives." In all these instances, a civilization that is different is judged by a kind of unconscious ethnocentrism. And of course a vicious circle is created. For the powerless do tend to imitate the powerful, and to "enjoy" degrading them.

Freud, as I have already noted, wanted "tractable" sons. So, in his psychoanalytic theory, he accused children of not wanting to renounce illicit goals—and emphasized less adults' reluctance to renounce their privileges vis-à-vis this helpless minority; in the same way, Freud viewed the Oedipus complex from the side of the adult who is the focus of the child's rivalry and love—more often than from the side of the child of whom the adult wants greedily to take possession.

That Freud sides with the authorities in this warfare is most sharply shown by his relative lack of indignation against the crimes parents commit on their children, even when those crimes have landed the children in his office. He takes for granted that that is how things are, and while he succors the victims he feels little fury against their oppressors. He never notes that the threat of castration is a more severe punishment than warranted even for the

52. *Wit*, p. 796.

Oedipal crimes which he believes children would like to commit. Even in the most extreme case, when a patient is taken from him by her parents who fear she will recover, he records the fact with only a marginal protest.[53] On the other hand, where he does have some control over an upbringing, as in the famous case of little Hans, he is critical of the mother for "spoiling" the boy, but much less of the prying father who pesters the child with psychoanalytic questions and interpretations from morning to night—a father who, as the report implicitly reveals, had no respect for the child's integrity, privacy, and idiosyncrasy.[54]

The Analyst as an Authority

A further example of Freud's attitude towards the powerless, lies in his treatment of neurotics, a minority, as against the "normal" majority. On one level, Freud consciously accepted the standards and outlook of the normal man and branded the neurotics as weaklings, constitutionally and psychically inadequate. These attitudes find their way into psychoanalytic therapy in Freud's primarily one-way concept of the transference. "Transference" means that the patient transfers to the analyst the constellations of love, hate, and other affects, which developed in his childhood; he treats the analyst, in feeling, as if the latter were his father or another significant figure. The theory, obviously, contains a great deal of truth. And, while Freud does deal with the "countertransference," in which the analyst's own resistances get in the way of his work, he does seem to set up an ideal in which only the patient is affected by the patient-analyst relationship, and where the analyst is merely a neutral figure.

But suppose the patient rebels, and refuses to accept the analyst's authority? Freud called this the "resistance," and set himself the methodical task of breaking it down. If a patient expresses a doubt about the content of a dream,

53. *A General Introduction to Psychoanalysis*, 1943, pp. 400–401; and cf. "The Psychogenesis of a Case of Homosexuality in a Woman," in *Collected Papers* 2:202, 206.
54. *Collected Papers*, 4:207.

Freud is apt to interpret this as a resistance.[55] If a patient is unable to give associations to a dream, Freud will supply the answers from the symbolic dictionary;[56] in other words, Freud, in effect, tells the patient, If you do not come across and reveal the mechanisms which I know to be at work within you, I will find them anyway. Once, he succeeded in producing from a patient the desired sexual key, after saying he would have to discontinue the analysis.[57] Though, theoretically, Freud called "resistance" anything which impeded the analysis, in practice he seems at times to have regarded such resistance as a personal attack: he said, in effect, to his patients, If you oppose me, that is your "resistance," your preferring to remain ill, and, perhaps, you wish to have me fail. In part, Freud thus avoided debate upon the merits of the case. A most striking single example of this outlook appears in the book on dreams. A patient knows Freud's thesis that all dreams are wish-fulfillments. Then she dreams of something so disagreeable—spending the summer with her mother-in-law—that it cannot be a wish-fulfillment, even in the most far-fetched interpretation. Freud replies that the patient wished to prove *"that I should be wrong, and this wish the dream showed her as fulfilled."*[58]

Though Freud insisted that the analyst should counsel and direct the patient as little as possible, he seems to have been not entirely aware of the degree of authority he exercised. In one of his earlier cases, he reports that he "expected her [the patient] to accept a solution which did not seem acceptable to her";[59] in the dream-associations he accuses her of showing him up by not getting well and responds by telling her that her symptoms are her own fault,[60] that he would prefer to have a more "docile" patient.[61] And, like God, there are no secrets from him; few

55. For example, *Interpretation*, p. 474.
56. For example, *Interpretation*, p. 381.
57. Ibid., p. 334.
58. Ibid., p. 229.
59. Ibid., p. 195.
60. Ibid., pp. 196–197.
61. Ibid., p. 199.

things so engaged his efforts as attempts of patients to hide something—this was "resistance" with a vengeance.[62] He prided himself that they could seldom, if ever, succeed. In this he had the advantage of a "phonographic memory";[63] if a patient got fuzzy about a dream, Freud could always catch him up.[64] Moreover, since not even the slightest error escaped him,[65] he must have given patients the feeling that they could not get away with anything.

This same congeries of attitudes towards the powerless—towards children, women, neurotics—is manifested towards the intellectual problems with which Freud was concerned; one might view this as sadism towards the (powerless) material of theory. Freud himself gives us, as one of his favorite quotations, a similar comparison which was once made by Lassalle:

> A man like myself who, as I explained to you, had devoted his whole life to the motto *Die Wissenschaft und die Arbeiter* (Science and the Workingman), would receive the same impression from a condemnation which in the course of events confronts him *as would the chemist, absorbed in his scientific experiments, from the cracking of a retort. With a slight knitting of his brow at the resistance of the material, he would, as soon as the disturbance was quieted, calmly continue his labor and investigations.*[66]

Freud's intellectual powers seem to have been excited by that very "resistance of the material," whether the "material" was the reception of his theories at the hands of the Vienna profession, the "resistance" of a patient in analysis, or the intractability of facts which he wished to order into a theoretical framework. "How many seemingly absurd dreams have we not forced to give up their sense!"[67] Freud

62. See, however, the benevolent attitude towards patients' denials Freud takes in "Constructions in Analysis" in *Collected Papers* 5:358.
63. *Psycho-analysis*, p. ix.
64. *Interpretation*, pp. 472–473.
65. Cf. *Psychopathology of Everyday Life*, in *The Basic Writings of Sigmund Freud.*
66. *Wit*, p. 682.
67. *Leonardo*, p. 65.

says of himself with pride. And elsewhere he refers to a type of dream which "stubbornly refuses to surrender its meaning."[68] In such a case, he advises the analyst to turn the inexplicable symbol into its opposite—say exchange night for day, or wet for dry—a technique that sometimes led him to great discoveries and sometimes simply to victory over a stubborn fact. One might even suppose that Freud's great admiration for Moses, Hannibal, Michelangelo, and others, may have sprung in part from his identification with the effort to shape and hew the hardest materials, physical or human.

Many illustrations could be given of this effort of Freud's to fit everything into a comprehensive system, even at the cost of distorting. When he deals, for instance, with dreams, he establishes that they are all wish fulfillments—and if, later on, a dream turns up which does not seem to fit this system, Freud can become very ingenious in nevertheless finding a wish. When he deals with Biblical history, as in *Moses and Monotheism*, his arbitrariness in selecting as true those narratives which fit, and rejecting as "tendentious" those which do not, strikes me as a somewhat aggressive handling of the data.

Moreover Freud was particularly attracted by anything which savored of mystery or challenged his powers of unmasking.[69] He was fascinated by the uncanny, by the dark and secret springs of life. But he was not awed; on the contrary, he responded by attack, by an insistence on penetrating the secret, coming to the heart of the artichoke.[70] The sign "Keep Out" has attracted many great thinkers, some of them Jews and other "marginal men" for whom exclusion touched a sensitive spot. But here we see that the material on which a thinker works is only apparently powerless; though it cannot talk back, it "resists," and it is "protected" by all the categories of convention. Sometimes

68. *Interpretation*, p. 352.
69. Speaking of the occult, Freud writes that "prohibitions will not stifle men's interest in an alleged mysterious world." *The Question of Lay Analysis*, 1950, p. 104.
70. See the "Dream of the Botanical Monograph," *Interpretation*, p. 243.

it seems as if a certain tendency to overpower is necessary for the creation of any radically new intellectual system; like Lassalle, the pioneer must be as deaf to the objections as the chemist to the cracking of his retort. Yet it is also this refusal to "listen" to the material which results in the distortions and overstatement of such a system.

FREUD AS PROMETHEUS

But all this is only one aspect of Freud's view. I have stressed this aspect because, for one thing, this hierarchical, reactionary side of Freud is just what attracts a number of contemporary intellectuals to him. Freud fits in with the current vogue of the "tough guy." And it is understandable that his tendency towards dogmatism should be admired by people who today force themselves to sound dogmatic even though they lack Freud's real self-confidence. However, in seizing upon the dogmatist in Freud, and upon the power-worshiper, they actually disregard his much more complicated view of things. In the remaining pages, I want to take up some of those themes in Freud that are liberating and equalitarian, and it will be seen, I think, that these themes are interwoven with their opposites. It is just such textures of ambivalence that Freud taught us to attempt to unravel.

Liberating Underprivileged Reality

I have already indicated that another way of looking at the elements of sadism in Freud's handling of data is to see them as a source of the energy and drive needed to liberate those aspects of reality that convention had submerged or hidden. And it cannot fail to strike us that the same man who intransigently sought to organize the material of experience into the shapes of his theoretical constructions also "listened" to that material with a rare attentiveness and respect. And what he listened to particularly were the little things—the unnoticed words, gestures, silences, and so on—which previous thinkers had considered too trivial for notice. And not only little things but despised things too:

"absurd" dreams, "debasing" perversions, "infantile" memories. Freud admitted them all into the structure of his thought and gave them all the credit of having meaning. Since, for Freud, these secret things are also the basic, the *Ursache*, they are even credited with an eminence over the more "powerful" and accepted data of experience. In other words, not only was no fact too humble to be lifted into the theoretical structure, but it might easily find itself outranking the more obvious and insistent facts which had been stressed by earlier thinkers.

Liberating Underprivileged Illness

It is the same with Freud's treatment of neurotics. Before his time, neurotics had generally been regarded as malingerers in whom no organic symptom could be found; or their ailment was credited to bad heredity. Instead, Freud insisted that psychic injuries ranked at least equally with the more obvious physical ones, were entitled to as much consideration, and were subject to the same causality. Everyone knows with what abuses the insane were treated before Freud's time, and how they are treated even today; the most innocent treatment for neurotics was to give them placebos, the harmless pills which swell the doctor's income. On the whole, medicine seemed to rank highest those specialists, such as surgeons, and eye, ear, nose, and throat men, who had the least close contact with the patient as a human being. And by and large when Freud started in psychiatric practice, only the hypnotists attempted to establish contact with the mentally ill; Freud soon rebelled against the authoritarianism of these men, with their inflexible "suggestions." He chose instead the far more respectful technique of "free" association. By this, he hoped to be able to listen to the voice of the id, freed from the supervision of the ego and superego, as well as from the surging noises of the external world.

Thanks to Freud, the powerless and despised neurotic finds himself, in the analytic situation, in a new relationship. Instead of being cursed out of the doctor's office with an accusation of malingering, or breezed out with a "why don't you just relax," or gentled out with a prescription for placebos, his every "thoughtless" word and act is taken with the utmost seriousness, and for a length of time—often years—unknown in any analogous professional relation. He can "make" the analyst listen to his stream of consciousness, his outcries, his silences, subject only to the injunction of sincerity, of keeping nothing back. But even this injunction bespeaks respect: not only the obvious respect for confidences, but the belief that what the patient seeks to hide is, after all, a human act or thought; and that, fundamentally, he has no thought or experience which cannot be matched among the dominant, the so-called normal.

Liberating Women and Children from Suffocating Piety

While in Freud's day the typical note in the treatment of the neurotic was brutality, the typical note in the treatment of women and children was sentimentality. In both cases, the powerless were treated with contempt; but in the second case the contempt, though it could be brutal enough, was veiled by hypocrisy and the assignment of angelic virtues to the group in question. Thus, Victorian middle-class womanhood—like the Southern white woman of today's romance—was put on a pedestal compounded of chastity, pity, and pretense. In showing up the falsity of this picture, Freud, despite acceptance of antifeminine bias, did much to put women in the same class with men. In the first place, his concept of bisexuality meant that women and men had come from the same original format—rather than from a male, as in the Adam and Eve myth; moreover, in the life of each sex, there existed elements from the other sex, one source of homosexual ties. In the second place, though Freud stressed the differences between the erotic and workaday roles of men and women, these after all are smaller than the similarities: both are subject on the whole to the same ontogenetic as well as phylogenetic destiny; both have the same internal structure of ego, superego, id; both may fall into the same characterological formations—both may fall ill of hysteria.

By similar leveling measures, Freud reduced the gap between the upper and lower classes of society. For him, the king was naked—with the ur-nakedness common to all mankind.[71] All women, of high and low degree, lost control of themselves in their destined labor of childbirth. Freud liked to tell the story of the obstetrician who played cards with a baron while the baroness was in confinement. When the latter called out, "Ah, mon Dieu, que je souffre," the husband jumped up, but the doctor said, "That's nothing; let us play on." Later she called, "My God, my God, what pains," but still the doctor said it was not yet time to go in. "At last, there rang from the adjacent room the unmistakable cry, 'A-a-a-ai-e-e-e-e-e-E-E!' The physician quickly threw down the cards and said, 'Now it's time.' "[72]

Likewise, in rescuing children from sentimentality, Freud in one sense put them on the same footing with adults. As I have pointed out, he credited them with vices, with rebellion, with lust and hate and murderous intent. His ur-thinking made every adult at heart a child, by the very process of debasement he himself described as central to the process of wit. Even the first difference—the one between animals and men—was broken down in the pattern of Freud's thought; he viewed men as, at bottom, animals and found the source of their most human traits in the sexual instincts which they share with the mammalian phylum.[73]

Furthermore, whatever markedly ambivalent deference Freud paid to the temporal authorities of his day—the upper classes, the males, the distinguished—he retained more than most men the obedience of the true scientist to the truth and to the scientific tradition which the Renaissance revived and glorified. While he was forced against his will to quarrel with scientists, he never broke faith with Science. The things he rendered unto Caesar are trivial

71. Ibid., pp. 293–296.
72. *Wit*, 5; p. 681.
73. Cf. Fenichel, *The Psychoanalytic Theory of Neurosis*, 1945, p. 213. "The child is not as arrogant as the adult person, who tries to believe in a fundamental difference between human beings and animals."

coin in comparison with the devotion he rendered to his fierce, yet fundamentally humane and passionately secular deity of Science.

Thus, we may compare his taking the side of the adult against the child in some of his views, such as the Oedipus complex, with his protest against adults who lied to their children. He realized quite clearly that children who can see through their parents' lies will become free of the parents, and he wrote that children who reject the stork fable begin their "psychic independence . . . from this act of disbelief. . . ."[74] Even more strongly, he denounced the "sadly antiquated" *patria potestas* which survives in modern society: "Even in our own middle-class families the father commonly fosters the growth of the germ of hatred which is naturally inherent in the paternal relation, by refusing to allow the son to be a free agent or by denying him the means of becoming so."[75] And the mother, too, he added, circumscribes her daughter when the latter's "budding beauty" reminds the envious parent "that for her the time has come to renounce sexual claims."[76] More searching still is Freud's awareness that the father's strictness evokes the child's criticism and the latter's close awareness of every weakness in the authority, but that this criticism is repressed and remains unconscious.[77] No truer statement as to the operation of authority has ever been written than this: that criticism is called into being by interest and need, and that the findings are then repressed and remain operative in the unconscious mind. Ambivalence towards the father, one may assume, is the inevitable outcome of this process, with conscious love and admiration acting as a cover for unconscious criticism and hate. Of this ambivalence, Freud's own attitude, which I have just reviewed, is an example; the phrases just now quoted hardly spring from an unequivocal worshiper of authority.

As one would expect, Freud's reported dreams indicate his ambivalence towards his own parents. He reports, with-

74. *Leonardo*, p. 47.
75. *Interpretation*, pp. 303–304.
76. Ibid., p. 304.
77. Ibid., p. 416.

out apparent indignation, his mother's deceiving him, her strict middle-class restraints.[78] But certain dreams are polemics against his father; Freud interprets these either to mean that the manifest father represents some other authority—when it could more easily refer both to the father and to the other authority—or by accusing himself, for example, of sexual curiosity, thus putting his father in the right.[79] Nevertheless, the dreams stand as proof that Freud rebelled against his father, but, like so many sons, did not carry the rebellion through.[80]

Promethean and constricting elements seem to me similarly intertwined in the thought and heritage of many great thinkers throughout history, whether one thinks of Confucius or of Marx, of Plato or of St. Simon. To be born is to be mortgaged; to live is to be crippled; to be socialized is to be limited as well as freed. And, as violent social revolutions have their Thermidors, so do violently original social thinkers look both forward and back. However, such an attempt at generalization will be misleading if it obscures the profound differences among thinkers in the degree to which they blend the prejudices of their class and age with means of escaping from those prejudices. Moreover, elements in a thinker which may have been peripheral in his own time may turn out to be decisive in his reception by later ages.

One can already see in Freud's case the divergent streams of social philosophy that trace their origins, more or less justly, to his work. I have spoken of the fashion among certain intellectuals to use Freud—along with Dostoevsky, Kierkegaard, and others—as a spokesman of man's irrationality, his need for mystery and authority. Among some psychiatrists, Freud's stress on reality-orientation can be read as justifying therapies aiming to adjust the patient to society as given, whether reality happens to be deserving of such sacrifice or not. And among a large lay

78. Ibid., pp. 266–267.
79. Ibid., pp. 416, 433. Cf. also the dream on p. 411.
80. Cf. "A Disturbance of Memory on the Acropolis," in *Collected Papers* 5:302, 311–312.

public, diluted Freudian interpretations are used by people to evaporate their own hostility; and to explain others' hostility to oppressive life-conditions as simple transfers of Oedipal rivalry to the social scene—or things of the same sort. There is a side of Freud that warrants these abuses of his contributions, just as there is a side of Marx that cannot completely disavow the atrocities committed in his name.

For Freud did share, in the ways which I have tried to trace, many attitudes which, in his epoch and in his class, were used to establish and support differences of value and rank. On one level, he sided with the authority and looked at the powerless through authority's eyes. But on another, and more characteristic level, he rebelled against authority. As in many such rebellions, his tactic was not to exalt the underdog but to degrade the top dog. "You are all the same," he seems to be saying, "princes and paupers, gentlemen and pimps, philosophers and babies." And, just as a lord has no secrets from his valet, so the illustrious could not dazzle Freud's eyes; in the very highest attainments of man —his art, his speculation, his juridical institutions—Freud found the cloven hoof of sex. As on the western plains the Colt revolver was called "Old Equalizer," so Freud saw the legacy each man carried on his person as the fundamental equalizer of the race.

The Themes of Heroism and Weakness in the Structure of Freud's Thought

Students of intellectual history tend to exaggerate, so it seems to me, the importance in contemporary life of the ideas whose derivations they trace. Since they are themselves intellectuals, for whom ideas are very important, they fall prey to the error of the specialist who sees the world from the angle of his own routines. Thus, one can find Nazism blamed on a congeries of alleged fathers from Machiavelli to Nietzsche, from Gobineau to Spengler or Carl Schmitt. Likewise, in much current discourse, William James and John Dewey are treated as the founts of all that is alleged to be shallow, manipulative, and complacent in American life. A whole school of critics, led by Van Wyck Brooks, blamed on the debunking writers of the twenties the cynicism and pacifism which they thought prevalent in the pre-World War II era. In this fashion, people whose trade is words cry their own wares even in the very act of claiming to be overwhelmed by the far more powerful words of their chosen enemies.

Obviously, it would be absurd to rush to the opposite extreme and to contend that words and ideas have only negligible influence on the stream of events. Indeed, a just appraisal in a concrete social context is always exceedingly difficult, as are efforts to isolate *any* single item in a cultural complex. We know well enough that institutions often come close to reversing their founders' intentions: that Christ was not a Christian, Marx not a Marxist (let alone a Stalinist), Dewey not a school principal in the Teachers College patronage network. And where a man's thought and

"The Themes of Heroism and Weakness in the Structure of Freud's Thought" was first published in Psychiatry, *Vol. 13, No. 3, 1950.*

action do not lead to creation of a new institution but mingle in a general climate of opinion, the tracing of the consequences of his work is even more a shadowy and impalpable task: no Mendelian law governs the unembodied transmission of ideas. Even when men acknowledge indebtedness, what does that prove? They often say they owe it all to their mothers. We are, I think, quite far from even knowing how to begin the job of evaluating the weight of any single person's ideas in the historical process. Conceivably, the sort of studies now undertaken by social psychologists concerning the impact of the mass media—radio, print, and film—on people will give us some clues as to the influence and social distribution of particular words and images.

Yet when all this is granted, it remains plausible to say that Freud has had tremendous impact on our popular culture. As radioactive tracers allow us to follow chemical substances in the physiologist's laboratory, so the verbal tags adopted by Freud and his followers give us some way of tracing the rapidity of the diffusion of his inventions. The number of psychoanalysts even today is a mere handful—in America, it would seem, less than 500—fewer than the number of "missionaries" who spread Marxist gospel as members of the International Workingmen's Association in the 1850's and 60's. And while the devotion, diligence, and productiveness of these analysts—who fill journals while treating patients and training the young—could scarcely be excelled by any band of missionaries, these qualities, without the aid of a powerful ideology, would not have given them their present place in popular discourse.[1]

1. Freud, in one of his moments of sober self-judgment—at other times, as I shall try to show, he was overmodest—ranked his contribution alongside those of Copernicus and Darwin: he saw it as reducing man's stature and self-pride. So he found it easy enough to explain why he had enemies, and could defend himself by explaining the "resistance" he met with. But he made less, at least in his published work, of the fact that after 1902 or so he attracted friends and followers—at a time when it still cost something to be a friend of Freud—and that before the Second World War his thought had spread to all industrialized or even semi-

It would be valuable to make a comparative study in detail, and to see how, in different countries and different social strata, Freud's thought has been received and modified, used and abused. Plainly, the process that Lasswell, with reference to political ideologies, termed "restriction by partial incorporation"[2] has also occurred with Freud. One would expect this process to occur when students in their courses read some watered-down or textbook version, but this process even occurs when students read Freud in his own words. For the revolutionary concepts of Freud can no longer have the same impact when they have their teeth drawn by the very nature of most classroom situations—when, moreover, students already come with some familiarity with major themes: the unconscious, childhood sexuality, the importance of dreams, slips and errors, and so on. But it follows from this that it makes little sense to blame Freud for the untoward consequences of some aspects of his thought as it is currently modified and received—if we find, for instance, "neurotic" used as a term of apology for the self and of vicious denigration against

industrialized lands. To be sure, in "The Future Prospects of Psychoanalytic Therapy," he allowed himself to speculate, as early as 1910, on the possibility that analytic thought would permeate education, would be made available to the poor, and would finally make therapy unnecessary by the progress of what would today be called preventive mental hygiene. (*Collected Papers* 2:285; London, Hogarth Press, 1925.) But he seems not to have realized that men were and would be attracted to his work, not only because it was socially useful, but because it was adventurous—that men would, in effect, trade their vanity for the pleasures of disinterested discovery and understanding. Indeed, it is striking that a number of the ideologies which are popular today, such as Marxism and Freudianism, cannot adequately explain the appeal they have for many of their devotees. A good many people embrace Marxism, for instance, in order to make sense of the world, or to contribute to it, and not only because of class consciousness; people embrace psychoanalytic thinking because it adds to the interest they find in observing human beings, and not only because of such motives as narcissism.

2. Harold D. Lasswell, *World Politics and Personal Insecurity*, 1935, p. 6.

others. That certain elements in Freud's view of life were narrow, class-biased, and reactionary is one of the points made in the preceding two papers and in this one. But this must not blind us to the fact that Freud expressed his views at a time when, in many quarters, democratic sentiments were powerful and when the "common man" was, in America especially, given a great deal of lip service. His opposition to those dominant trends, even when the latter happened to be progressive, was stimulating and productive; and this is not altered by the fact that today some of his views on work, on authority, on heroism, may no longer liberate thought but, in the present context of Freud's reception, may confine it.

It is, then, up to each generation to read Freud as if it were for the first time, much as men in the sixteenth and seventeenth centuries sought—and even today such men as Schweitzer and Buber still seek—to approach the Bible anew. I would like to succeed in sending at least some of the readers of these articles back to Freud to see whether the themes I trace in his work actually exist and, if so, whether they can be stated in a more fundamental and searching way. By such ever-renewed readings, I hope that Freud can be saved from the fate of "partial incorporation," and that his power to challenge, inspire, and perplex can be retained. If so, we need worry less about tendencies to put his work to manipulative uses and his authority behind socially regressive ideologies.

In depicting Freud's view of human nature and social organization in the previous articles, I have already touched on Freud's ideal of human life—what he admired in people and, conversely, what he despised. Indeed, such ideals, explicit or implicit, are ordinarily part of that image of human nature from which everyone makes judgments as to the meaning of life and the value of, and possibilities for, social relations. Here I want to examine Freud's ideal and its counterimage of weakness in more detail.

Note that I have taken heroism and weakness—not heroism and villainy—to be polar opposites in Freud's view. Such a polarity ostensibly eliminates ethical considerations.

It accompanies a view which sees men as divided into a strong elite and a numerous but vacillating mass. But here again one finds ambivalence in Freud's outlook. For while he shared with thinkers such as Nietzsche and Carlyle elements of an elitist position, he also emphasized, as I have indicated before, the fundamental similarity of all men, their obedience to the same instinctual laws and infantile survivals.

PORTRAIT OF A HERO

Freud's ideal man is harmonious within and successful without. He has conflicts and meets obstacles but they are all in the external world. Out of polymorphous infantile sexualities he has developed a definite genital supremacy; the hero neither lingers at the childhood way-stations of sex nor returns regressively to them. His potency is unproblematical and his choice among sexual objects is unrestricted by fetish or fixation. Freud, in commenting on a statement by Leonardo that "great love springs from great knowledge of the beloved object," declares that people in love "are guided by emotional motives which have nothing to do with cognition; and their consequences are rather weakened by thought and reflection."[3] In this light, "genital maturity" means for Freud lesser rather than greater complexity and differentiation of emotions. But one must qualify this by observing that such maturity involves a man's ability to make love to women of the same social class and refinement as his mother and sister; he remains immature so long as, hounded by the incest taboo, he can let himself go only with women whom he socially despises—that is, who do not forcibly remind him of the forbidden objects of his childhood. By implication, therefore, mature love involves more than mere ability to secure genital heterosexual release.[4]

3. *Leonardo da Vinci,* 1947, p. 40. Hereafter this citation will be referred to as *Leonardo.* All books cited are by Freud, unless otherwise noted.

4. One must remember, moreover, that more was involved in such ability in the days before the advent of

Nevertheless, the course of the hero's sexual gratification, as one senses it from Freud's writings, takes the shortest line between the unconscious wish and the conscious gratification; there is no occasion for the procrastination of daydreaming nor, indeed, for the 'waste' of dream-stimulated emissions.[5] There is none of "the tendency to reflection and delay" that Freud noted in Leonardo's art.[6] Freud attributed a similarly uncomplicated quality to the dreams of the normal person. "Indeed," he writes, "the natural dreams of healthy persons often contain a much simpler, more transparent, and more characteristic symbolism than those of neurotics, which, owing to the greater strictness of the censorship and the more extensive dream-distortion resulting therefrom, are frequently troubled and obscured, and are therefore more difficult to translate."[7]

The hero, viewed economically, follows, without scruple, without hesitation, without doubt, the hedonistic calculus in his sexual life. Freud declares:

> The man who in consequence of his unyielding nature cannot comply with the required suppression of his instincts, becomes a criminal, an outlaw, unless his social position or

easy and reliable contraceptives and of easy and reliable women who were not courtesans. While at one point Freud pleads for the spread of contraceptive knowledge among married couples ("Sexuality in the Aetiology of the Neuroses," in *Collected Papers* 1:237–239), this is not inconsistent with his statement in which he speaks of nongenital forms of sexuality: "ethically they are reprehensible, for they degrade the love-relationship of two human beings from being a serious matter to an otiose diversion, attended neither by risk nor by spiritual participation." "'Civilized' Sexual Morality and Modern Nervousness," in *Collected Papers* 2:95. Hereafter this citation will be referred to as *Papers*.

5. The dreamer, Freud writes, "thinks in his sleep: 'I don't want to continue this dream and exhaust myself by an emission; I would rather save it for a real situation.'" *The Interpretation of Dreams*, in *The Basic Writings of Sigmund Freud*, Modern Library, 1938, p. 514, cited hereafter as *Interpretation*.

6. *Leonardo*, p. 116.

7. *Interpretation*, pp. 381–382.

striking abilities enable him to hold his own as a great man, a 'hero.'[8]

Moreover, the hero is a person of great energy potential: "psychic greatness like somatic greatness is exhibited by means of an increased expenditure."[9] Viewed topologically, this pattern means that the ego of the hero is in unquestioned command, and that conflict between the conscious and unconscious levels of the personality is at a minimum. As the wise statesman never veers too far from the demands of the mob he leads, but controls and channels them in the very process of carrying them out, so the hero's ego is in the closest touch with the wishes of the id, of which it is in one sense a most effective "public servant."[10]

Plainly, all this does not mean that the hero is as completely free of internal superego restraints as he is unintimidated by society's efforts at repression. While his ego does not cringe before an internalized father-imago, the superego functions to provide an ideal to which the narcissistic elements in the personality can aspire and to demand a high level of performance in line with that ideal. The restraints so imposed may perhaps be compared to the concept of "noblesse oblige." For they are voluntarily accepted—even though their original imposition may have been far from voluntary—as a nobleman's code is supposed to be, rather than submitted to through the operation of the bureaucratic internal machinery based on fear of castration, of God, of public opinion. The hero has a certain Spartan, uncomplaining attitude towards life, and a sportsmanlike adherence to the rules of good breeding. Freud's heroes are at farthest remove from the spoiled Bohemian

8. *Papers,* 2:82.

9. *Wit and Its Relation to the Unconscious,* in *The Basic Writings of Sigmund Freud,* p. 777, hereafter cited as *Wit.*

10. Even so, Freud pointed out that "the subjection of the *Ucs.* by the *Pcs.* is not thorough-going even in perfect psychic health; the extent of this suppression indicates the degree of our psychic normality." *Interpretation,* p. 520. See also *The Ego and the Id,* 1927, pp. 81–83.

attitudes, seemingly free of superego and of inhibition, which Freud detested.[11]

Nevertheless, there is, I feel, something romantic and parochial in Freud's image of the ideal type of man as one who goes directly at what he wants, including sexual objects, without getting lost in the toils and discontents of thought.[12]

With a different outlook, one might describe neurotics as people for whom life is insufficiently complicated; they over-simplify it by seeing new events within the stereotype of old ones; they find nothing new under the sun. The ideal of a mentally healthy person would then be someone able to differentiate his experience in every field; to see other people, for example, in terms of subtle changes in them so that they are never the *same* people. Such a person would make only minimal use of the categories and conventions which culture provides in order often to simplify life to the point of bareness.

We may make the comparison more concrete by another glance at Freud's picture of genital love. For him, "two on an island" was the ideal; he wrote in *Civilization and Its Discontents* that a pair of lovers needed no one else to complete their happiness but wished to withdraw their libido from the task of building civilization.[13] This is an adolescent moviegoer's dream of love, but not something which mature lovers actually seek: love rather leads them to widen and complicate their dealings with other people, with art, and with other civilized matters. In those cultures, whether 'civilized' or 'primitive,' where human relations are marked by subtlety of feeling, sexual love can become

11. Cf. his well-known remark that "revolutionary children are not desirable from any point of view." *A New Series of Introductory Lectures on Psycho-analysis*, 1933, p. 206. Hereafter this citation will be referred to as *Psychoanalysis*.

12. There is a similar note in Elton Mayo's critique, based on Janet, of "obsessive thinking" in modern industrial society. See, for example, Mayo, *The Human Problems of an Industrial Civilization*, 1933.

13. *Civilization and Its Discontents*, 1930, p. 80, hereafter cited as *Civilization.*

filled with overtones. Moreover, one may today observe, among the groups where Victorian morality has waned, that love can become even more complex and, if you please, more 'intellectual,' precisely because it lacks the artificial spur of taboos and inhibitions.[14] Contrary to what many think, romantic love does not depend on delayed gratification but on gratification and mutuality which occur on many levels of the love relationship. Indeed, as Simone de Beauvoir has so well observed in *Le Deuxième Sexe*, such love can grow only when women are emancipated, when they no longer, as in Freud's day, have "only the choice between unappeased desire, infidelity, or neurosis."[15]

For other elements in Freud's picture of the hero, one may turn to his two loving studies of Moses. In his essay on "The Moses of Michelangelo,"[16] Freud describes the hero admiringly—his great frame and impressive beard, his noble brow and piercing, inscrutable glance, his fiery anger and his equally powerful restraint. In *Moses and Monotheism*, Freud pays more attention to the hero's intellectual than to his physical qualities. The hero is shown to be a proud Egyptian nobleman, his monotheism the product of the kingly temper of Ikhnaton, which brooked no illusions and required no orgies of belief. This Egyptian Moses is undeterred by the resistance of the image-worshiping masses; he is unafraid of the fate of pioneers. This intransigence, so similar to his own, appeals to Freud. Likewise, as he indicates obliquely in his book on dreams, Freud admires "those powerful personalities who, by their sheer force of intellect and their fiery eloquence, ruled" the course of the

14. Cf. Freud's remark that "the view may also be accepted that the differentiation of individual character, now so much in evidence, only becomes possible with sexual restraint." *Papers* 2:91. It depends, of course, on what one means by "restraint."

15. *Papers* 2:93. Since writing the foregoing, I have been glad to find the searching article by Edith Weigert, "Existentialism and Its Relations to Psychotherapy," in *Psychiatry* (1949) 12:399–412, which takes much the same attitude as the text.

16. *Papers* 4:257.

French Revolution; and he also admired the eloquence and virility of Garibaldi.[17]

Views of this sort, largely implicit in Freud's pre-World War I writings, became of course much more explicit in his *Group Psychology and the Analysis of the Ego,* where he writes:

> . . . from the first there were two kinds of psychologies, that of the individual members of the group and that of the father, chief, or leader. The members of the group were subject to ties just as we see them to-day, but the father of the primal horde was free. His intellectual acts were strong and independent even in isolation, and his will needed no reinforcement from others. . . .
>
> He, at the very beginning of the history of mankind, was the *Superman* whom Nietzsche only expected from the future. Even to-day the members of a group stand in need of the illusion that they are equally and justly loved by their leader; but the leader himself need love no one else, he may be of a masterly nature, narcissistic, but self-confident and independent.[18]

Evidently, there is a solipsistic tendency in this Freudian hero. In his contempt, in the style of his idealism, in his egocentric insistence on having his way, he reminds one of certain Hollywood types, or of the Hero Roark in Ayn Rand's best-selling novel, *The Fountainhead,* which was later made into a movie. This hero is tall, dark, handsome, and young.[19] But it would be manifestly unfair to push the comparison with Hollywood too far. Freud's hero is no rich

17. *Interpretation,* pp. 461, 410–411.
18. *Group Psychology and the Analysis of the Ego,* 1922, pp. 92–93. It is interesting to note, in this connection, one of the charges that Freud brings against the United States; namely, that in this country "leading personalities fail to acquire the significance that should fall to them in the process of group-formation." *Civilization,* p. 93. In other words, America in Freud's eyes lacked dominating leaders, through identification with whom the masses could be bound to one another and to the system.
19. Several of Freud's dreams or dream-associations refer to his feeling of aging. *Interpretation,* p. 220 (his black beard turning color); p. 447 (growing grey); p. 446 (youth as a time of many loves).

playboy; his orientation is entirely toward reality, toward serious tasks in this world. He is in fact quite grown up; like Leonardo in his later years, he has attained "the resignation of the man who subjects himself to the *'Ανάγκη*, to the laws of nature, and expects no alleviation from the kindness or grace of God."[20] He has faced the fact that "dark, unfeeling and unloving powers determine human destiny," or, again, that "the world is not a nursery."[21] In other words, the hero is one who is able to live without illusions —but this includes an end to illusions about the self, an end to vain regrets, wasteful mourning,[22] feminine pity, and sentimentality.[23]

This stern reality-orientation of the hero includes the related element of steadiness and practicality in the pursuit of goals. Subject to "storming passions of the soul-stirring

20. *Leonardo*, p. 105.

21. *Psycho-analysis*, pp. 229, 230. Perhaps it should be added that, in Freud's view, the nursery becomes very like the world.

22. Freud again and again returned to the problem of mourning and sought to explain its "wastefulness" in terms of mental economics. See, for example, "Mourning and Melancholia," in *Papers* 4:152. It is typical of his outlook that he was baffled whenever men seemed to extend themselves, whether in grief, in love, or in work, without the pressure of apparently overwhelming need. With a different outlook, one would find a problem in an inability to mourn, as in affectlessness generally.

23. Finding that Leonardo was "kind and considerate" to his young male disciples, Freud regards this as a correlate of his homosexuality. (*Leonardo*, p. 77.) Freud also notes his "exaggerated sympathy for animals" (pp. 114, 36). He may, of course, be right with regard to Leonardo; my point is that he seems to accept, though not without qualification, conventional definitions of masculinity.

To be sure, Freud criticizes German Army leadership in the First World War as too harsh, resulting in a failure to create sufficient libidinal ties between officers and men, hence among the men *inter se;* but this seems really to be a critique not of harshness as such, but of unskillful manipulation of men. *Group Psychology and the Analysis of the Ego*, p. 44, n. 1.

and consuming kind"[24] though he may be, he is nonetheless able to hold his fire, even to sublimate if need be. While he seeks, by the exercise of his "manly creative power,"[25] to change the course of the world, he faces the delays and frustrations of his self-appointed task with stoicism. Freud admired the insouciance in the face of death of aristocrats in the French Revolution,[26] or indeed of any criminal who could go to the gallows with a laugh.[27]

But to enter Freud's Valhalla it is not enough to be brave; one must also succeed. Sexual achievement is, in fact, the sign of success as of maturity. Freud writes:

> A man who has shown determination in possessing himself of his love-object has our confidence in his success in regard to other aims as well. On the other hand, a man who abstains, for whatever reasons, from satisfying his strong sexual instinct, will also assume a conciliatory and resigned attitude in other paths of life, rather than a powerfully active one.[28]

Freud agrees with those critics of Leonardo, the homosexual, who object that the latter did not finish all the work he started; and he comments on Leonardo's "lack of ability to adjust himself to actual conditions."[29] And yet in writing about Leonardo, Freud states that he himself "succumbed to the attraction which emanated from this great and mysterious man, in whose being one seems to

24. A phrase Freud uses in explaining why the over-ratiocinative Leonardo missed those loves and hates that "others experience [as] the best part of their lives. . . ." *Leonardo,* p. 43.
25. Ibid., p. 115.
26. *Interpretation,* p. 461.
27. Cf. *Wit,* p. 798.
28. *Papers* 2:93–94. Freud goes on in the same passage to point out that since women are intimidated from sexual curiosity, they are likewise rendered submissive in other spheres of life: "the undoubted fact of the intellectual inferiority of so many women can be traced to that inhibition of thought necessitated by sexual suppression." Such observations on Freud's part must be taken as a counterpoise to what has been said earlier about the exclusively masculine qualities of the hero.
29. *Leonardo,* pp. 101, 116.

sense forceful and impelling passions, which nevertheless evince themselves in a remarkably subdued manner."[30] There are, moreover, other heroes of Freud who were in the long run unsuccessful; he admired Hannibal and Ikhnaton. Thus, plainly enough, the men whom Freud looked up to are not cast in a single stereotype. They must leave a mark on the world, but there are different types of marks which count.

Perhaps the most important evidence of this is Freud's lifelong reverence for "the immortal Goethe."[31] He writes that his decision to become a medical student came about through reading, at seventeen, Goethe's essay on Nature;[32] and quotations from Goethe, meant to illustrate the latter's psychological wisdom, are scattered throughout his writings. Moreover, with his own desire "to fathom with coldest reflection the deepest secret,"[33] he was preoccupied with the "secret" of Goethe's genius, as with that of Leonardo and of other artists. In "A Childhood Recollection from *'Dichtung und Warheit'*" Freud traced the early source of "that victorious feeling, that confidence in ultimate success, which not seldom brings actual success with it"[34]—that

30. Ibid., pp. 117–118. Cf. his reference to "the magic of his [Charcot's] aspect and his voice," in "Charcot," *Papers* 1:15.

31. See Freud's dream of Goethe, *Interpretation,* pp. 418–420, 352.

32. *An Autobiographical Study,* 1935, p. 14.

33. A phrase Freud quotes with reference to Leonardo. *Leonardo,* p. 39.

34. *Papers* 4:367. Freud, like many worshipers, failed to see the bitter tensions and surrenders in Goethe's life, which are dealt with in a fine, and to me convincing, essay by Ortega y Gasset, "In Search of Goethe from Within," reprinted in *Partisan Review* (1949) 16:1163–1188. Possibly, Freud was taken in by his envy of just those phases of Goethe's life that Ortega y Gasset finds suspect—his role as a courtier, his inability to commit himself to his art. Freud would not call this last an inability, but rather an ability to lead a well-rounded life. However, from this other point of view, Goethe's sunny freedom seems to be more apparent than real.

smiling destiny which Freud felt he himself perhaps lacked.

While Freud, not unlike Goethe, took for his subject matter all of human life and history, and many of the sciences, social and physical, while he wrote with the style of a novelist and ran the psychoanalytic movement with the style of a statesman, he continued to view himself as a restrained and plodding specialist. He speaks of "an inclination to concentrate my work exclusively upon a single subject or problem," and seems to accept, as I noted in a previous paper in commenting on his "Dream of the Botanical Monograph," the charge of being "one-sided."[35] In a way, this is quite fantastic: it is hard to think of anyone in the last seventy-five years who has roamed and rummaged so widely in so many different fields. Yet this modesty, whatever its source, saved Freud from supposing that when he had analyzed the "family romance"—that is the Oedipal constellation—of a great artist, he had also fathomed the latter's gift for writing romances. Artistic gift and artistic technique Freud felt to be beyond the reach of psychoanalytic scrutiny. Since he had no similar hesitation in explaining other great human attainments psychoanalytically, one may suppose that his deference to the artist shows by implication that he retained to the end of his life what he felt at seventeen: unquestioning admiration for talent and achievement, such as Goethe exemplified for him. Whatever one may say of the limitations of the qualities Freud sometimes admired, the fact is that, in spite of his growing pessimism, he continued to be able to admire.

A further and quite remarkable example of this ability appears in Freud's *Festschrift* essay, "My Contact with Josef Popper-Lynkeus." There Freud quotes a story of Popper's, published in 1899, which described a man so pure and

35. *An Autobiographical Study*, p. 17. One may perhaps speculate as to what claims to grandiose versatility may lie concealed behind this self-image—or what truth in the sense of Freud's recognition of his unremittingly rational and intellectualized rhythm of life; that he did not care for music, an art whose meanings are difficult to seize by means of intellect, may be of some relevance here. Cf. *Papers* 4:257.

whole in heart that his dreams lacked opacity. He adds:[36]

> And if Science informs us that such a man, wholly without evil and falseness and devoid of all repressions, does not exist and could not survive, yet we may guess that, so far as an approximation to this ideal is possible, it had found its realization in the person of Popper himself.

Here we find Freud admiring, though not without a characteristic touch of irony, a utopian reformer, a mere scribbler of impractical plans for social amelioration! At the close of the essay, Freud refers to the disappointments he had suffered when great men whom he had "honoured from a distance" turned out to be unsympathetic to psychoanalysis. With such experiences, it is surprising that Freud did not become more soured on those heroes, such as Popper, who were his contemporaries.[37]

FREUD'S ATTITUDE TOWARD HIS OWN QUALITIES

This brings us to inquire directly how far Freud himself, in his own eyes, measured up to his portrait of a hero. It is hard to say, but there are a few stray remarks which we may take as clues. Unlike Leonardo, he is not the son of a "great gentleman,"[38] and while in his dreams he compares his father to Garibaldi, or to the statesman Szell who

36. *Papers* 5:300–301. It is interesting to recall that Edward Bellamy once described in his story, "To Whom This May Come," a society in which people would know each other's inmost thoughts, hence have no need for guile. See Arthur E. Morgan's *Nowhere Was Somewhere;* Chapel Hill, Univ. of North Carolina Press, 1946; p. 142. Cf. the pungent observations of Harry Stack Sullivan concerning an anthropological report about an isolated Malay tribe whose members engage in mutual dream interpretation. "The Study of Psychiatry," *Psychiatry* (1949) 12:326.

37. Cf., for example, Freud's warm tribute to Romain Rolland, in "A Disturbance of Memory on the Acropolis," in *Papers* 5:302.

38. *Leonardo,* p. 100. In fact, Freud notes that his very name—"*Freude*" means "joy" in German—is the butt of jokes. *Interpretation,* p. 268.

leads the unruly Magyars,[39] his father seems to have been a somewhat small-minded and unsuccessful man who could not imagine great things for his son.[40] Freud's boyhood and youth, moreover, were anything but glamorous. Instead of killing insolent Egyptians, he was a "good boy" at the *Gymnasium;* later, in Brücke's laboratory, he was afraid of arousing the master's ire by being unpunctual.[41] In contrast with those of his heroes who were courtiers or leaders of great armies, Freud spent what he terms "this unfruitful and actually somewhat humiliating period of my student days" at the Chemical Institute.[42] Compelled to wait five years before he could afford to marry,[43] he settled down with a prudent *Hausfrau,* remaining, he implies, sexually "above reproach."[44] In his daily life, he trained himself to wear a mask of politeness.[45] Nor was his routine varied by wild drinking bouts or Dionysian orgies. Freud was plagued, as I have already noted, by aging; and also by the Job-like but quite unheroic afflictions of boils, swellings in the nose, rheumatism,[46] and finally cancer. He bore these painful afflictions, as he bore the approach of death, with an extraordinary stoicism, but one feels that he was far from thinking himself a hero on this account.

Despite his family's poverty, Freud appears, moreover, to have been a sheltered lad, educated among the profes-

39. *Interpretation,* pp. 410–411. In another dream (p. 418) he makes his father "a professor and a privy councillor."

40. Cf. Freud's discussion of his feeling of guilt for having outdistanced his father, in "A Disturbance of Memory on the Acropolis," *Papers* 5:311–312.

Even as a student at the University, Freud felt that, as a Jew, he could look no higher than for "some nook or cranny in the framework of humanity" from which to make a contribution. *An Autobiographical Study,* p. 14.

41. *Interpretation,* p. 407 (see also p. 450): "What overwhelmed me was the terrible gaze of his [Brücke's] blue eyes, before which I melted away. . . ."

42. Ibid., p. 445.
43. Ibid., p. 418.
44. Cf. ibid., p. 221.
45. Ibid., p. 223.
46. Ibid., pp. 199, 201, 220, 284.

sional and business classes. And this diligent student, though he went through medical school, seems to have been astonished at his later realization of the prevalence of sex and sadism. For it is with a certain recollected innocence that he tells us of his surprise that other highly esteemed doctors—Breuer, Charcot, Chrobak—knew about the sexual etiology of neurosis all along;[47] they took for granted what for Freud was a discovery—one that landed him, as it were by default, into greatness and controversy. In one respect, however, these discoveries did not disillusion Freud. For he seems never to have shed the illusion, perhaps typically middle class, that there *are* people who experience the wildest sensuality, or who abandon themselves in orgies of destruction. In *Civilization and Its Discontents* there are passages about intense pleasures of this sort which culture has forced us to surrender.[48] Such passages remind me of the newspaper advertisements several years ago for the movie "Anna and the King of Siam": "A strange, barbaric world of unendurable pleasures . . . infinitely prolonged." This is language to arouse excitement, to suggest experiences from which we, a humdrum people in a workaday world, are inevitably cut off and can only share by sublimation. If such pleasures are to be won by the adventuring hero, Freud was in his own eyes no hero.

Yet such romanticism about sexual conquest is of course only one aspect of Freud's complicated view of things. Though there was no pleasure to compare with sexual excitement, Freud convinced himself that even this delight was fundamentally unsatisfying in the long run: it had to contend not only with obstacles in the external world but with the fact that in the civilizing process, sexual energy itself seemed, in Freud's view, to be diminishing. And true lasting greatness, Freud believed, was generally paid for by libidinal sacrifice. Indeed, the tragedy implicit in this outlook runs through his last long philosophic essay, *Civilization and Its Discontents,* in which he argues that since

47. "The History of the Psychoanalytic Movement," in *The Basic Writings of Sigmund Freud,* Modern Library, 1938, pp. 937–938; also in *Papers* 1:294–296.
48. *Civilization,* p. 80.

men can only be happy in a state of idleness and sexual gratification, no conceivable culture can meet their requirements: both biology and culture forbid. The reader is led to conclude that the earth is a trap, for it tempts men to have wishes which it cannot satisfy, and the adult's only realistic course is that of Odysseus: to stop the ears of others and tie oneself firmly to the mast of sublimation, until in old age and finally in death the wishes lose their power to torment.

Work, then, and especially science and art are surer bets than sex. But how did Freud regard himself in his chosen field of scientific work? One of his dream associations is quite poignant evidence of his unsatisfied wishes to be uncontroversially great and famous. He imagines himself going anonymously to be treated for glaucoma by a doctor in Berlin; the doctor applies cocaine which makes the operation possible; and Freud takes pleasure in the secret knowledge of his share in discovery of the drug.[49] Thus Freud in this fantasy plays the role of a prince of science in disguise. Since he came close to being in fact the discoverer of cocaine's anaesthetic uses and never forgave himself for missing the opportunity, the fantasy, with its image of eye illness, is obviously touched with self-pity. Today, many people learn of the discovery of cocaine only through Freud!

One may find similar notes of self-pity based on a quite

49. *Interpretation*, p. 241. While Freud would himself tend to assume that, once we have found the wish that was motive to a dream we must take it at face value, I would prefer to argue that the dream- or day-wish may be of much less weight in the total personality than explicit conscious considerations. Dreams may represent the husks, rather than the vital centers, of one's contemporary life, and it is far from decisive proof of childish ambition that one has a dream or daydream, perhaps in a mood of depression, such as Freud here reports and interprets. Today, indeed, dream-interpretation often permits people to discount themselves unduly and to take a passing thought, whether libidinal or aggressive, as better evidence of their "true" selves than a lifelong commitment.

understandable feeling of isolation in Freud's long essay "On the History of the Psychoanalytic Movement."[50] Freud speaks there of those "lonely years" when he alone *was* the Movement—when he thought "science would ignore me entirely during my lifetime," though he believed that at a much later time his discoveries would be found and honored. While on the one hand he regards those years as "a glorious 'heroic era,'" on the other hand he seems to have been unduly impressed by his invitation to accept an honorary degree and to deliver lectures at Clark University, in Worcester. In his *Autobiographical Study,* he writes:[51]

> As I stepped on to the platform at Worcester to deliver my *Five Lectures upon Psycho-Analysis* it seemed like the realization of some incredible day-dream: psycho-analysis was no longer a product of delusion, it had become a valuable part of reality.

Even as of 1909 this seems slightly excessive, as does Freud's overgratefulness for the Goethe prize bestowed on him by the City of Frankfort—"the climax of my life as a citizen."[52] When disciples came, he accepted them, by his own later avowals, somewhat uncritically, and he worked with them to give to the minuscule "psychoanalytic movement" those congresses, journals, reports from abroad which one might expect from a world-wide organization of many thousands.

How is one to explain this disparity between Freud's altogether extraordinary achievements, which in the main he evaluated justly, and these scarcely heroic concerns? I think that here again one is confronted with the problem of Freud's ambivalence toward authority. To the extent that Freud irrationally admired the powerful and illustrious of his day and had not completely freed himself from his

50. *Basic Writings of Sigmund Freud,* p. 943; *Papers* 1:304–305.
51. *An Autobiographical Study,* p. 95.
52. Ibid., p. 135.

"innocent faith in authority"[53] it was almost impossible for him to avoid viewing himself and his work through their eyes, even or perhaps especially where that judgment was a negative one. Thus, though Freud's own method gave him an exceptional weapon for understanding the hostility and irrationality with which he was surrounded, a weapon which, ironically, distracted him from seeing in equally full light the friends who flocked to him, he nevertheless seems to have felt to some slight extent: *After all, my enemies are right; I am, like so many other Jews, a disturber of the peace and it is only right if I am badly treated.* He was anything but the rebel who likes to *épater les bourgeois* and who consciously feels worried only if he has the admiration of conventional circles. In spite of himself, Freud could not help his preoccupation with questions of rank within the institutions of solid-seeming Vienna[54] and, beyond Vienna, solid-seeming 'official' German science and chauvinistically hostile but culturally reputed Parisian science.

Elsewhere, I have briefly discussed the problem of the "nerve of failure," by which I mean the ability of a lonely thinker, or other minority-figure, to remain unimpressed by the judgments passed on his views, his personality, his system of values by the dominant authorities of his day.[55] Some thinkers defend themselves by a kind of paranoia, as Fourier did; others minimize their deviations, as for a time Robert Owen did; still others, such as Marx or Rilke, take refuge in understandable but hardly amiable dependency on a few loyal patrons. Very few men seem to have been able to rest secure in the knowledge of their qualities and conviction of their achievement without some support from authoritative contemporaries. Freud possessed the nerve of failure in great measure. To sustain himself, he depended on his reason, on his ability to trust his own experience—

53. Ibid., p. 27.
54. Cf. his dream of the memorial at the University, *Interpretation*, pp. 407–408.
55. "The Ethics of We Happy Few," "A Philosophy for 'Minority' Living," "Some Observations on Community Plans and Utopia." All are found in previous chapters.

even after this ability was temporarily shaken by the dramatic disproof of the stories of seduction his early patients had told him and he had believed.[56] He thought, not that he was crazy nor that the authorities were, but that he was a laborious worker and discoverer, while they were bigoted, frivolous, and hypocritical. Freud wrote in 1921 that "he who knows how to wait need make no concessions";[57] such a man may also, with good friends and good luck, avoid the fate of a Semmelweiss.

Furthermore, Freud was able to discover in his own case how the oppression of the child by the authority of the father, or other parental figure, can be prolonged in the obeisance of the adult toward father-surrogates. He recognized, in connection with the memory on the Acropolis, his unconscious feeling that to become unequivocally great would amount to an act of impiety toward his own father.[58] Freud therefore had to laugh at himself when, in interpreting a dream, he found that he compared himself with Hercules, with a superman.[59] Even at the age of 40, with distinguished contributions to neurology and related sciences behind him, and well started on his unique psychoanalytic enterprise, he dared not think he had grown so big.

Nevertheless despite the great distances which Freud felt separated him from his heroes, it is clear that he never surrendered his quite justified hope that he would be as great as they. This may be one factor overdetermining the devotion of his last major work to the story of Moses. As Freud pictured him, Moses found his "clients" among the weak and alien tribe of Jews, as Freud found his among the neurotics who were treated as hereditary pariahs by the medical profession of his day. Moses, in Freud's view,

56. *An Autobiographical Study*, pp. 60–62; also "My Views on the Part Played by Sexuality in the Aetiology of the Neuroses," *Papers* 1:275–281.

57. *Group Psychology and the Analysis of the Ego*, p. 40.

58. *Papers* 5:302.

59. *Interpretation*, pp. 440–41.

sponsored an ego-deflating system—a tight, logical monotheism which made no concessions to human frailty by the route of superstition or animism; here again the parallel to Freud's own contribution seems clear. Moses, according to Freud's account, was reviled and eventually killed by those whose illusions and indulgences he attacked; Freud, as we have seen, was intensely and continuously conscious of an ever-widening area of hostility—from the infuriated psychiatrists of Vienna, to the wider reading and writing public,[60] and finally even including the Austrian Church, the Nazis, and other bitter enemies of his science, his outlook, and his Jewishness. And while, in Freud's view, the killing of Moses by the Jews only fastened them eventually more fully to his teachings of grim renunciation, so Freud hoped for the eventual victory of the persecuted wisdom of science and truth, including psychoanalytic truth.[61] To the end, so far as his writings show, Freud was not for any length of time impressed by the seeming strength of his opponents; he did not come to think that his own soft voice would be *spurlos versenkt.*

At no point, indeed, was Freud's consciousness of his enemies that of a timorous man; perhaps it was rather that of an ambitious one. It was precisely the most exposed and criticized positions in his theory to which Freud ardently held. He refused, as he says again and again, to play down the role of sex, either in the life of children or of adults, whatever might be gained by the concession; and, after the "defections" of Jung and Adler, he felt even more committed to holding the fort. In his book on dreams, he wrote: "An intimate friend and a hated enemy have always been indispensable to my emotional life; I have always been

60. For early references, see, for example, ibid., pp. 420, 429; for later ones, for example, *Psycho-analysis*, pp. 186–191. Note also the form of his book, *The Question of Lay Analysis*, 1950: the discussion proceeds, as so often in Freud's writing, by an argument with an untutored critic and, with other evidence, makes me think that Freud constantly internalized the voices of his foes.

61. Cf. *The Future of an Illusion*, 1928, p. 93, quoted below, p. 292.

able to create them anew. . . ."[62] In the same book he declared that it was decades since he had had any anxiety dreams,[63] and in all probability this did not change with the further passage of years.

Freud had the courage to pursue his way in the face of common opinion and of the in some ways more substantial obstacle of congealed scientific opinion paraded as common sense. He learned, despite his university training, to pay more attention to what was said by an hysterical woman patient than to what was said in books and lectures by professors of psychiatry. At the same time, he rejected neither the vested institutions nor the impalpable traditions of science; though he felt compelled in self-defense to found his own movement, he hoped eventually to rejoin the mainstream of scientific thought and communication. If one judges the heroes of mankind not in terms of the power they wielded over masses of men but in terms of their contribution to the control of nature, including human nature, and to the enrichment of the human spirit; if one adds consideration of the courage, the nerve of failure, needed to achieve that contribution in the face of obstacles, then surely Freud deserves to be regarded as one of the great intellectual heroes of all time. It is not the least of his triumphs that he was willing and able to go on to the very end of his long life reopening questions and laying himself open to criticism by writing; perhaps his failure fully to see and foresee his laurels was in part a way to avoid any resting on them.

WEAKNESS AND NEUROSIS

In sketching Freud's portrait of a hero, I have already very largely indicated his portrait of the weakling; it remains only to review several cumulative themes. The weakling, as Freud depicts him, comes of "poor stock"; he possesses a

62. *Interpretation,* p. 451.

63. Ibid., p. 522. He worried (see p. 420) about the future his own children would meet as Jews, but not about the hostility he himself encountered.

quantitatively small libido and has other constitutional inadequacies.[64] This hereditary taint is magnified by a poor educational environment. The weakling is apt to be overgratified as a child: Freud traced one type of homosexuality in part to a boy's having "too much love" from the mother.[65] To at least some degree, he seems to have believed that only a rigorous training would produce a manly sexuality. And indeed one can agree that there is something to this view if the love of the mother is actually the smothering pseudo-love of overprotection, which neither gives the child a basic sunniness and security nor gives him the chance to free himself by fighting a patently oppressive parental authority.

At any rate, Freud felt that the combination of poor heredity with poor training or supervision in childhood expressed itself in adult sexual inadequacies which might take form either as neurosis (repression of libido from heterosexual object-choice) or perversion (wrong object for libido). In either case there is a failure to surmount the Oedipus complex, to break with the father and at the same time to identify with his masculine role, and this may show up in a Hamlet-like wavering as in a Leonardian overreflectiveness. This attitude of considering the unaggressive as weak appears with special clarity in Freud's famous letter to Einstein. There he writes:

> Why do you and I and so many other people rebel so violently against war? Why do we not accept it as another of the many painful calamities of life? After all, it seems

64. It is evident that, behind the argument over "constitutional" factors in neurosis, lurk many social struggles, just as most eugenic considerations hide class or ethnic bias; today a similar argument rages over William Sheldon's studies of delinquency but, thanks partly to Freud, the weight of scientific opinion has shifted and "hereditary factors" are viewed with great (perhaps excessive) skepticism.

65. *Leonardo*, p. 73. Freud also believed, at least in his early practice, that strict watch should be kept over children to prevent "excessive" masturbation, as well of course as sexual assaults by relatives, nurses, and tutors. But cf. footnote 29.

> quite a natural thing, no doubt it has a good biological basis and in practice it is scarcely avoidable.[66]

He adds that the pacifists' attitude "is not merely an intellectual and emotional repudiation; we pacifists have a constitutional intolerance of war, an idiosyncrasy. . . ."[67] And while he ends on the note of hope that the rest of mankind, with the growth of culture, may become equally organically intolerant of war, the whole essay assumes that it is pacifists who need to be "understood," while warlike people can, on the basis of the death instinct, be taken for granted. We may compare with this Freud's essay on "The Taboo of Virginity,"[68] in which he seeks to explain on grounds of fear, and not at all on other possible grounds (such as culturally organized sympathy), those customs which in some tribes have a maiden deflowered before marriage by an instrument—again the point at issue is not the facts of preliterate psychology but the trend of Freud's mind.

Yet there is more to Freud's view of the matter than a mere criticism of "over-refinement" and a readier understanding for those who take easily to blood and thunder. As one can see by studying his essay on "'Civilized' Sexual Morality and Modern Nervousness," written in 1908, he was preoccupied with the loss of individual enjoyment as well as racial vitality that he felt accompanied Victorian sexual repressions. In this same essay he suggested that neurotics are those who only partially succumb to such repression:[69]

> Neurotics are that class of people, naturally rebellious, with whom the pressure of cultural demands succeeds only in an apparent suppression of their instincts, one which becomes ever less and less effective.

The neurotics, in this view, were those who had too much

66. "Why War?" in *Papers* 5:285; see also "Thoughts for the Times on War and Death," in *Papers* 4:288.
67. Ibid., 5:287.
68. Ibid., 4:217.
69. Ibid., 2:76, 86. Cf. the development of the point by Erich Fromm, *Man For Himself*, pp. 22–23, 36–37.

libido to permit them to surrender completely to the cultural ideals of sexual restriction, and too little fortitude to resist the hypocritical social norms imposed on them by the beguiling authority, first of the father and later on of society at large. It is, therefore, not only out of weakness of will but out of strength of libido that the neurotic falls ill. It seems that Freud does not maintain a wholly consistent position regarding the source of the neurotic's inability to attain heterosexual success.

Later experience led Freud to considerable skepticism as to the ability of such people to overcome their dependence; instead, he saw that in the analytic situation they often only renewed it in a new form.[70] However, despite his awareness of the contrast between the neurotic's irresolution and stubbornness in remaining ill, and the mastery of self and others which he admired in his heroes, Freud never for a moment doubted that neurotics suffer, that they are oppressed, that society bears on them much more harshly than it does either on the elite who succeeded discreetly in getting their way or on the mass of men who have very little to get. In other words, Freud, in his daily work, took the neurotic with complete seriousness, and one must set this consistent behavior over against the passages in his writings where he glorifies the strong and ruthless male.

Indeed, I think that one of Freud's greatest contributions, though it is one he took more or less for granted, lay in his willingness to spend years if necessary with patients who were neither fatally ill nor important people,[71] without, moreover, any great confidence on his part that they would inevitably get well. To be sure, he declared that "a certain measure of natural intelligence and ethical development may be required of him [that is, the person amenable to psychoanalytic therapy]; with worthless persons the physician soon loses the interest which makes it possible for

70. See "Analysis Terminable and Interminable," in *Papers* 5:317 *et seq.*
71. Erich Fromm takes a very similar position in *Psychoanalysis and Religion,* p. 98.

him to enter profoundly into the mental life of the patient."[72] Nevertheless, without a great deal of willingness to "enter profoundly into the mental life" of people who were very far from his image of the hero, he could easily have gotten rid of his "interminable" patients, as other doctors did. Today, it is just this luxury aspect of psychoanalysis—its prolonged concern with individuals as such, and for their own sake—that is sometimes under attack. Popularly, analysis is often regarded as occupational therapy for wealthy women; hostility to the neurotic is easily disguised by charging him with the crime of being middle-class, or the double crime of being middle-class and a woman.

Unquestionably, efforts to hasten analysis, and to broaden its scope beyond the middle class and beyond the well-to-do, are desirable, but I cannot conquer the suspicion that some psychiatrists—not to speak, of course, of medical men who are not psychiatrists—share to a degree the popular impatience, sometimes dimly veiled by fascination, with the seemingly endless talkfest of individual analysis. Among the many motives which impel the physician to resort to shock therapies (and the community to consent to this), a lack of Freud's generous concern with the well-being of a single all-too-human person may perhaps be one. Indeed, one cannot read Freud's article, "Sexuality in the Aetiology of the Neuroses,"[73] written in 1898, as well as other writings of this early period, without seeing how passionately Freud protested against injustice in the treatment of neurotics, and the medical hypocrisy which veiled that

72. "Freud's Psycho-Analytic Method," *Papers* 1:270–271. Since Freud's day, a number of his followers have been trying to widen the bounds of what they find "interesting" and endurable in patients. See, for example, Frieda Fromm-Reichmann, "Notes on the Personal and Professional Requirements of a Psychotherapist," *Psychiatry* (1949) 12:361, and the insistence of O. Spurgeon English that manic-depressives are not as insensitive as they seem and can be reached by therapy, "Observation of Trends in Manic-Depressive Psychosis," *Psychiatry* (1949) 12:125.

73. *Papers* 1:220.

injustice; he adds that "the layman is deeply convinced inwardly of the unnecessariness, so to speak, of all these psychoneuroses, and therefore regards the course of the disease with little patience. . . ."[74] Nearly forty years later, in one of his last papers, he recurs to a similar theme; he begins "Analysis Terminable and Interminable," published in 1937, with these remarks:

> Experience has taught us that psycho-analytic therapy—the liberation of a human being from his neurotic symptoms, inhibitions and abnormalities of character—is a lengthy business. Hence, from the very beginning, attempts have been made to shorten the course of analysis. Such endeavours required no justification: they could claim to be prompted by the strongest considerations alike of reason and expediency. But there probably lurked in them some trace of the impatient contempt with which the medical profession of an earlier day regarded the neuroses, seeing in them the unnecessary results of invisible lesions. If it had now become necessary to deal with them, they should at least be got rid of with the utmost dispatch.[75]

This outlook made Freud a "rate-buster" among his medical colleagues—a person, that is, who violated "production norms" as to how much sympathy and time were to be given to patients; and it seems not unlikely that hostility based on this ground may sometimes have been rationalized as based on the *content*, especially the sexual content, of Freud's discoveries.

Conversely, one should expect that Freud himself, with his ambivalence toward authority, would be to some degree affected by such medical attitudes. Just possibly, his tough, 'masculine' talk might therefore be considered, among other things, as a defense mechanism against so 'unmanly' a drain on his sympathy for the weak and oppressed as, on one level, he may have felt his therapeutic work to be—a drain he could not, however, avoid as his experience with free association and transference problems developed. In this interpretation, I suggest that he may have been

74. Ibid., 1:247.
75. Ibid., 5:316.

frightened by the dangers for him of what he regarded as sentimentality, of identifying too closely with his patients. He justified his conduct to himself and others by stressing his preoccupation with research—research which, by his bad luck, had to be done with patients.[76] But that he was haunted by the problem appears in his discussions of the analyst's role, in which he concluded that complete neutrality and impassivity of behavior in the transference situation were not always tolerable.[77]

A number of those analysts who belong to what one might term the third generation from Freud are, perhaps especially in America, not much interested in his ethical concerns and 'metaphysical' explorations. For example, they dismiss the death instinct as a late aberration and do not inquire into the latent tragic import behind its manifestly dubious biology. They strenuously avoid 'jargon' or any other eccentricity and try to become indistinguishable from the other hard-boiled medicos from whose ranks they have sprung. By insisting on medical training, they tend to eliminate at the outset some of the more sensitive spirits who might seek careers in analysis. The *American Imago* struggles on largely supported by some of the old-timers; many of this new generation prefer to report clinical findings. This tendency among some analysts is part of the process of 'normalizing' Freud which I have referred to earlier. Such a development is perhaps inevitable when

76. Cf. also the following remarks from *The Question of Lay Analysis:* "Not every neurotic whom we treat may be worth the trouble of analysis, but there are many valuable personalities amongst them. The goal of our achievement must be to secure that as few human beings as possible are left to confront civilized life with such defective psychical equipment; and to that end we must collect much material, and learn to understand much. Every analysis is instructive and can be made to yield fresh elucidation, quite apart from the personal worth of the individual patient." P. 78.

77. See, for example, "Observations on Transference-Love," in *Papers* 2:377; and cf. "Recommendations for Physicians on the Psycho-analytic Method of Treatment," in *Papers* 2:327, 331.

what has begun as a sect becomes an institution with a more approved and lucrative cultural niche.

But such analysts make a mistake if they suppose that they can avoid the metaphysical issues Freud raised by a matter-of-fact focus on therapy and clinical research. The words they use, to describe to their patients or to each other what is going on in the patients, are inevitably loaded with cultural meanings and ethical judgments. No matter how they may duck the issue of the goals of therapy, their own ideals of heroism, their own views of what is weakness, will affect whom they accept or seek out as patients, what they say to them, and the tacit models they themselves are for their patients. Since they want to be just like other doctors, they try to push all problems of ethical responsibility under the tent of 'professional [that is, medical] ethics,' an ethics which less friendly critics of the profession might see as principally a code of trade secret and trade association tactics.[78] In his writings on lay—that is, nonmedical—analysis, Freud showed himself fully aware of the dangers of medical incorporation and regularization of his work. As I have tried to show in this paper, he very much wanted official recognition—but not at the price of emasculation.

78. However, the therapeutic duty of the doctor was a strong support to Freud in his early days when he was attacked in medical circles for prying into sexual matters. See, for example, *Papers* 1:220, 221–224.

Freud, Religion, and Science

I want to begin by saying a few words about the social setting in which such a series topic as ours—Attack and Counter-attack in Religion—occurs. Then I want to say something about the use made of Freud in the religious counter-attack before turning more explicitly to Freud's own views. Finally, I shall touch on possible rapprochements between certain tendencies in religion and certain tendencies in psychoanalysis.

I. We may take it as a principle of social observation that, when we find the words "attack" (or "counter-attack"), we must always ask, who is really hitting whom? If we listen to the rhetoric of Southern whites, they talk as if the Negroes, and Northern "do-gooders," were hitting *them*. The Nazis gave it out that the Jews were the attackers. Any child learns to say, "He hit me," to justify an attack. Obviously, we cannot accept at face value the clamor of many religious organizations that they are under attack from psychoanalysis, Marxism, secularism, and so on: we must examine the power relations actually involved. It may be that the very rhetoric of being attacked used by these groups is a sign of their crescence and of the weakening of the allegedly attacking groups.

In *Patterns of Culture*, written in 1934, Ruth Benedict

"Freud, Religion, and Science" was first delivered as a lecture to the Channing Club of the University of Chicago, January 9, 1950. It was later (as "Freud: Religion as Neurosis") reprinted in part in the University of Chicago Roundtable on Psychoanalysis and Ethics, *No. 638, June 18, 1950, and in* The American Scholar, *Vol. 20, No. 3, 1951. It was later reprinted in full in* The Chicago Review, *Vol. 8, No. 1, 1954.*

discussed the problem of criticism of contemporary American institutions and how such criticism might be advanced and enlightened by anthropological and comparative studies. We have accustomed ourselves, she observed, to shedding our ethnocentrism when it comes to religion; nobody gets into trouble because he attacks religion; we have not done that, however, with respect to our economic institutions, with respect to capitalism. Here we have remained ethnocentric, and an attack may be dangerous.

Now I wonder if you will agree with me that, fifteen years after this book appeared, the situation is very nearly reversed. The massed social pieties which ranked themselves behind the economic order in the pre-Roosevelt era now seem to rank themselves behind religion and nation. The economic order is today nothing one has to be particularly pious about—unless one is a Communist and then, indeed, religion and nationalism are both involved. But one has to be (and, more important, feels one ought to be) considerably more careful about the religious order. To give an interesting example which comes to mind, the magazine *Commentary,* published by a secular and on the whole conservative group, the American Jewish Committee, has contained many profound critiques of capitalism, articles for instance by John Dewey and Karl Polanyi. These caused no trouble for anybody. But when the gifted novelist Isaac Rosenfeld wrote an article suggesting a psychoanalytic interpretation of Jewish dietary laws, noting a possibly sexual undertone in separating meat from milk, a violent storm broke out upon him and the magazine and it became necessary for the editors to print a disclaimer and apologia.

The movies, with their extraordinary sensitivity to pressure, provide another illustration. In the twenties or thirties there was a Lillian Gish picture in which a minister seduced a young girl who was his ward. I doubt if such a movie would be made, or could be made, today. Religion, much more than free enterprise, is sacred in the movies—many films are devoted to sentimental glorification of churchly figures—and in popular culture generally. Even capitalists enjoy going to plays and reading books which either make fun of business or, as in *Death of a Salesman,* make tragedy of it; and, so far as I know, no one has criticized the play, *The Madwoman of Chaillot*, for the silliness, let alone the offensiveness, of its handling of the bourgeois class.

If we wanted to give a psychoanalytic interpretation, we might think of the image of the rebellious son who carries out a partial, not wholly successful, rebellion against his father. Because of his ambivalence and partial failure, the son feels guilty; because of his partial success, the father gives in; and there is a reconciliation on a new level. Similarly, the revolt against the Hoover economic order (or, more accurately, the radical change in economic conditions) carried out since 1934 has been partly successful—too successful to allow the "father" to hope more than nostalgically for the restoration of "free enterprise." But father and son have come to terms on religion and nation, and the continuing and perhaps even increasing social anxieties and rigidities, displaced from economics, have found a new, "spiritual" fold. This shift permits religious organizations today, which in some ways are much stronger than in the thirties, to feel themselves aggrieved by any scientific and intellectual tendency which is at all outspokenly irreligious. Such a tendency can then be attacked as an "attack on religion," without violating the code of fair play.[1] We can

1. When I expressed this tentative view of the shift in power positions between "science" on the one side and "religion" on the other, in the course of my lecture, many in the audience questioned my interpretation. Some pointed to Blanshard's *American Freedom and Catholic Power* as evidence that the older Mencken attitude toward organized religion is still strong. A more important argument, in my opinion, was raised by those who contended that the *lack* of strong scientific attacks on religion today was caused, not by the strength of religion and the weakness of the scientific temper, but by its opposite: religion is no longer an issue which the young, emancipated by science, find worth arguing about. And to be sure, scientists now go their way with less worry than ever before about those theological issues which developed in the great battles between science and organized religion from the sixteenth to the beginning of the twentieth century; the turmoil in which such a man as the biologist Gosse was caught by Darwinism is today hardly conceivable. But one reason for this "peace

recall that when the psychiatrist Brock Chisholm stated in a lecture to the Washington School of Psychiatry that the myth of Santa Claus was a swindle on children, the Canadian cabinet was forced to meet, and he very nearly lost his job as health minister.

I may be mistaken—and certainly there are countertendencies which indicate the weakening of organized religion. But assuming that I am right, how are we to explain this alteration in the climate of discussion concerning religion? Obviously, in this article I can touch on only a few of the many factors involved. One factor is the increasingly sympathetic attitude toward religion taken among avant-garde groups. Intellectual anti-clericalism, like anti-clericalism in the labor movement, is out of fashion; and it is not surprising that psychoanalysts—even those "orthodox" in other respects—seem to have fallen in with the general trend, and either stick to their clinical work or claim religion as an ally.

To be sure, the avant-garde has little social power and less political influence. Nevertheless, its loss of the barbed and merrily agnostic elan of a Mencken, a Veblen, a Haldeman-Julius is not without effect, especially among those who are or want to be young. The avant-garde had power enough during the twenties to put religion on the defensive among those upper-class and upper-middle-class Catholics and other communicants who wanted to feel socially and intellectually accepted and up-to-date. Such people did not want to appear backwoodsy and bigoted. Today, however, it is backwoodsy to be anti-religious, and in fact I find among my students that only, on the whole, small-town, especially Southern, boys will go whole hog with Freud's view of religion. The revival of interest in religion (if not in church-going) among intellectuals means that many in the upper social strata who are affili-

of Westphalia" is that religionists are at last resigned to leaving natural science alone—it is only philosophers, humanists, and psychologists who, dealing with man, face even the possibility of jurisdictional dispute with organized religion.

ated with organized religion need no longer flinch in pressing the claims of religion and in attacking its few remaining outspoken foes. They can now accept without embarassment the anti-scientific position of the devout of lesser social standing.

This alliance of the classes in defense of religion is facilitated by a development much more important in its bearing on our topic than the altered mood of the avant-garde—namely, the rise in the social position of American Catholics in the last several decades. Everett C. Hughes, a very thoughtful and sympathetic student of church institutions and especially of Catholicism, has pointed out that one of the greatest sources of anxieties among middle-class Catholics is the problem of the relation between their church affiliation and their social mobility. Because they are mobile, these Catholics have looked for the definition of "good American" in the past largely to non-Catholics: to high-status Protestants, to Jewish intellectuals and mass-media opinion leaders, and (to a degree) even to the "leakage," as those are called who seep away from the Church. But as Catholics have increasingly moved into the managerial and professional classes, they have been able greatly to influence the definition of "good American," and have taken the lead, since they were among the "earliest arrivals" in the crusade against Communism, in defining the "bad un-American" as well. At the same time, non-Catholic opinion leaders, for the reasons given earlier, do not define the middle- and upper-class style of life in such a way as to exclude good Catholics—save, perhaps, for the still differentiating and hence exceedingly anxiety-provoking issue of birth control.

Yet, while the Catholics have risen substantially, they have not yet gained full social security on the American scene—and the same, of course, is true of the Jews, whose "religious" revival deserves a chapter to itself. Consequently, they are not yet able to laugh off such criticisms of religion as, despite religious censorship of the mass media, continue to crop up. It is unlikely that, fifteen years ago, a high Catholic churchman would have dared to attack an Eleanor Roosevelt after the recent fashion of

Cardinal Spellman; it is unlikely that, fifteen years hence, a high churchman will find such a polemic fitting and needful.

So far, I have stressed the tendencies to censor science and intellectual discourse that are implicit in the new "united front" of religionists and intellectuals. But in this same development there are liberating aspects. The seriousness with which religion is now taken has made an interest in it respectable among many scientists who would earlier have considered an irreligious attitude—a village atheist's outlook—an essential mark of emancipation. While William James was considered by many of his professional colleagues to be a kind of nut for concerning himself with religious experience, especially of a mystical and sectarian sort, no such scorn would greet a similar student, for instance Gordon Allport, today. Nor do I think we should bemoan the passing of the village atheist, with his easy monotone of a debunking approach to questions of faith and morals.

II. It is important to realize, in the light of this changing political and social context, that Freud, when he wrote on religion, seems generally to have thought of himself as the attacked, not the attacker. In *The Future of an Illusion,* written in 1928, he showed his sensitivity to the charge that he was robbing people of their faith. He pointed out that *he* had no such faith in his own arguments: people, he said, were capable of great "resistance" to unacceptable thoughts; their emotional bonds had shown enormous tenacity which even the great Voltaire, let alone Freud, could not shake. Hence, Freud argued, he and his movement were the only ones likely to suffer from an attack on religion. Likewise, when he wrote *Moses and Monotheism* ten years later, he for a while did not dare publish the last chapters—though these raised no new points against or about religion—because he thought it would give the Austrian Church an excuse for closing down the psychoanalytic movement in Nazi-threatened Vienna. Beyond that, Freud felt that whenever it was attempted to put bounds on the inquiries of science—to confine it, for example, to the "material" universe—this actually constituted an attack on science's right to deal with everything. No matter how small the enclave which, like some Vatican City, was preserved against the inquiries of science, Freud felt a real challenge to the total claim and method of empirical investigation.

Now it is ironical that, in the continuing campaign of organized religious thought against organized scientific thought, Freud is today frequently thrown into the fray on the side of the campaigners. It is worth devoting some attention to this paradox, because it will help both to illuminate Freud and the kind of orthodoxy which currently makes use of him. We may consider four themes: the allegation that Freud has dethroned reason and crowned irrationality and mystique; the emphasis on anxiety in Freud's writings; his pessimism about man's fate; and his concept of original sin.

In thinking about these uses of Freud, I was reminded of the figure of Squire Gaylord in William Dean Howells' novel *A Modern Instance,* written in 1881. Gaylord is the crusty village atheist, and also the lawyer, of a small Maine town which Howells calls Equity. A cantankerous man, with a low opinion of mankind. "For Liberal Christianity," Howells writes, "he has nothing but contempt, and refuted it with a scorn which spared none of the worldly tendencies of the church in Equity. The idea that souls were to be saved by church sociables filled him with inappeasable rancor; and he maintained the superiority of the old Puritanic discipline against them with a fervor which nothing but its re-establishment could have abated." There is something of the Squire in Freud. As he says in *Civilization and Its Discontents* (pp. 23–24), he is happier with, or at least more respectful of, the old-time religion than with its liberal variants which have pretensions to accommodate science. And yet, as we shall see, the "hard" religion which often appeals to Freud for support would be considered by him quite as comfortable and lacking in real strength as a church social.

The first such appeal to Freud is made on the basis that

he dethroned the claims of rationalism and positivism and upheld those of the dark, irrational forces in man. The neo-orthodox today like to talk about such forces as a way of slapping down the liberals who are alleged to believe that man is good and his life a feast of reason. They cite Freud's findings as evidence for man's daemonic powers and also for his need for unquestioning faith. This view, I think, comes from a misunderstanding of Freud—and it is probably also a misunderstanding of the "liberals" such as John Dewey who are set up as straw men on the other side. Freud is fundamentally a rationalist—in fact, it would be difficult to find anyone in the Enlightenment who was more so. His whole effort as a scientist was to make the irrational understandable—to capture it for rationality—while as a therapist he had the same goal for the patient—that he should gain control over his irrational strivings by an understanding of them. To a degree (and perhaps we tend to overestimate the degree) the Enlightenment had overlooked and Victorian hypocrisy had buried the *materials* which Freud drew attention to; but the *method* of Freud was invariably the method of science, of positivism if you like, and the morality he demanded of himself and shepherded in his patients was a modified, but far from rebellious and Bohemian, Victorianism.

If we look at the whole body of Freud's work, we can see that he was attracted, like many great scientists, by puzzles, by mystery, by what was veiled and hidden whether by prevailing medical doctrine, by religious dogma, or by the uncanny and perplexing nature of the material itself. Yet always his effort was to order this material, sometimes with pedantic rigor, and he sharply criticized those who used "intuitive" methods in dealing with symbolic data. As other nineteenth-century entrepreneurs took upon themselves the white man's burden of subduing foreign customs and procedures which seemed irrational from the standpoint of Ricardian economics, so Freud sought to subject to laws—for which he often used the term "economic"—all the seemingly irrational phenomena he uncovered. In *Beyond the Pleasure Principle*, there is a typical passage where he expresses these scientific goals. He is arguing that the purpose of an instinct is the restoration of an earlier state in the history of the human race, and that since living matter was once inorganic, there must be an instinctive drive to restore that earlier condition; the goal of life must therefore be death. Yet in the middle of this highly speculative flight, Freud writes as follows:

"If what results gives an appearance of 'profundity' or bears a resemblance to mysticism, still we know ourselves to be clear of the reproach of having striven after anything of the sort. We are in search of sober conclusions of investigation or of reflections based upon it, and the only character we wish for in these conclusions is that of certainty."

Moreover, it is interesting to see that, when he dealt with religion—and he recurred to it again and again in his work—he analyzed only its more rational forms. Despite his discussion of the "oceanic feeling" in *Civilization and Its Discontents*, a discussion which ends in dismissal, he seems nowhere to have dealt with Western mysticism in its wide variety of expressions. Unlike William James, he was less interested in the religious *experience* than in the meaning of the rules and rituals laid down under religious auspices. (There are some partial exceptions to this, as we shall see.) In general, he looked for this meaning in terms of a disguised statement of an historical truth. Like an archaeologist, he asked, "What does this religion say about these people's past?" And he found the answer in, for example, a father-murder at an earlier point, followed by guilt and remorse, and the deification of the slain. Here, typically, we find Freud asking rational questions of, and giving rational answers about, data whose source lay in the unconscious of men and in what he regarded as their irrational feelings. Since he concluded that the source of religion lay in the repressed, irrational childhood of the race, he was able to interpret religion, as he did myths and dreams, in a genetic and "economic" rational way.

True, Freud was not very sanguine about reason. He thought that to trust it might sometimes be to trust in an illusion. But at least it was capable of disproof as an illusion, according to the canons of reason itself; and therefore it was superior to the illusion of religion which did not offer itself to proof or disproof. In other words, while Freud was skeptical about how much science could explain, he was far more skeptical about the claims to explanation of any other system, including occult practices and religion.

Another theme in Freud which makes him appealing to some of the more sophisticated among the neo-orthodox is his repeated emphasis on anxiety. But here again, there is I believe a misapprehension of Freud, some of it perhaps of a semantic sort. Freud's "anxiety" has only a peripheral connection with the "anxiety" of the fear-and-trembling school. Far from being a sign of potential grace or of any religious significance, it is a sign of weakness and sexual inadequacy. Freud did not admire those who trembled in contemplation of the problems of living and dying. He himself did not tremble, but steeled himself in Stoic fashion against isolation, illness, and impending death. To be sure, he counselled resignation. But this was the resignation of the strong and not the resignation of the weak—moreover quite different in quality from the haughty self-abasement whose long religious tradition can be traced in St. Paul, St. Augustine, and their successors.

There is even perhaps a certain Philistinism in Freud's view, like that of the self-made man impatient with anyone unwilling to come up the hard way. What Freud admired in the Jews—and it seems to me he gives them just a bit too much credit—was their stiff-necked pride in the face of the universe, in the face of persecution. Skeptical as he was of religion, traces of his admiration for the tough, uncompromising monotheism of the Jews appear again and again in his work. The Jews in repressing the memory of having killed Moses, their "Father," could never enjoy the expiation of their guilt, as the Christians could in the Son's atonement for their sins.

I think it follows from this that Freud would interpret the seeming toughness of Christian neo-orthodoxy as not tough at all, but a new form of comfortableness: a refusal to defy the father, as all must do who wish to grow up; a refusal to face uncertainty; a wallowing in anxiety, rather than a resolution of it through action. Thus he would find a secondary gain of surrender hidden under the only apparent harshness of contemporary revivals of old-time religion.

Still another theme where some religious thinkers trace affinity with Freud is that of pessimism. Freud was undoubtedly a pessimist, but of a different brand from most religious writers. Not only did he have little faith in social reform or in man's innate goodness, he also had no faith at all in eschatological visions, let alone in any doctrine of election. In this sense his pessimism is more thoroughgoing than that of his new religious allies. Moreover, as we have already seen, Freud did have a qualified confidence in reason; through strengthening of man's ego—the wise arbitrator seeking to balance and control the passions—he hoped for a better future. More important, perhaps, than these statements of *Weltanschauung* or ideology is the fact that one cannot read Freud's work without realizing the passionate and sanguine admiration he had for human achievement, for human curiosity, for human mastery. What delighted him in monotheistic religion was its intellectual achievement, even if he saw elements of illusion in it.

The final theme in Freud to which some religious people point is his emphasis on original sin. Somewhere Freud writes, "Psychoanalysis confirms what the pious are wont to say, that we are all sinners." Certainly, there is something here from which the orthodox may take comfort, but it is less than they think. Freud's thought is filled with paradoxes and ironies and we must use his own method to make sure that we do not take him at face value: his text, like that of a dream, challenges us to interpret it. When we do this, Freud's concept of original sin appears at best as an analogy to the religious concept. For Freud saw its origin in biology, rather than in a religious framework. Its biological base was the death instinct, followed by the primal crime, the killing of the father, but this chronologically original sin was for him the source of god-making rather than the result of God's prior existence. More meaningful, perhaps, than these differences in the nature of the concept are the differences in the metaphorical use made of it by Freud and by some of the neo-orthodox. The latter, as Arthur Murphy and Gardner Williams have pointed out with reference to Reinhold Niebuhr, in saying that all men are sinners are creating a preferential position for those who recognize this fact. For Niebuhr, those men are in some ways the worst who think themselves good; those the most arrogant, who think they understand society.[2] This position elevates those who abase themselves, who acknowledge man's intellectual and moral limitations. Freud, on the contrary, used original sin as a democratizer of men. He liked to see the symptoms of sex and aggression in the work of the high and mighty, and in the very good of the "good" men who scorned his theory. And not only men, but men and animals and men and gods were equalized by Freud's view: his interpretation of the totem animal as both a sign of the original crime and as destined to become a god may be thought of as the symbol for this. So we must conclude that for Freud the phrase "original sin" is tinged with irony —and beyond irony, compassion.

2. In correspondence, Dr. Niebuhr has pointed out that I have been unjust to him here, and I accept his criticism. Quoting Pascal's remark that "Discourses on humility are a source of pride to those who are proud," he declares: "I have again and again insisted that such are the powers of human self-deception that those who have what I believe to be a correct analysis of human nature may use it as a source of pride. . . . There is a sense of course in which everybody who strives for the truth gives implicitly a 'preferential' position to those who perceive the truth, as you do for instance, in your article. I cannot help but feel, though this may be quite unjust, that you had to make some critical remark like that in order to establish the preferential position of irreligion as against religion in the matter of truth, for it would be embarrassing to grant that any truth could come out of a religious position. . . ." Dr. Niebuhr referred me to statements in *Faith and History* and *The Children of Light and the Children of Darkness* to show how thoroughgoing a foe of pretence and arrogance, in and out of theology, he has been; I needed no references for his zeal on democracy's behalf.

III. The fundamental premise of Freud's view of religion is that we can understand it, not in its own terms, but only by understanding men and their human situation. For him, then, religion is a shared neurosis, having its origin, like any neurosis, in the Oedipus complex, that is, in hostile and rivalrous attitudes towards the father which have been replaced by identification and submission. Equally interesting and significant, however, is Freud's idea that neurosis is a private religion. One of his most interesting case studies is that of Schreber, a German jurist who, at the end of the nineteenth century, developed highly elaborate and quite original religious views while he was confined in a mental hospital. Through his conversion into a woman, Schreber felt God would "get into him," and he would found thereby a new race of Schrebers. Schreber's religion was socially defined as paranoia because, unlike the great religious leaders of history, he could not make others renounce claims in favor of his God as he had offered to renounce his masculinity. (In the nineteenth century and since, as we know, many cults hardly less fantastic have flourished in America.)

Furthermore, both private religion and shared neurosis resemble each other for Freud in that both seek to escape from reality, and as we have seen he criticizes those who, by whatever route, try to avoid facing life and pressing their claims. Once he allowed himself to say of the priests: ". . . they are spoilt, they have an easier time of it with their revelation." What he meant was that he himself was a scientist, arduously digging in the murky, the disapproved, the controversial, while at the same time obedient to the traditions and procedures of science. As against this, the priests took the easy way out of "*ipse dixit.*"

Freud's analysis of the monastic reports of the troubles of a seventeenth-century painter, Christopher Heitzmann, is revealing. It appears that, when Christopher was around thirty or forty his father died, and the son had tough going economically and psychologically. He could not work, could not paint, and was depressed. In a vision, the Devil appeared to him, and Christopher made a deal with him that, if the Devil would take him as his son for nine years, then he, Christopher, would belong to the Devil thereafter. When the nine years were up, Christopher wanted to welch (as Freud viewed it) on the bargain, and so hied himself to a monastery where he underwent conversion and was saved by the intercession of Mary. Much else is involved in Freud's essay, but important here is his position that Christopher-become-monk took the easy way out.

Freud had something of the same tough approach to the person who escapes through suicide and through mental illness—and even to the artist who, in Freud's eyes, deals with fantasy, not with the "real." Conversely, those whom he admired were those who were able to make others renounce, those who "civilized" others while remaining strong and unbowed themselves. Thus he admired Ikhnaton, the Egyptian monarch whom he credited with founding monotheism, the worship of an abstract sun god, and with forcing the Egyptians, at least for a time, to give up their comfortable beliefs in immortality and in a plenitude of gods. He admired Moses, whom he regarded as an Egyptian follower of Ikhnaton, who succeeded in imposing on the Jews the monotheism of his King. These were men who left an impress on the world, but for their followers—those who gave in to fear, to guilt, to remorse—Freud had scant respect.

Both the religious man and the neurotic in Freud's eyes are cowards who compromise the search for the meaning of life and the truth of social relations. The religious man is inhibited by the power of his racial memory, by collective authority. This blocks his inquiries in certain areas and this blockage spreads over other areas. Likewise, the neurotic is blocked in his search by his inability to rebel against parental authority. This inhibits his sexual curiosity; and this blockage, too, spreads over other areas. Similarly, Freud found analogies in obsessional ritual between religion and neurosis: the same compulsiveness, the same driven need to carry out acts the meaning of which had been repressed—meaning related in the case of the individual to his own childhood, and in the case of the religious man to the childhood of the race.

There is, however, in Freud's estimation an important

difference between religion and neurosis, resulting from the fact that the former is *shared.* He speaks, for instance, of a compulsion neurosis as a caricature of a religion. It is this because it lacks the companionship, the close touch with others, secured by the religious devotee. The latter finds his way to others—and hence to a part of reality—through religion, while the neurotic is isolated by his very rituals, often practiced in secret, which he cannot and dare not share with others. This ability to share, even if it is only the sharing of a collective illusion, puts the religious man on the same psychological footing as the successful artist. The latter is one who, in Freud's eyes, is originally alienated from reality but who, through success in selling his private fantasies to the public, wins his way to fame, money, and beautiful women—and so at least to the realities of social existence. Thus, the privacy of neurosis endangers the individual escape, while the publicity of religion brings the devout into contact with others, even though reality be mutually distorted.

Now we must stop for a moment to ask again, what kinds of religion is Freud talking about here, what aspects of religion? In the first place, he is preoccupied with the search for origins that was so characteristic of nineteenth-century scientific thought. In company with the early evolutionary anthropologists, he was concerned with tracing religion back to a presumptive starting point. This led him to examine the beginnings of totemism and of monotheism—the latter interested him mainly in its Jewish and Christian forms. When he talks about modern religion, he seems to be referring to its more puritanical Victorian versions. I have already pointed out that he left out of account anything which might be called genuine religious mysticism. In this latter tradition, in some of its Christian, Jewish, and also Oriental forms, the religious man is placed on a footing of a certain equality with God. He is made in God's image, and God in his. They communicate with one another; the mystic may even talk back to God—recall Joseph wrestling with the angel. This kind of mysticism is, to be sure, rather individualistic, but its attitudes are not unknown to some of the Protestant sects of the seventeenth century and later that emphasize love, such as the Dutch cult of the Family of Love. Freud seems to have been unaware of these minority phenomena and, indeed, in view of his system it is somewhat hard to see what he would have made of them.

In fact, I am afraid that these kinds of religious experience are but infrequently considered. Perhaps we have a kind of bias in the sorts of religion we talk about, when we discuss the relations of religion to science and philosophy. We are influenced by what is powerful, rather than by what might teach us something.

However that may be, Freud did not grant a great future to religion, in his own limited definition. This collective neurosis would not last. For, if the individual can grow up, can overcome his Oedipal ties, so can the race. He arrives at this conclusion after a magnificent dialogue with himself in *The Future of an Illusion.* We may call his alter ego in this dialogue the Grand Inquisitor, though Freud does not call him that.[3] When Freud suggests that perhaps the human race can grow up, then comes the Inquisitor and denies it. Religion is useful, the latter says, useful to force the mob to renounce and to console it for having renounced, and to reconcile them to the culture from which they reap so little gain. Moreover, the Inquisitor adds, religion has this great advantage over science, that high and low strata of society can come together in its folds, as in the Catholic Church, with the high strata making their own sublimatory refinements yet remaining in the same house with the low. Freud answers that we can hope that all men (not merely some) will become rational and face reality. The Grand Inquisitor returns and says, what is this reality? If you know it, you know that most men cannot face it, and that religion, though untrue, is useful and will if it passes be re-

3. In his essay on "Dostoevsky and Parricide," Freud pays his respects to the great scene in *The Brothers Karamazov,* and points out that Dostoevsky, out of his neurosis, allowed his fine intelligence to be humbled by the Little Father of the Russians and the Great Father of the Russian Orthodox Church. Nowhere does Freud make sharper remarks about the intellectual's "turn to religion."

placed by doctrine not calling itself religion but equally untrue, equally constricting for the masses, and equally consoling to them. Freud replies:

"You shall not find me impervious to your criticism. I know how difficult it is to avoid illusions; perhaps even the hopes I have confessed to are of an illusory nature. But I hold fast to one distinction. My illusions—apart from the fact that no penalty is imposed for not sharing them—are not, like the religious ones, incapable of correction, they have no delusional character. If experience should show—not to me, but to others after me who think as I do—that we are mistaken, then we shall give up our expectations."

And then he adds:

"We may insist as much as we like that the human intellect is weak in comparison with human instincts, and be right in doing so. But nevertheless there is something peculiar about this weakness. The voice of the intellect is a soft one, but it does not rest until it has gained a hearing. Ultimately, after endlessly repeated rebuffs, it succeeds."

So Freud ends the story.

We must take full account of Freud's tentativeness here. He is often criticized as a dogmatist, and I am one of those who have made this criticism of him. But concerning religion and its future, Freud says that he may be mistaken, and that the last word will be said by others besides himself. With this let us turn to look at some of the elements in Freud's view of religion that may be overstated or mistaken.

IV. In what has just been said, I have adverted to the analogy Freud draws between ontogenesis and phylogenesis, between the life-cycle of the neurotic individual who succumbs to the Oedipus complex and the history of humanity which has succumbed, in the form of religion, to the guilt of the prehistoric Oedipal crime. Obviously, all such "organicistic" analogies are as dangerous as they are alluring. Freud, though well aware of this, repeatedly resorted to such analogies and metaphors and, like many scientists, put more weight on them than was warranted. To be sure, when he came to study in *Moses and Monotheism* the history of the Jews, he abandoned the historical universalism which would have given all human beings the same phylogenetic experience and racial memory; instead, he traced those particular events of Jewish religious experience which, to his mind, gave the Jews a distinct national character and a distinct racial memory—one which the Christian world only repeated in considerably chastened and modified form. Those Jews who could not endure this guilt of the murder of the father, Moses, accepted Christ as the Messiah, the Son who came to atone for their racial crime, to expiate their guilt. It is plain, however, that Freud did not similarly differentiate between the historical experience of different social classes within a society, though in his day-to-day work he recognized of course that the lower classes suffered less from sexual inhibitions—and therefore should presumably have "inherited" a different set of Oedipal memories. Any attempt at racial, or "human-racial" interpretation of history, such as Freud builds on his analogy between individual and group, inevitably "declassifies" societies and runs into trouble in dealing with the stratification and divisions of any complex social order such as that of the Western world, or even of the Jews of Biblical times. It follows, therefore, that Freud's approach to religion will prove unsatisfactory to the more sociologically-minded investigator.

To illustrate this, and to show the limitations in Freud's method, I should like to review briefly a discussion in the psychoanalytic periodical *Imago* concerning the development of Christian dogma. An orthodox Freudian position was taken by Theodor Reik; a more sociological view was taken by Erich Fromm, and it is from the latter's article on "The Origin of the Dogma of Christ" that I primarily draw.[4] Both Reik and Fromm were struck by the fact that there is a change in the image and symbolism of Christ in the early Christian era. He appears in early representations as a

4. On this problem I am indebted to Murray Wax for many helpful suggestions.

young man, sometimes a young man suffering on the Cross; in later representations He appears as a babe in the arms of His mother, the Virgin Mary, who had been very much in the background in the early period.

The orthodox psychoanalyst looks at this development and says, in effect: oh yes, we know all about such alterations; that is simply ambivalence; people cannot make up their minds whether they wish Jesus to be a man or a baby. Moreover, we often see such ambivalence in our patients; they, too, cannot make up their minds whether to be a man or a child. So again mythology confirms what we find in the study of the neuroses.

Erich Fromm's critique of this kind of psychoanalytic analogizing is, I think, sound. He points out that such a view does not take religion seriously enough, does not take society seriously enough, does not even take the individual seriously enough. For the development of Christian dogma can tell us much, not about the psychological complexes of individual men who may have been ambivalent in one respect or another, but about the social struggles which shook the Roman Empire at this period—struggles in which, despite their individual ambivalences, men took sides and developed important religious and social institutions. We cannot dismiss such struggles without examining them historically, any more than we can dismiss the tragedies of individual decision and indecision in a social setting by speaking only of ambivalence.

Thus, Fromm observes that the young Christ of the early decades represents the Messianic hopes of the peasants, of the oppressed classes. They identify with Him as a man, as a focus of social protest—and as a man who becomes God. True, He does not replace God—the movement is a Messianic one, not an actual and successful social revolution—but He joins God on high. Much later, when Christianity has become a state religion and when the Messianic hopes have evaporated, we find an entirely different image of Christ. He is the Son who is consoled and protected by His mother; moreover, He was God all the time, rather than attaining to Godhood by His own manly efforts. This shift is a sign, at one and the same time, of psychological regression among large social strata and of the defeat of these same strata. The peasants no longer challenge the Empire even in fantasy, and their religion mirrors their situation as earlier it mirrored their hopes for social change. Fromm notes that it is only with the coming of the Reformation that God re-emerges as a father-figure, while during the medieval epoch the challenge to the father, to authority, is muted and the mother-figure predominates. Thus the Reformation's change of Christian imagery presages new social stirrings and new possibilities of rebellion. In this analysis, the emphasis is on *social* authority, which is reflected both in the structure of the family and the structure of religious doctrine; whereas in Freud's or Reik's analysis, the emphasis is on the family—on the individual domestic constellation—from which the racial and religious imageries are developed.

I want, however, to warn you that Fromm's argument is a very complicated one—so, for that matter, is Reik's discussion of religious rituals—and I have presented it only in oversimplified form. I would not want to leave the impression that Fromm takes an entirely Marxist position, of saying that religion is a mere superstructure—a narcotic in the class struggle. Fromm criticizes Kautsky's view as to the origin of Christianity quite as sharply as he criticizes Reik's. For Fromm sees religion as playing an important part in social struggles, and not merely as a reflection or distortion of those struggles.

Taking religion seriously as a factor in man's long effort to free himself, Fromm also differs from Freud in the role he assigns religion within the individual's psychic economy. Freud, as we have seen, considers religion to be crippling for the individual, crippling to his intellectual curiosity and his emotional claims alike—and this holds for all religion which deserves the name. In contrast with this, Fromm sharply differentiates among religions in terms of their specific social functions. Some doctrines which are not *called* religion may be far more crippling than some which are called religion. That is, while all of us, by virtue of the socialization we have undergone, are crippled to some degree, we cannot differentiate the more crippled from the less crippled by the tags of church identification. If we look at the whole person and the interpretations he puts on his religion—the specific quality of his religion—we may very well find that a devout person is far more "free"—far less deluded—than a man who claims he has outgrown belief in God.

Religion, in other words, can tell us a good deal about the individual believer and the social system in which he exists. We can, in socio-psychological terms, interpret the part religion plays in the life of men and groups. But this part is seldom simple and monolithic. Paradoxically, Freud seems to have taken too much at face the religious opposition to science, and failed to see, at least in this particular, that we have not said the last word about a man's rationality when we have stamped him as a believer—his religion may be the very sign of his rationality, though a disguised one.

This leads me to a further criticism I would like to make of Freud's view of religion, namely concerning the problem of motivation. When Freud found a religious man, he was likely to assume that his altruism, for instance, covered something up—perhaps it was a reaction-formation to anal-erotic sadism. Surely, that often happens, and the time when Freud lived was particularly noted for its pious frauds, its hypocrites who concealed their meanness consciously or unconsciously under a cloak of fervent religious devotion or obsessive attention to ritual. But it seems to me that today we face an altered situation, in which the limitations of Freud's view have become more apparent. Partly as the very result of Freud's work, we have invented a new kind of hypocrisy in which we have to cover over anything decent in ourselves, and call it tough. If we do an altruistic or decent act, we don't dare admit it, even or perhaps especially to ourselves. We rationalize away what is good and genuine in us. The businessman, for instance, chalks it up to public relations if he does something generous. The student, if let us say he does not cheat or is not aggressive, will chalk it up to timidity, to his fear of what people might think—he will certainly not give himself credit for any nobility of impulse. This new hypocrisy strikes me as in some ways quite as displeasing, and socially perhaps considerably more dangerous, than the old.

It would seem to follow from this that we cannot regard religion as simply a method for controlling libidinal and aggressive drives in the interests of society or of some other ultra-individual power. Religion is not, as Freud thought it to be, a kind of tax collector that collects from everybody the energy necessary to power civilization, and to keep it going. Nor will we necessarily find in religious practices what Freud called "the return of the repressed," that is, the reappearance in distorted or symbolic form of the very tendencies that religion had served to inhibit. Freud's whole position here, while it contains much that is true for certain epochs and for certain social groups, rests on his "scarcity economics," his view of man as having only so much libido, so much benevolence, to go around. And if this structure of motivations, with its tendency to biological reductionism falls, with it does Freud's view that religion on its ethical side represents, in the individual, no more than a reaction-formation, and, in the society, no more than a method of social control. As Freud saw an obsessional neurosis as a caricature of a religion, so we may regard Freud's picture of religion itself as a caricature of certain reactionary Augustinian tendencies within the Christian denominations—where the establishment comes close to being a method of social control and a reaction-formation against hatred and lust in whose very practices and doctrines hatred and lust reappear.

Furthermore, as I have already implied, there is in Freud's analysis of religion a somewhat pedantic treatment of religious symbolism. Freud does not, like Durkheim, study a religious ritual with the feeling that the ritual is trying to say something to him in another language—something which may be quite as rational as any scientific text. For example, he fails to see how a whole group, like the American Negroes, could guard their aspirations for liberation under a religious guise. Though far less heavy-handed than some of his followers, he nevertheless handles symbolism, whether in religion, in dreams, or in works of art, a bit too literally—not rationally so much as rationalistically. He wants to force it into a certain framework, and to pierce through the manifest symbol to its genetic origin. But the search for origins, which we have already seen to be characteristic of his approach to religion as to so much else, may tend to lead one to miss both artistry and overtones of contemporary meaning. In a way, the origins of a religious doctrine are relevant to contemporary men only insofar as they have incorporated those origins in their reinterpretations of what they do. Hence even if it were true that religion invariably arose out of men's fear and guilt, it would not necessarily follow that it is today propelled by fear and guilt.

V. Having made these criticisms of Freud's view of religion, I think we must grant his tremendous contribution to our understanding of it. As in so many other fields of his boundless curiosity and passionate moral courage, he succeeded in his effort to win a new territory for science, or at least a new angle of approach to the new territory. It is an approach which, when combined with other approaches, can be very fruitful, as I think Fromm's work indicates. Indeed, to make the study of religion (apart, of course, from Biblical criticism and other ongoing nineteenth-century efforts) respectable among scientists was perhaps as hard when Freud wrote as it was to make science respectable among religious fundamentalists.

Another contribution Freud has made to the study of religion leads me to introduce a kind of dialectic argument with the views of Malinowski. Malinowski takes a functional view of religion. This "functionalism" means that, if the investigator finds religion as an element in the life of a man or a group, he will assume it has a function, will seek to discover what it is, and will not consider it part of his task to criticize the function. Whatever is, functions; whatever functions, is part of the ethnographic picture. Many cultural anthropologists—partly because of the almost inevitable contemporaneity of field work, the lack of historical data—will not assess the historical weight of anything that functions in the present, and will perhaps overinterpret functions which may, in fact, no longer matter very much. They may be simply relicts.

Freud erred in the other direction by putting his emphasis almost exclusively on origins and relicts. This, however, provides him with the perspective from which he says—whether he is right or wrong in his prediction is not the question here—that the religion which seems to have such a strong hold on mankind will very likely disappear with the adulthood of the race. For he can look back historically and conclude that the hold of religion was not always what it now is; that there have been decisive historical events, such as the reign of Ikhnaton, or the Jews' killing of Moses, or the Crucifixion of Christ, which altered the social and individual function of religion. Malinowski finds it hard to do this with the Trobriand Islanders.

But Freud's look forward is not only based on his look backward into history. He also looks into himself, and asks: do I need religion, can I get along without it; and if I can, why not all men? By assuming the unity of men's psychic constitution, he was enabled by self-analysis to subject social institutions to criticism, whereas an anthropology that follows functionalism literally cannot criticize what it finds, if it "functions." In other words, Freud found within himself a scientific *Weltanschauung* which transcended religion in its historical givenness, and from this base he could criticize religion and look forward to its demise while granting its functional role in the development and cementing of Western civilization.

VI. Let me turn finally, in the light of what has just been said, to the question of possible meeting grounds between psychoanalysis and religion. . . .

Within both fields, within psychoanalysis and within religion, there is an increasing preoccupation with meaning, with values. We must be as careful not to confuse psychoanalysis with one brand of it as we must be not to confuse religion with one brand of it. Indeed, I think it fair to say that the differences in attitude towards fundamental questions *within* religion and *within* psychoanalysis are greater than the differences between like-minded schools of religion and analysis.

As I have said, religion is today for many no longer the formal, often hypocritical shell that it frequently was in the nineteenth century. Great numbers of people can no longer coast on nineteenth-century religious observances, and they have been driven by modern life out of the religious communities that once held them fast. In the name of religion, they therefore meet together to consider where they are. It should not disturb or confuse us that these people put their quest for meaning in religious terms; he would be a bold person indeed who would allege that these terms cannot hold and develop new meanings.

A number of analysts have come to the same conclusion by a different route. In his therapy, Freud rejected the notion that he was a moral or ethical guide; he thought this would be a concealed dictatorship and that his job was done when he had helped the patient to find his own ego-ideals, free from compulsive obedience to, or flight from, a parental imago. Actually, he could largely coast on the implicit ends of the nineteenth century, and assume that his patients were on the whole sensible people whose neurosis did not itself originate in a moral conflict. Moreover, he was able to solve most moral problems which came up in his research and therapy by one ethical principle we have already seen at work in him: passionate devotion to the truth. Psychoanalysis in fact constitutes a great ethical achievement in its invention of a human relationship whose cardinal principle is scrupulous, or if you please ruthless, honesty *on both sides*. Freud's early patients, at any rate, were hysterics or obsessional people who had obvious symptoms and who wanted to be free of them, in order simply to lead good Victorian lives.

Perhaps it was Jung who first saw, in the immediate generation of analysts after Freud, that this (or training) was not the only reason people came to analysis. His patients seemed to be mainly men of middle age who were "in search of a soul"—who asked the analyst, "What is the purpose of my life? What should I do with it?" Their neuroses seemed to be bound up with moral problems,

problems of choice. Increasingly today, this new type of analytic work with people who are not obviously ill—whose "symptom" is their malaise, their whole way of life—people who are troubled about moral issues, or who ought to be troubled about them, forces analysts to become concerned with problems of casuistry, of values, as part of the very task of therapy. Neurosis then appears, not so much as a conflict between "natural" libidinal demands and society's restraints, but as a conflict among moral strivings within the individual himself—though these, of course, reflect the conflicts within society. And, in terms of technique, the analyst's task may no longer lie in coaching sexual frankness. The analyst may have to help patients confront repressed moral issues about which they ought to be, but are not consciously, troubled.

In two books, *Man For Himself* and *Psychoanalysis and Religion,* Erich Fromm has made an effort to grapple with these moral problems as they present themselves in analysis, within an evaluative framework that finds much in common with what he terms "humanistic" religion. He takes religion much more seriously as a source of illumination for psychotherapy than most psychoanalysts (including Jung) have hitherto done. At the same time, he employs the Freudian methods to understand the hold over men of both humanistic and "authoritarian" religion, and its value for them. Thus he regards himself, not incorrectly, as working in the tradition of Freud, but (like John Dewey) he regards as truly religious certain elevated ethical attitudes and cosmologies, which Freud, when he adverted to them at all, regarded as too highbrow to be given the name of religion. Fromm speaks for a number of contemporary analysts who are preoccupied with theological questions, not simply as Freud was—i.e., as "evidence" of human weakness and as sources of historical data—but on their merits and in their own terms. At the same time, theologians, turning the tables, can look to psychoanalytic developments for evidence concerning basic human "needs" and the psychic mechanisms which give rise to problems of an ethical and religious sort.

Such reconciliations, however, are not likely to get very far in the prevailing atmosphere where people are afraid of criticizing religion. For if the onslaughts of organized religious groups succeed in putting psychoanalysis, along with other inquisitive sciences, on the defensive, psychoanalysis—far from joining in the possible creation of new, syncretistic religious patterns—will either leave religion alone, as too hot to handle, or will form expedient alliances and make expedient obeisances and denials of any claim to ethical and religious relevance. If, in other and more "emancipated" circles, psychoanalysis, in the form of a diluted popular Freudianism, can still put people on the defensive who would like to know how to live decent lives, they will look to analysis only for debunking cliches and for symptom-therapy, not for its moral illumination.

Indeed, if we are to get beyond such sterility and defensiveness on both sides, we must abandon the misleading notion that there is such a thing as pure science or pure religion. All thought—that of religion and psychoanalysis alike—is impure, or, as Freud would say, ambivalent; all thought must be constantly removed from its wrappings of this time or that place. This is true of Freud's views concerning religion, as their paradoxical uses traced here would seem to indicate. It is also true, I venture to say, not only of our religious inheritance as a whole, but specifically of our traditional religious way of dealing with the temerities of science.

No doubt, future developments in the relation between psychoanalysis and religion (including Fromm's attempt to break down this distinction and to develop new ones) will depend rather more on such larger issues of social structure as the fate of the Catholic middle class than on the success of the intellectual adventure of a handful of theologians and analysts. But religious and scientific advance must usually occur as relatively powerless movements within a precarious setting. Freud, like other innovators, started as a minority of one.

CONRAD, JOSEPH Victory A106
———— Youth: A Narrative and Two Other Stories A173
COULANGES, FUSTEL DE The Ancient City A76
CRANE, HART The Complete Poems of Hart Crane A128
CROMBIE, A. C. Medieval and Early Modern Science: I, II A167a, A167b
DANTZIG, TOBIAS Number, the Language of Science A67
DICKINSON, EMILY Selected Poems and Letters A192
DIDEROT, DENIS Rameau's Nephew and Other Works A61
DOLLARD, JOHN Caste and Class in a Southern Town A95
DOSTOEVSKY, FYODOR Three Short Novels A193
DOUGHTY, C. M. Travels in Arabia Deserta A50
DUMAS, ALEXANDRE Adventures in Spain A211
DUPEE, F. W. Henry James A68
EDEL, LEON Literary Biography A188
FERGUSSON, FRANCIS The Human Image in Dramatic Literature A124
———— The Idea of a Theatre A4
FINCH, JAMES K. The Story of Engineering A214
FLORES, ANGEL (Ed.) An Anthology of French Poetry A134
———— An Anthology of German Poetry A197
———— Nineteenth Century French Tales A217
———— Nineteenth Century German Tales A184
FLORNOY, BERTRAND The World of the Inca A137
FORTUNE, EDITORS OF The Exploding Metropolis A146
FRANKFORT, HENRI The Birth of Civilization in the Near East A89
FREUD, SIGMUND Civilization and Its Discontents A130
———— The Future of an Illusion A99
———— A General Selection from the Works of A115
———— The Origins of Psychoanalysis A112
FRY, ROGER Transformations A77
GALILEO Discoveries and Opinions A94
GARNETT, DAVID Pocahontas A157
GASTER, T. H. The Dead Sea Scriptures in English Translation A92
GOFFMAN, ERVING The Presentation of Self in Everyday Life A174
GOGOL, NICOLAI Tales of Good and Evil A120
GONCOURT, EDMOND and JULES DE The Goncourt Journals A158
GOYA, FRANCISCO DE The Disasters of War AA1
GRANVILLE-BARKER, H. and HARRISON, G. B. A Companion to Shakespeare Studies, A191
GRAVES, ROBERT Good-Bye to All That A123
———— The Poems of Robert Graves—Chosen by Himself A139
GREEN, HENRY Loving A18
HADAS, MOSES (Ed.) A History of Rome A78
————(Ed) The Stoic Philosophy of Seneca A148
————(Trans.) Three Greek Romances A21
HAGGIN, B. H. The Listener's Musical Companion A183
HAHN, WALTER F. and NEFF, JOHN C. American Strategy for the Nuclear Age A224
HALL, ROBERT A. JR. Linguistics and Your Language A201
HANDLIN, OSCAR Race and Nationality in American Life A110
HENDERSON, HAROLD An Introduction to Haiku A150
HERBERG, WILL Four Existentialist Theologians A141
———— Protestant, Catholic, Jew A195
HOLT, ELIZABETH GILMORE A Documentary History of Art: I, II A114a, A114b
HUIZINGA, J. The Waning of the Middle Ages A42
IBSEN, HENRIK Brand A215
———— When We Dead Awaken and Three Other Plays A215b
JAMES, HENRY The Ambassadors A154
———— The Awkward Age A138
———— In the Cage and Other Tales A131
———— Selected Letters, A204
———— What Maisie Knew A43
JARRELL, RANDALL (Ed.) The Anchor Book of Stories A145

JASPERS, KARL Man in the Modern Age A101
JESPERSEN, OTTO Growth and Structure of the English Language A46
JEWETT, SARAH ORNE The Country of the Pointed Firs A26
JONES, ERNEST Hamlet and Oedipus A31
JUNG, C. G. Psyche and Symbol A136
KAFKA, FRANZ Amerika A49
KAUFMANN, WALTER From Shakespeare to Existentialism A213
KAZIN, ALFRED On Native Grounds A69
KEATS, JOHN Selected Letters A70
KIERKEGAARD, SOREN Either/Or, I, II A181a, A181b
———— Fear and Trembling and The Sickness Unto Death A30
———— Selections from the Writings of Kierkegaard A210
KISSINGER, HENRY Nuclear Weapons and Foreign Policy A152
KITTO, H. D. F. Greek Tragedy A38
KRAMER, SAMUEL NOAH History Begins at Sumer A175
LASKY, MELVIN J. (Ed.) The Anchor Review: Number One A64, Number Two A109
LAWRENCE, D. H. Sea and Sardinia and Selections from Twilight in Italy A39
———— Studies in Classic American Literature A5
LEAVIS, F. R. The Great Tradition A40
LERMONTOV, MIHAIL A Hero of Our Time A133
LEWIS, D. B. WYNDHAM François Villon A147
LEWIS, W. H. The Splendid Century A122
LUBELL, SAMUEL The Future of American Politics A71
LYNN, Kenneth S. The Comic Tradition in America A187
MALINOWSKI, BRONISLAW Magic, Science and Religion A23
MARX, KARL and ENGELS, FRIEDRICH Basic Writings on Politics and Philosophy A185
MATTINGLY, HAROLD Roman Imperial Civilisation A160
MAURIAC, FRANCOIS Thérèse A79
MELVILLE, HERMAN Redburn: His First Voyage A118
MEREDITH, GEORGE "An Essay on Comedy" in Comedy A87
MEYERHOFF, HANS (Ed.) The Philosophy of History in Our Time A164
MILLER, PERRY (Ed.) The American Puritans: Their Prose and Poetry A80
————(Ed.) The American Transcendentalists: Their Prose and Poetry A119
MONTAIGNE, MICHEL DE The Complete Essays, Vols. I, II, III A227a, A227b, A227c
MURASAKI, LADY The Tale of Genji A55
———— The Tale of Genji, Part II A176
MURRAY, GILBERT Five Stages of Greek Religion A51
MURRAY, MARGARET The God of the Witches A212
NEALE, J. E. Queen Elizabeth I A105
NEHRU, JAWAHARLAL Discovery of India, A200
NIETZSCHE, FRIEDRICH The Birth of Tragedy and The Genealogy of Morals A81
ORTEGA Y GASSET, JOSE The Dehumanization of Art A72
ORWELL, GEORGE A Collection of Essays A29
PANOFSKY, ERWIN Meaning in the Visual Arts A59
PEIRCE, CHARLES S. Values in a Universe of Chance A126
PETERSEN, WILLIAM (Ed.) American Social Patterns A86
PIERSON, GEORGE W. and LUNT, DUDLEY C. Tocqueville in America A189
PIRENNE, HENRI A History of Europe: I, II A156a, A156b
———— Medieval Cities A82
POLYA, G. How to Solve It A93
POWER, EILEEN Medieval People A32
PRAZ, MARIO The Flaming Heart A132
PROUST, MARCEL Pleasures and Days and Other Writings A97
RAHV, PHILIP Discovery of Europe A208

RIESMAN, DAVID Constraint and Variety in American Education A135
——— The Lonely Crowd A16
——— Selected Essays from Individualism Reconsidered A58
RILKE, RAINER MARIA Selected Letters A223
ROUGEMONT, DENIS DE Love in the Western World A121
ROURKE, CONSTANCE American Humor A12
RUSSELL, BERTRAND Mysticism and Logic A104
SANTAYANA, GEORGE Character and Opinion in the United States A73
——— Three Philosophical Poets A17
SCHRODINGER, ERWIN What Is Life? A88
SCOTT, GEOFFREY The Architecture of Humanism A33
SHAW, BERNARD Shaw on Music A53
SHERRINGTON, SIR CHARLES Man on His Nature A15
SIGERIST, HENRY E. The Great Doctors A140
SNOW, C. P. The Masters: A Novel A162
STEEGMULLER, FRANCIS The Grand Mademoiselle A205
STENDHAL The Charterhouse of Parma A1
——— Five Short Novels of Stendhal A153
——— On Love A103
STRINDBERG, AUGUST Six Plays A54
——— Five Plays A219
SUZUKI, D. T. Zen Buddhism A90
SYPHER, WYLIE (Ed.) Comedy A87
——— Four Stages of Renaissance Style A45
TAYLOR, A. E. Socrates A9
TITCHMARSH, E. C. Mathematics for the General Reader A169
TOCQUEVILLE, ALEXIS DE The European Revolution and the Correspondence with Gobineau A163
——— The Old Regime and the French Revolution A60
TOKLAS, ALICE B. The Alice B. Toklas Cook Book A196
TRAVERSI, D. A. An Approach to Shakespeare A74
TRELAWNEY, E. J. The Last Days of Shelley and Byron A225
TREVELYAN, G. M. History of England I, II, III A22a, A22b, A22c
TRILLING, LIONEL The Liberal Imagination A13
——— The Middle of the Journey A98
TROTSKY, LEON The Russian Revolution A170
TSAO HSUEH-CHIN Dream of the Red Chamber A159
TURGENEV, IVAN Selected Tales A203
TURNER, W. J. Mozart: The Man and His Works A24
VAN DOREN, MARK Shakespeare A11
VERGA, GIOVANNI The House by the Medlar Tree A47
VIDICH, ARTHUR J. and BENSMAN, JOSEPH Small Town in Mass Society A216
VIRGIL The Aeneid A20
WADDELL, HELEN The Wandering Scholars A63
WALEY, ARTHUR Three Ways of Thought in Ancient China A75
WESTON, JESSIE From Ritual to Romance A125
WHYTE, WILLIAM H., JR. The Organization Man A117
WIENER, NORBERT The Human Use of Human Beings A34
WILDER, THORNTON Heaven's My Destination A209
WILLEY, BASIL The Seventeenth Century Background A19
WILLIAMS, RAYMOND Culture and Society 1780–1950 A220
WILSON, EDMUND Eight Essays A37
——— A Literary Chronicle: 1920–1950 A85
——— A Piece of My Mind A143
——— To the Finland Station A6
WOODWARD C. VANN Reunion and Reaction A83
WRIGHT, G. ERNEST and FULLER, REGINALD H. The Book of the Acts of God A222
YEATS, WILLIAM BUTLER The Autobiography of William Butler Yeats A142
YARMOLINSKY, AVRAHM (Ed.) Soviet Short Stories A218
YOURCENAR, MARGUERITE Hadrian's Memoirs A108